The Foundations
of Human Experience

[I]

FOUNDATIONS OF WALDORF EDUCATION

RUDOLF STEINER

The Foundations
of Human Experience

Translated by Robert F. Lathe

& Nancy Parsons Whittaker

✑ Anthroposophic Press

*The publisher wishes to acknowledge the inspiration
and support of Connie and Robert Dulaney*

❖ ❖ ❖

Foreword © Henry Barnes, 1996
Introduction © Robert F. Lathe and Nancy Parsons Whittaker, 1996
Text © Anthroposophic Press, 1996

This book is a translation of *Allgemeine Menschenkunde als Grundlage der Pädagogik* (GA 293), published by Rudolf Steiner Nachlassverwaltung, Dornach, Switzerland, 1992. The appendix is a translation of lectures 4 and 5 of *Geist und Stoff—Leben und Tod* (GA 66), published by Rudolf Steiner Nachlassverwaltung, Dornach, Switzerland, 1961.

Published by Anthroposophic Press
www.anthropress.org

Library of Congress Cataloging-in-Publication Data

Steiner, Rudolf, 1861–1925.
   [Allgemeine Menschenkunde als Grundlage der Pädagogik. English]
   The foundations of human experience / Rudolf Steiner ; translated by
Robert F. Lathe & Nancy Parsons Whittaker.
      p. cm. — (Foundations of Waldorf Education ;1)
   Includes bibliographical references (p. 317) and index.
   ISBN 0-88010-392-2 (pbk.)
   1. Educational psychology. 2. Educational anthropology. 3. Waldorf
method of education. 4. Anthroposophy. I. Title. II. Series.
LB1051.S71313 1996   96-12551
370.15—dc20   CIP

10 9 8 7 6 5 4 3

Printed in the United States of America

CONTENTS

Opening Address, August 20, 1919.. 29

The Waldorf School as a cultural deed. The Waldorf School as a unified
school. The necessity of making compromises. Schools and politics.
Bolshevik schools as the grave of teaching. A republican administration
of the school. The composition of the pedagogical course: general
pedagogy, methodology, practice. The Waldorf school is not a parochial
school. The relationship of Anthroposophy to instruction. Religious
instruction. Necessary characteristics of teachers: interest in world events,
enthusiasm, flexibility of spirit and devotion to the task.

Lecture One, August 21, 1919... 33

The moral-spiritual aspect of teaching. The founding of the Waldorf
School as a "ceremony in Cosmic Order." The question of immortality
as an example of the relationship of modern culture to human egotism.
Education as a continuation of "what higher beings have done before
birth." Concerning the problem of "prenatal education." The connection of the two doubled trinities upon entering Earthly existence? Spirit
Human, Life Spirit, Spirit Self and Consciousness Soul, Comprehension
Soul, Sentient Soul? with the astral, ether and physical bodies and the animal, plant and mineral kingdoms (temporal body). The task of the
teacher is to harmonize the spirit soul with the temporal body through

1) harmonizing the breathing with the nerve-sense process; 2) teaching the proper rhythm between waking and sleeping. The importance of the inner spiritual relationship between teacher and child.

Psychology based upon Anthroposophical world view as a foundation for teaching. Concerning the empty concepts of modern psychology. The central meaning of thinking and willing. The pictorial character of thinking: reflection of prenatal experience. The will as a seed for spirit-soul reality after death. The transformation of prenatal reality into thoughts through the power of antipathy; the increase of this power to memory and concept. The increase of the sympathetic power of willing to imagination and living pictures. Blood and nerves: the tendency of the nerves to become material, the tendency of the blood to become spiritual. The intertwining of sympathy and antipathy in the brain, in the spinal cord and in the sympathetic nervous system. The threefold aspects of the human being: head, chest and limbs. The interactions of these three aspects and their relationship to the cosmos. The development of willing and thinking through pedagogy.

A comprehensive view of cosmic laws as a basis for being a teacher. The duality of the human being as the greatest error of modern psychology. The misleading law of The Conservation of Energy; the formation of new energy and matter in the human being. Understanding what is dying in nature through the intellect and what is becoming through the will. How perceiving the I is based in the physical body. Freedom and sense-free thinking. Nature without the human being: the danger of extinction. The function of the human corpse for the development of the Earth. The prevalence of death-bringing forces in the (dead) bones and (dying) nerves and life-giving forces in the blood and muscles. Rickets. The relationship of geometry to the skeleton. Geometry as a reflection of cosmic movements. The human being is not an observer of the world, but its "stage." The creation of new matter and forces through the touching of blood and nerves. Concerning the scientific method: postulates instead of universal definitions.

Feeling in relationship to willing. The nine aspects of the human being as a willing being. The expression of will as instinct in the physical body, drive in the etheric body, desire in the astral body; the absorption of will into the I as motive in the soul; as wish in Spirit Self, intent in Life Spirit and decision in Spirit Human. Psychoanalysis seeks the unconscious willing of the "second person" in us. Intellectualism as will grown old and feeling as developing will. Concerning socialist education. The formation of feeling and will in education: cultivation of feeling through unconscious repetition and cultivation of the will and strengthening the power of decision through conscious repetition. The importance of artistic activity in this connection.

The convergence of the three activities of the soul. The connection of cognitive and will activities in the antipathetic and sympathetic processes of seeing. The greater isolation of the human being from the environment in contrast to that of animals. The necessity of an interpenetration of thinking and willing. Isolation from the world in seeing and connection with the world in doing. The struggle against animalistic "sympathetic" instincts through the integration of moral ideals. The intertwining of soul activities exemplified by the argument between Brentano and Sigwart about the nature of human judgment. Feeling as retained cognition and willing: the revelation of hidden sympathy and antipathy in willing and thinking. The rise of feeling in the body through the touching of blood and nerves exemplified by the eyes and ears. The argument between Wagner and Hanslick concerning feeling and cognition in musical hearing. The erroneous position of modern psychology exemplified by sense theory. Errors in Kantianism.

An overview of the lecture cycle. Until now, consideration of the human being from the point of view of the soul and the body and now from the point of view of the spirit: levels of consciousness. Thinking cognition is fully conscious and awake, feeling is half-conscious and dreaming, willing is unconscious and sleeping. Working with dreamy and numb children. The completely wakeful life of the I is possible only in pictures of the world, not in the real world. The life of the I in activities of the soul: pictorial and awake in thinking cognition, dreaming and unconsciously inspired in feeling, sleeping and unconsciously intuitive in willing. Nightmares. The rise of intuition exemplified by Goethe's creation of *Faust, Part 2*. The close connection of intuitive willing with pictorial cognition contrasted to inspired feeling. The existence of the head separate from sleeping willing.

The human being from a spiritual standpoint: observations of consciousness levels. Concerning comprehension. The loss of the capacity of the body to absorb the spiritual with increasing age. From the child's feeling will to the elderly person's feeling thinking. Observation of what is purely soul in adults. Freedom. The task of education is to separate feeling from willing. The nature of sensation: the misleading view of modern psychology and Moriz Benedikt's correct observations. The sleepy-dreamy nature of the body's surface as the realm of sensing: the willing-feeling nature of sense perception. The difference of sensations in children and elderly people. Waking, dreaming and sleeping in human spatiality: a sleeping-dreaming surface and inner core and the wakeful nervous system lying between. The nerves in relationship to the spirit-soul: the formation of voids for the nerves through continual dying. Sleeping and waking in connection with human temporality: forgetting and remembering.

Comparison of the processes of forgetting and remembering with those of falling asleep and awakening as exemplified disturbances in sleep. The process of remembering. Training the power to remember and the will through the effects of repetition. Strengthening memory through awakening intense interest. Comprehending human nature through division into components on the one side and the integration of components on the other. The twelve senses. Concerning the sense of I and the difference between the perception of another I (cognitive process) and the perception of one's own I (will process). The sense of thought. The division of the twelve senses into will oriented senses (touch, life, movement and balance), feeling oriented senses (smell, taste, sight and temperature) and cognitive senses (I, thought, hearing and speech). The division of the world by the twelve senses and their reintegration through judgment. Comprehension of the spirit through levels of consciousness (waking, sleeping, dreaming), of the soul through states of life (sympathy, antipathy) and of the body through forms (sphere, crescent moon and lines).

The first three seven-year periods of life. The three aspects of logical thinking: conclusion, judgment, concept. Healthy conclusions live only in completely awake aspects of life. The descent of judgment into the dreaming soul and concepts into the sleeping soul. Development of the habits of the soul through the type of judging. The effects of concepts which have descended into the sleeping soul upon the formation of the body, in particular the uniform common physiognomies. The necessity of living concepts: characterizations instead of definitions. Flexible and fixed concepts. The structure of a human idea. The child's unconscious basic tenor: 1) In the first seven years "the world is moral," and therefore to be imitated; the impulse of the prenatal past. 2) In the second seven-year period, "the world is beautiful"; life in art, enjoyment of the present. 3) In the third seven-year period "the world is true"; systematic instruction and an impulse toward the future.

The spherical form as a foundation of the three bodily aspects: 1) head (only physical), spherical form completely visible; 2) chest (physical and soul), only visible as a crescent shaped spherical fragment; 3) limbs (physical, soul, spiritual), only visible as radii. The head as an expression of intellect and the limbs as an expression of will; the tubular and bowl-like bones in this connection. The skull as a transformed vertebra. The tubular bones as transformed head bones. The centers of the head, chest and limb spheres. Head and limbs in connection with cosmic movement. The imitation of cosmic movement in dancing and its translation into music. The origin of sense perceptions and their connection with sculpture and music. Body, soul and spirit in connection with the head, chest and limb spheres. The Council of 869: the Catholic Church as the source of scientific materialism. The development of the head from the animal world. The importance that the teacher have a feeling of the connection of human beings with the cosmos. Pedagogy as an art.

Human physical nature in relationship to the world of the soul and the spirit: head? developed body, dreaming soul and sleeping spirit; chest? wakefulness in the body-soul, dreaming of the spirit; limbs? wakefulness in the still unformed body, soul and spirit. From this perspective the task of the teacher is to develop the limbs and partially the chest and to awaken the head. The educational effect of language in the early stages of childhood and of the mother's milk in the first part of childhood: awakening of the sleeping human spirit. Awakening the intellect through artistic involvement of the will during elementary school. The influence of education upon the child's growth forces: accelerating growth through too much emphasis upon memory and inhibiting growth through too much emphasis on imagination. The necessity that the teacher observe the bodily development of the child over a period of years and the senselessness of the commonly practiced frequent changes in teachers. Children who tend toward memory or imagination.

The inner connections between the physical body and the environment. The physical structure of the human being: the continual overcoming by the torso and limbs of animalistic forms emanating from the head; thoughts as their supersensible correlation. The relationship of the torso to the plant kingdom. The opposing processes of human breathing and plant assimilation. The development of plantlike tendencies in human beings as a cause of illness. The plant kingdom as a picture of all illnesses. Human nutrition as the central portion of the combustion processes occurring in plants. Breathing as an anti-plant process. The relationship of breathing and nutrition to the physical body and the soul. The future task of medicine and healthcare. Modern medicine's search for bacteria. The relationship of the limbs to the mineral kingdom. The continual dissolving of minerals by the limbs. Illnesses such as diabetes or gout as a beginning of the crystallization process in the body. The I lives in forces. The task of the human physical body: dissolving what is mineral-like, reversing what is plantlike, spiritualizing what is animal-like.

The form of the human head aspect (from within outward) compared to the form of the human limb aspect (from outside inward). The human being as a "dam" for the spirit-soul. The absorptive tendency of the spirit-soul process. The creation of superfluous matter (formation of fat) by the chest-digestive system; how this matter is consumed by the spirit-soul working through the limbs. The pooling of the spirit-soul in the head and its coursing along the nerve paths. The opacity of living organic matter to the spirit and the transparency of the physically dead skeletal and nervous system to the spirit. The overabundance of spiritual activity in physical work and of bodily activity in mental work. Purposeful and senseless activity and its effects upon sleep; calisthenics and eurythmy in this context. Extreme sports as "practical Darwinism." Insomnia as a result of too much spirit-soul activity and drowsiness as a result of too much physical work. The senselessness of cramming for exams. Healthy and unhealthy kinds of thinking activity. Importance of spiritualizing external work for teaching and social life and importance of bringing blood to inner work for teaching and health.

The three aspects of the physical body. The three aspects of the head: the head, the chest (the nose as metamorphosed lung) and the limbs (jaws); the limbs as metamorphosed jaw. The chest-torso between the head and the limbs: the tendency of the upper chest aspect toward the head aspect (larynx and speech) and the lower chest aspect toward a coarsened limb formation (sexuality). Appealing to imagination through teaching material in the last elementary school years. Example of the Pythagorean theorem. The conditions of the teacher: permeate the teaching material with feeling will and maintain a lively imagination. Pedantry is immoral. Nineteenth century views concerning the use of imagination in teaching; Schelling. The teacher's motto: Imagination, Sense of Truth, Feeling of Responsibility.

Henry Barnes

A long and terrible war had just ended, a war that caused untold suffering and was to set the stage for the twentieth century. During those years, Rudolf Steiner, restricted in his outer movements, was able to conclude three decades of intense inward, spiritual-scientific research into the nature of the human being. In 1917, around the time that the German High Command secretly sent Lenin into Russia, and Woodrow Wilson led the United States into war, it finally became clear to Rudolf Steiner how the human soul and spirit are engaged in the human physical organism. That the brain and nervous system are the instrument of consciousness had long become evident to natural-scientific research, as well as to those who sought to understand the human being from the aspect of soul; but the question of how human feeling and human volition were grounded organically was, at best, a matter of speculation. There were schools of thought that attributed feeling to a subtle sympathetic vibration of the nervous system, and it was assumed that the will was merely a function of the motor nerves, controlled and stimulated from corresponding centers in the brain. But, even if an objective existence to the soul were admitted, the possibility that either feeling or will might be independent functions of the soul and have direct access to the organism as their bodily instrument was not even given theoretical consideration.

Into this situation Rudolf Steiner introduced the results of his years of research. These described the threefold human organism as the basis for the soul's life of willing, feeling, and thought. Only in thinking, he maintained, can we look to the brain and nervous system as the physiological instrument. If we look for the instrument of willing, Steiner said, we must look for it in the activity of the *metabolism*, while the bodily basis for feeling should be sought in the rhythmic pulsation of *breathing*, which is closely intertwined with the circulation of the blood. Therefore, to understand how the soul—and through it also the human spirit—works into earthly life through the instrument of the body, we must come to recognize that the soul, as a being of thinking, feeling, and willing, engages itself *as a whole with the whole physical organism* as metabolism, rhythmic breathing organism, and nerve sense system.

Summarized in this way, these conclusions appear highly theoretical and remote from life; but as Steiner first presented them in two lectures in Berlin during March 1917 (included in their first English translation in this volume), and which he reformulated in the autumn of that same year in his book *Von Seelenrätseln* (*Riddles of the Soul*),[1] and further developed in far greater detail in the fourteen lectures newly translated for this edition, his research results provide an anthropological basis for understanding the soul, spirit, and bodily nature of the human being. Thereby we come to realize that these challenging, difficult concepts are what made possible the development of a radically new approach to education, medicine, the arts, and many other fields. And it was just these insights that enabled Steiner, in May 1917, to respond to the

---

1. Translated and edited by Owen Barfield in *The Case for Anthroposophy*, Rudolf Steiner Press, London, 1970.

appeal by a keen observer of the political and social situation in Germany[2] for ideas on which a genuine and lasting peace might be founded when the war finally came to an end. Thus not only did the results of this research make it possible for Rudolf Steiner to describe what he saw as the direction in which forces were working beneath the surface of the chaos and desolation in Central Europe at the time, but it also yielded the conceptual basis for building a practical art of educational renewal—embodied two years later in the founding of the first Waldorf school in Stuttgart, Germany, in the autumn of 1919.

Steiner saw beneath the social chaos accompanying the war's end the striving of the social organism to re-constitute itself as the working together of three independent, but inter-active, spheres of life. He recognized that economic life on one hand, and cultural-spiritual life on the other, were struggling to free themselves from the centralized political control of the state. Steiner saw the same threefoldness of forces at work in the social body that he had come to recognize as working in the form and function of the human organism. The social struggle into which Steiner plunged in a heroic effort to awaken his contemporaries in German-speaking Middle Europe during the months immediately following the end of the war, led his long-time student Emil Molt,[3] the owner-director of the Waldorf-Astoria cigarette factory, to ask Rudolf Steiner the fateful question: Would he be willing to guide and direct a school for the children of the workers in

---

2. Otto von Lerchenfeld, at that time secretary to the Bavarian ambassador to the imperial court in Berlin.
3. Dr. Emil Molt (1876–1936), was an industrialist with a deep concern for social conditions, and was well-regarded by his employees. See *Emil Molt and the Beginnings of the Waldorf School Movement: Sketches from an Autobiography*, Floris Books, Edinburgh, UK, 1991.

his factory? This question led directly to the founding of the Waldorf School four and a half months later.[4]

The coming together of these two streams—the stream of insight and research, and the stream of outer social action—bore fruit in Steiner's immediate and wholehearted acceptance of the challenge implicit in Emil Molt's question. His response was based on the understanding that four basic conditions would be met. These conditions were, first of all, that the school be open to *all* children; second, that it be co-educational; third, that it be a comprehensive school—in contrast to the prevailing system where the intellectually gifted were sent to academic schools around the age of eleven, while their schoolmates completed their education at fourteen and then entered into apprenticeships or vocational training—and, fourth, that the conduct of the school be entrusted to those who would work with the children every day—that is, the children's teachers.

It was Molt's immediate, unhesitating agreement to these conditions and his rapid, practical engagement in bringing about the school that enabled Steiner—in such an astonishingly short time—to meet the group of prospective teachers who responded to his call, and to begin the work with them that culminated, sooner than anyone could have believed possible, in the opening of the school. The teachers gathered on August 21, 1919, in what had been a favorite restaurant-cafe for the citizens of Stuttgart until Molt bought it for the site of the new school. The two weeks that followed were weeks of almost unimaginable concentration.

Every day during this time Rudolf Steiner gave three courses of fourteen lectures each, and these three courses, together, constitute the initial cornerstone upon which the

---

4. For a detailed account of the development of Waldorf education see Gilbert Childs, *Steiner Education in Theory and Practice*, Floris Books, 1991.

new educational venture was to be built.[5] The course presented in this volume was, it might be said, "the cornerstone of the cornerstone." It introduced its hearers to the radically different way through which one can come to understand human nature by striving to know the human being not only from a physiological-biological point of view—with certain psychological attributes deriving from the physical—but also from an open-minded consideration of the results of spiritual-scientific research. To do so, however, requires that one be prepared to extend the scope and method of scientific inquiry into realms of experience beyond sense perception and ordinary intellectual analysis. In fact, such extended spiritual-scientific inquiry, as practiced by Rudolf Steiner for many decades, leads to the recognition that human beings, after a life of earthly experience, enter after death into a world of spiritual being from which they descend once more into a new birth. It is from this perspective then that Rudolf Steiner describes how human individualities gradually penetrate and take possession of their inherited organisms, and thus prepare—through the educational process—to awaken as morally responsible human beings who become capable of finding their own direction in life. Indeed, reading these lectures, it becomes clear that Rudolf Steiner saw the essence of teaching as service to this process of human incarnation in our time.

With one exception, the first Waldorf teachers-to-be had been students of Rudolf Steiner and anthroposophy before gathering in Stuttgart to prepare for the founding of the school. Nevertheless, the three courses in which they participated each day—and especially the course presented here—challenged them to think and experience anew everything for which their own education

---

5. These three courses include, in addition to the lectures in this volume, *Discussions with Teachers* and *Practical Advice to Teachers* (see bibliography for the complete list of Rudolf Steiner's educational courses).

and training had prepared them. They had to "turn themselves inside out," as it were, in order to re-enter in imagination, as conscious, intellectually-oriented adults, the world out of which they had been born, which was the world of experience from which the children, soon to be entrusted to their care, were just in process of emerging. And this task, they soon discovered, required the awakening of meditative, artistic capacities that had, perhaps, long been dormant in them. Yet it is just these artistic, meditative capacities that we, as students of this work over seventy-five years later, must also awaken within us if we are truly to serve the children who come to meet us.

Yet, for Rudolf Steiner, the honest struggle for self-transformation on the part of every individual—which, in a real sense, was what qualified them to assume their places as colleagues in this initiative—was only part of a greater whole. For Steiner himself, the school that was coming into being was called upon and intended to demonstrate that men and women could unite in free initiative to create and guide an enterprise for which they carried inner and outer responsibility. In other words, it was Steiner's hope that the Waldorf School would pioneer the establishment of an independent life of the spirit within the totality of modern social life. He saw clearly that the renewal of culture—for which four and a quarter years of World War I had convincingly and cruelly demonstrated the desperate need —could originate only in a society in which creative individuals were free to work together out of insight in institutions that owed their existence to neither political nor economic control. Only from such initiatives—whether educational, artistic, scientific, or religious—could one hope for the ideas on which a genuine and lasting peace—rooted in social justice—might eventually be founded. And because he saw all too clearly that Western society was headed in the opposite direction, Steiner during the last years poured all his energies, indeed his very life, into the renewal of both education and social life as a whole. The mere fourteen years that it took to bring Adolf Hitler to power in Germany and to virtually guarantee an even more terrible war, tragically confirms the realism of Rudolf Steiner's reading of the direction of world events.

Steiner saw that his was a time for far-reaching decisions— decisions that all individuals would have to make for themselves. Either Western humanity would continue to commit itself blindly to one-sided materialism—the Nazi doctrine of *Blut und Boden* (Blood and Land) was only one crude example of such commitment—or humankind would have to wake up to its own innate human spiritual potential. The chips were down: there was truly no other option than to come to terms with this radical choice. This was the challenge with which Rudolf Steiner initiated his new educational effort, and with which he greeted the prospective teachers on the first morning of the course:

> Dear Friends, we can accomplish our work only if we do not see it as simply a matter of intellect or feeling, but, in the highest sense, as a moral spiritual task. Therefore, you will understand why, as we begin this work today, we first reflect on the connection we wish to create from the very beginning between our activity and the spiritual worlds.

In this same lecture he characterized the basic task of education as overcoming egoism. "When you turn to your work, do not forget that all of modern culture, right into the spiritual areas, is based upon human self-interest. . . . We live in a time when we must combat this appeal to human selfishness in all areas if people are not to go even farther down the declining cultural path they now tread."

Steiner saw that to accomplish this task humanity must turn from its self-absorbed preoccupation with death and the significance of death for one's personal existence, must turn its attention toward the other end of life, toward the process of birth. "We must become increasingly conscious of the other end of earthly human development—birth." He saw that this would lead to the recognition that the task of teachers is to learn how to continue the work of higher spiritual beings, done before birth, within the life of the children we have to teach.

> Although we can physically see children only after their birth, we need to be aware that birth is also a continuation. We do not want to look only at what the human being experiences after death, that is, at the spiritual continuation of the physical. We want to be aware that physical existence is a continuance of the spiritual, and that what we have to do in education is a continuation of what higher beings have done without our assistance. Our form of educating can have the correct attitude only when we are aware that our work with young people is a continuation of what higher beings have done before birth.

Thus, without mincing words, Steiner directed the attention of his listeners to the fullness of human existence where the soul, spirit, and body must be engaged at every step of the way. Students of these lectures, following this challenging beginning, are led, through characterizations of soul life, to considerations of how the spirit awakens in the soul as human beings mature and, finally, in the concluding lectures, to an entirely new way of seeing the body as instrument for both soul and spirit.

At the conclusion of this arduous conceptual pilgrimage, Rudolf Steiner reminds us that what we know is not what truly educates, but *who* we are; this is what awakens, within children, the human beings toward which they are struggling to grow, struggling to *become*. For the teacher, three qualities are essential if the relationship with the child is to be alive and, in the true sense, educational. The first is *imagination,* which transforms the intellectual content of one's teaching into a language of experience that speaks directly to the child's soul; the second is *courage for the truth* of world realities; and the third is a *feeling of responsibility* toward what is truly human in the children entrusted to our care. At the end of the final lecture, Steiner expresses it this way:

What forms human intellectuality has a strong tendency to become slow and lazy, and it becomes most lazy when people constantly feed it with materialistic ideas. However, it will take flight when we feed it ideas received from the spirit, but we receive these into our souls only through the indirect path of imagination.

How people ranted and raved against including imagination in education during the late nineteenth century! In the first half of the nineteenth century we had such brilliant people as Schelling, for example, who thought more soundly about education. You should read Schelling's exciting discussions in *Concerning the Method of Academic Study,*—which was, of course, not intended for elementary school, but the early nineteenth-century spirit of pedagogy lives in it. During the second half of the nineteenth century, people understood this spirit in a masked form. Then, people were cowardly about the life of the soul and complained about whatever entered the human soul through the indirect path of imagination, because they believed that if they accepted imagination, they would fall directly into the arms of untruthfulness. People did not have the courage for independence, for freedom in their thinking and, at the same time, for a marriage to truth instead of lies. People feared freedom in thinking because they believed they would immediately take lies into the soul. To what I just said—that is, to filling their lessons with imagination—teachers must therefore add *courage for the truth*. Without this courage for truth, teachers will achieve nothing with the will in teaching, especially with the older children. We must join what develops as courage for truth with a strong sense of responsibility toward truth.

A need for imagination, a sense for truth and a feeling for responsibility—these are the three forces that constitute the nerves of pedagogy. Those who would take up education should write this as their motto:

> Enliven imagination,
> Stand for truth,
> Feel responsibility.[6]

From what has been said, it will have become evident that the lectures published here require a different kind of reading than a text that makes no demands on the reader beyond intellectual comprehension. If readers are to gain anything of real value from the study of this material, it will have to be digested and transformed into their own experience. When this effort is brought to them, however, students may well discover what many others have already discovered—that it becomes a source of life within the soul and leads toward the wellspring of creative teaching.

---

6. This motto has also been translated as:
> Imbue yourself with the power of imagination,
> Have courage for the truth,
> Sharpen your feeling for responsibility of soul.

Robert F. Lathe & Nancy Parsons Whittaker

This volume contains some of the most remarkable and significant lectures ever given by Rudolf Steiner. If you follow Steiner's
developing presentations of the threefold nature of the human
being and the dynamic relationships of our inner world to all of
creation, two essential facts become apparent. The first is that
with this seminar Rudolf Steiner finally succeeded in bringing
together, clarifying and synthesizing his many profound insights
into the reality of human nature.[1] *The Foundations of Human
Experience* presents the core of anthroposophy; it is the deepest,
most integrated and most active picture of the human being
Rudolf Steiner ever presented. Here we have a truly fundamental anthropology in which the vibrantly *alive* human being steps

---

1. Steiner began to make his work on these questions public as early as 1904,
although he does not appear to have coined the term "threefold human
being" until 1917. We encourage the reader to sample the way his understanding and capacity to communicate it unfolded by reading in this order
Theosophy, Chapter 1 (1904); *The Wisdom of Man, of the Soul and of the
Spirit,* Part 1 (1909); *Anthroposophy, A Fragment* (1910); The two lectures
included in this volume: "The Human Soul and the Human Body" and
"Riddles of the Soul and Riddles of the Universe (1917); and then *The
Foundations of Human Experience* (1919). After 1919, Rudolf Steiner continued to develop specific aspects of the insights contained in *The Foundations
of Human Experience,* but never again presented such an all-encompassing
picture.

forth to reveal the dynamic nature and active relationships of our threefold being. But, there is something more.

The Foundations of Human Experience represents a qualitative change in the nature and intent of Steiner's presentation. His earliest writings and lectures on the subject are clearly hoping to achieve understanding, a new way of thinking. The lectures of the middle period incorporate an element of warmth: Steiner gave them with the hope of not only evoking a new way of thinking, but of eliciting a warmth and concern for human life.

This seminar offers a profound deepening of Steiner's manner of presentation. In giving these lectures, Rudolf Steiner expected those attending the seminar to *use* them to rethink their acquired viewpoints, to reshape their feeling responses and then to forge new deeds into the fabric of human development. Steiner intended to engage not only our thinking and feeling (for now, we attend the seminar also), but also our will. *The Foundations of Human Experience* was intended to be used.

An unfortunate, though very understandable, outcome of the fact that Steiner delivered this seminar to those people preparing to teach at the Waldorf School has been the misconception that these lectures are for teachers only. An active understanding of their contents is certainly essential to any teacher desiring to teach in a way that addresses the underlying needs of the whole child. But, this understanding is also essential to parents wishing to be wise and effective guides for their children, to counselors seeking to assist clients along the pathways of growth and healing, or to anyone desiring to place his or her talents at the service of the progress of other human beings.

An active understanding of the contents of these lectures, an understanding deep enough to attain a useful mobility, is also necessary for any striving person who desires to further his or her own growth and development. In our opinion, it is in this regard that these lectures have their greatest value, for how can you become wise and effective for anyone else until you have wisely and effectively understood and undertaken to *change* yourself?

The information contained in this volume can lead you to an enriched self-awareness that can become the starting point along the road to heightened self-development. You can use *The Foundations of Human Experience* in exactly the same way you might use a road map. That is, discover quite precisely where you are in your capacities of thinking, feeling and willing and determine a path that will lead toward your further development. As you find your personal starting point, you can continue by taking up the path described in *How to Know Higher Worlds*. This is not the only effective guidance available, but it does have the advantage of addressing a very general readership with exercises given in such a form that makes it possible to weave balancing activities and attitudes into the surging events of daily life.

With *The Foundations of Human Experience* as a beacon and *How to Know Higher Worlds* as the pathway, you can discover in the most intimate ways the depth of the ancient admonition, "Know thyself." You will find that every step in self-awareness is the result of an increased experience of the manifestations of creation, and that to experience the world as it approaches you, you must first experience yourself. Ultimately, you will also find that, whether you look within yourself or direct your gaze outward, the source of all things resonates throughout the past and into the distant future. You will find that all things have their true life in eternity, and eternity, that is, Spiritual Intent, will become the basis of all your experience. Then whatever your vocation or life situation, you will be able to actively participate in the currents of a positive future.

A Note of Appreciation from the Waldorf School Faculty

The first edition of this volume, published in 1932, contained a note of appreciation from the faculty of the Waldorf School in Stuttgart describing the situation in which this course was held.

At the end of the World War, in response to the request of some members of the Anthroposophical Society, Dr. Steiner held a series of comprehensive lectures about the threefold nature of the social organism which form the content of his book *Towards Social Renewal*. The thoughts presented by Dr. Steiner prompted the industrialist Emil Molt to decide to found a school that was to be a germ for the free spiritual life. At his request, Dr. Steiner took over the leadership of this school and was continuously concerned with its success.

Prior to the opening of the Waldorf School, Dr. Steiner held a pedagogical course for three weeks in August and September of 1919 that was attended by the teachers and by a number of other people who desired to work with this new pedagogy.

The course was made up of three parts. The fourteen lectures of the first part, which appear in this volume, presented the anthroposophical understanding of the human being as a basis for a pedagogy, reflecting the needs of our time and the near future. Connected with these was a series of lectures on utilizing this anthroposophical perspective as a teaching methodology. The two series of lectures are closely related and form a unified whole.[1]

---

1. *Practical Advice to Teachers*, Rudolf Steiner Press, London, 1988 (GA 294).

A series of discussions followed the lectures in which Rudolf Steiner, together with the teachers, worked out the practicalities for particular areas of instruction and discussed solutions of specific pedagogical problems.[2]

Although this course took place quietly among a small circle, the participants experienced a spiritual event intended to help humanity reach a higher stage of development. As this work of Rudolf Steiner is now sent out into the world, the teachers of the Waldorf School wish to accompany it with a deep feeling of gratitude and the desire that it be taken up with understanding so that it may fructify education everywhere.

_____

2. *Discussions with Teachers*, Rudolf Steiner Press, 1992 (GA 295).

Opening Address
Given on the Eve of the Teachers' Seminar

STUTTGART / AUGUST 20, 1919

This evening I wish to make some preliminary remarks. To achieve a renewal of modern spiritual life, the Waldorf School must be a true cultural deed. We must reckon with change in everything; the ultimate foundation of the whole social movement is in the spiritual realm and the question of education is one of the burning spiritual questions of modern times. We must take advantage of the possibilities presented by the Waldorf School to reform and revolutionize the educational system.

The success of this cultural deed is in your hands. Thus, you have much responsibility in working to create an example. So much depends upon the success of this deed. The Waldorf School will be living proof of the effectiveness of the anthroposophical orientation toward life. It will be a unified school in the sense that it only considers how to teach in the way demanded by the human being, by the totality of the human essence. We must put everything at the service of achieving this goal.

However, it is necessary that we make compromises, because we are not yet so far developed that we can accomplish a truly free deed. The state imposes terrible learning goals and terrible standards, the worst imaginable, but people will imagine them to be the best. Today's policies and political activity treat people like pawns. More than ever before, attempts will be made to use people like cogs in a wheel. People will be handled like puppets on a string, and everyone will think that this reflects the greatest progress imaginable. Things like institutions of learning will be created incompetently and with the greatest arrogance. We have a foretaste of this in the design of the Russian Bolshevik schools, which are graves for everything that represents true teaching. We have a difficult struggle ahead of us, but, nevertheless, we must do this cultural deed.

We must bring two contradictory forces into harmony. On the one hand, we must know what our ideals are, and, on the other hand, we must have the flexibility to conform to what lies far from our ideals. It will be difficult for each of you to find how to bring these two forces into harmony. This will be possible to achieve only when each of you enters into this work with your full strength. Everyone must use his or her full strength from the very beginning.

Therefore, we will organize the school not bureaucratically, but collegially, and will administer it in a republican way. In a true teachers' republic we will not have the comfort of receiving directions from the Board of Education. Rather, we must bring to our work what gives each of us the possibility and the full responsibility for what we have to do. Each one of us must be completely responsible.

We can create a replacement for the supervision of the School Board as we form this preparatory course, and, through the work, receive what unifies the school. We can achieve that sense of unity through this course if we work with all diligence.

The course will be held as a continuing discussion of general pedagogical questions, as a discussion of the special methods concerning the most important areas of instruction, and as a seminar to practice teaching. We will practice teaching and critique it through discourse.

We will take up the more theoretical aspects in the morning and the seminar in the afternoon on each day. We will begin at

9:00 A.M. with general pedagogy, then undertake instruction concerning special methods at 11:30, and in the afternoon do seminar exercises from 3:00 until 6:00.

We must be completely conscious that we have to accomplish a great cultural deed in every sense of the word.

Here in the Waldorf School we do not wish to create a parochial school. The Waldorf School will not propagate a particular point of view by filling the children with anthroposophical dogma. We do not wish to teach anthroposophical dogma; anthroposophy is not the content of the instruction. What we want is a practical utilization of anthroposophy. We want to transform what we can gain through anthroposophy into truly practical instruction.

The anthroposophical content of instruction is much less important than the practical utilization of what we can create out of anthroposophy, generally in pedagogy and particularly in the special methods; in other words, how we can bring anthroposophy into teaching practice.

Representatives of the confessions will give religious instruction. We will use anthroposophy only in the method of instruction. Therefore, we will divide the children among the religion teachers according to their confession. This is another part of the compromise. Through justifiable compromises we can accelerate our cultural deed.

We must be conscious of the great tasks before us. We dare not be simply educators; we must be people of culture in the highest sense of the word. We must have a living interest in everything happening today, otherwise we will be bad teachers for this school. We dare not have enthusiasm only for our special tasks. We can only be good teachers when we have a living interest in everything happening in the world. Through that interest in the world we must obtain the enthusiasm that we need for the school and for our tasks. Flexibility of spirit and devotion to our tasks are necessary. Only from that can we draw out what can be achieved today when we devote our interest to the great needs and tasks of the times, both of which are unimaginably large.

1

We can accomplish our work only if we do not see it as simply a matter of intellect or feeling, but, in the highest sense, as a moral spiritual task. Therefore, you will understand why, as we begin this work today, we first reflect on the connection we wish to create from the very beginning between our activity and the spiritual worlds. With such a task, we must be conscious that we do not work only in the physical plane of living human beings. In the last centuries, this way of viewing work has increasingly gained such acceptance that it is virtually the only way people see it. This understanding of tasks has made teaching what it is now and what the work before us should improve. Thus, we wish to begin our preparation by first reflecting upon how we connect with the spiritual powers in whose service and in whose name each one of us must work. I ask you to understand these introductory words as a kind of prayer to those powers who stand behind us with Imagination, Inspiration and Intuition as we take up this task.

[*The words that followed were not recorded by the stenographer—see the Notes of Three Participants at the end of this lecture.*]

It is our duty to see the importance of our work. We will do this if we know that this school is charged with a particular task. We need to make our thoughts very concrete; we need to form our thoughts so that we can be conscious that this school fulfills something special. We can do this only when we do not view the founding of this school as an everyday occurrence, but instead regard it as a ceremony held within Cosmic Order. In this sense, I wish, in the name of the good spirit whose task it is to lead humanity out of suffering and misery, in the name of this good spirit whose task it is to lead humanity to a higher level of development in education, I wish to give the most heartfelt thanks to this good spirit who has given our dear friend Mr. Molt[1] the good thoughts to do what he has done for the further development of humanity at this time and in this place, and what he has done for the Waldorf School. I know that he is aware that what can be done in this work now can only be done with weakened strength. He sees things in this way. However, because we are united with him in feeling the greatness of the task and of the moment in which it is begun, and in feeling that this is a festive moment in Cosmic Order, he will be able to work in our midst with the necessary strength. We wish to begin our work with this in mind. We wish to see each other as human beings brought together by karma, who will bring about, not something common, but something that, for those doing this work, will include the feeling of a festive Cosmic moment. At the end of our course I will say what I would like to say following today's festive commencement of our preparation. Then much will have been clarified, and we will be able to stand before our task much more concretely than we can today.

Emil Molt: If, in this festive moment, I may say a few words, I do so to express my heartfelt thanks that it has been possible for me to experience this moment. I vow to do what lies within my weak powers to help in this great task we begin today.

* * *

Dr. Steiner: My dear friends, We will begin with discussions about our pedagogical task. Today I wish to introduce these discussions. We must differentiate our pedagogical task from those previously set by humanity. Our task is not different because we believe in vain arrogance that we should establish a new direction in pedagogy, but because, through spiritual science, we are clear that each period in the development of humanity always sets itself new tasks. Humanity had a different task in the first post-Atlantean developmental period, another task in the second, and so forth, right up into our fifth period. However, the tasks of a human developmental era now come to consciousness only some time after the era begins.

The present developmental period began in the middle of the fifteenth century, but the recognition of the educational task of our era is only now emerging from its spiritual basis. Until now, people, even though they worked in education with the best of intentions, still worked in the manner of the fourth post-Atlantean developmental period. From the very beginning, much depends upon our ability to correctly address our work and to understand that we must give ourselves a particular direction appropriate to our time. This direction is important, not because it is valid for all humanity in all times, but because it is valid specifically for our time. Materialism has resulted in the fact that, among other things, people have no awareness of the particular tasks of a particular period. The first thing I ask you to understand is that specific times have their specific tasks.

You will be teaching children (of course, children of a particular age) and you must consider that you will be receiving these children after they have undergone the upbringing (or perhaps the neglect) of their parents during the first period of their lives. What we desire can first be completely accomplished when humanity has progressed so far that parents understand that, even in the first period of upbringing, modern humanity has special tasks. We will be able to correct much of the neglect of the first period of life when we receive the children at school.

Each one of us must be especially conscious of how we comprehend our teaching.

When you turn to your work, do not forget that all of modern culture, right into the spiritual areas, is based upon human self-interest.[2] When you objectively observe the most spiritual area to which modern people devote themselves, the religions, ask yourself if the basis of modern culture, particularly in religion, is not human self-interest. It is typical of modern sermons that the preacher criticizes people for their selfishness. Take, for example, something that should affect people most deeply, namely the question of immortality, and consider that today nearly everything, even sermons, is directed by an understanding of humanity that focuses upon a self-centered view of what is supersensible. Due to this self-centeredness, people want to continue to exist when they go through the gates of death: they want to retain their I. Although very refined, this is one form of egotism. Today, every religious confession appeals broadly to this egotism when addressing the question of immortality. Thus, the religions speak to people so that they forget one end of earthly existence and take only the other into account. That is, they place their focus upon death and forget birth.

These things are not normally said so clearly, but they do lie at the foundation of people's thinking. We live in a time when we must combat this appeal to human selfishness in all areas if people are not to go even farther down the declining cultural path they now tread. We must become increasingly conscious of the other end of earthly human development— birth. We must be conscious that human beings develop for a long time between death and a new birth, and that during this development they come to a point where, in a certain sense, they die in the spiritual world. They come to a point where conditions in the spiritual world are such that they can no longer live there without going into another form of existence. Humans receive this other form of existence when they clothe themselves with physical and etheric bodies. What they can receive through this taking on of physical and etheric bodies they could not receive if they continued to develop in the spiritual world. Although we can physically see children only after their birth, we need to be aware that birth is also a continuation. We do not want to look only at what the human being experiences after death, that is, at the spiritual continuation of the physical. We want to be aware that physical existence is a continuance of the spiritual, and that what we have to do in education is a continuation of what higher beings have done without our assistance. Our form of educating can have the correct attitude only when we are aware that our work with young people is a continuation of what higher beings have done before birth.

Today, when people have lost their thinking and feeling connection with the spiritual worlds, they often ask abstract questions that have no real meaning for the spiritual world view. People ask how we should guide prenatal education.[3] There are many people today who take things too abstractly. If we take things concretely, we cannot endlessly pursue questions. I once used the example of seeing wheel tracks in the street.[4] Then you can ask, "Where did they come from?" "A wagon drove

by." "Why did the wagon drive by?" "Because the people sitting in it wanted to go someplace." "Why did they want to go
there?" At some time this questioning must stop. So long as
you remain in the abstract, you can always ask, "Why?" You
can always continue this line of questioning. Concrete thinking
always comes to an end; abstract thinking continues in an endless circle. It is the same with questions concerning a not-so-
common area. People think about education and ask about
prenatal education. Before birth, the human being is still in the
care of beings above the physical plane. We must leave the
direct individual connection between the world and the individual to them. Thus, prenatal education is not a task for the
child. Prenatal education can only be an unconscious result of
what the parents, particularly the mother, do. If, until the child
is born, the mother acts in such a way that she expresses what is
morally and intellectually correct, then what she accomplishes
in her own continuing education will transfer to the child. The
less we think about teaching the child before it has seen the
light of day, and the more we think about leading a correct life,
the better it will be for the child. Education can first begin
when the child is really integrated into the cosmic order of the
physical plane, and that is when the child begins to breathe
physical air.

When children step out onto the physical plane, we must
be conscious of what actually happens to them in the transition from the spiritual to the physical.[5] We must be quite
aware that the human being consists of two parts. Before the
human being steps upon the physical earth, the spirit and the
soul connect. What we understand as the spirit remains hidden in the physical world today and is what we in anthroposophy call Spirit Human, Life Spirit and Spirit Self. In a certain
sense, these three aspects of the human being already exist in
the supersensible sphere into which we must work our way.[6]

Between death and a new birth we stand in a certain relationship to Spirit Human, Life Spirit and Spirit Self. The strength
that emanates from this trinity permeates the human soul—
the Consciousness Soul, the Comprehension Soul,[7] and the
Sentient Soul. If you consider the human being preparing to
step down into the physical world after having gone through
the existence between death and a new birth, then you will find
what I have just described as the spirit bound with the soul.
Human beings step from a higher sphere into earthly existence
as spirit-souls or soul-spirits. They cloak themselves with
earthly existence. We could also describe this other part of the
human being that connects with the part I have described by
saying that what results from the processes of physical inheritance is brought to the spirit-soul on earth. The temporal body[8]
meets the spirit-soul[9]—once again, two trinities are connected.
In the spirit-soul, Spirit Human, Life Spirit and Spirit Self are
bound together with the soul consisting of the Consciousness
Soul, the Comprehension Soul, and the Sentient Soul. These
are all connected, and in stepping into the physical world bind
themselves with the feeling or astral body, the etheric body, and
the physical body. However, these are first united in the body of
the mother and then in the physical world with the mineral,
plant and animal kingdoms, so that here, as well, two trinities
are united.

If you observe children with sufficient objectivity as they
grow into the world, then you will perceive that children's temporal bodies are still not fully connected with the spirit-soul.
The task of education, understood in a spiritual sense, is to
bring the soul-spirit into harmony with the temporal body.
They must be brought into harmony and they must be tuned
to one another because when the child is born into the physical
world they do not yet properly fit each other. The task of the
teacher is to harmonize these two parts to one another.

Now let us look at this task more concretely. Of all the relationships humans have to the physical world, the most important is breathing. Breathing begins the moment we enter the physical world. Breathing in the mother's body is a preparatory breathing; it does not bring people into complete relationship with the physical world. What we properly call breathing begins only when the human being leaves the mother's body. This breathing is extremely important for the human essence, since the entire three-part system of the physical human is connected to it.[10]

We include the metabolic system as one of the members of the three-part physical human being. However, the metabolism is intimately connected with breathing—the breathing process is connected metabolically with blood circulation. In the human body, the blood circulation absorbs the material of the external world that has been brought in through other means, so that, on the one hand, breathing is, in a sense, connected with the metabolism. Breathing has its own functions, but in this way it is also connected with the metabolism.

On the other hand, breathing is also connected with human nerve-sense life. When we breathe in, we press in upon the brain fluid;[11] when we exhale, it springs back into the body. In this way, we transfer the breathing rhythm to the brain, and breathing is connected with nerve-sense life in the same way that it is connected to the metabolism. We can say that breathing is the most important human connection to the outer physical world. However, we must also be aware that breathing does not yet fully function such that it can support physical human life. When the human being enters physical existence, the proper harmony, the proper relationship between the breathing process and the nerve-sense process, has not yet been created.

In observing children, we must say in regard to their being that they have not yet learned to breathe so that breathing properly supports the nerve-sense process. Here is a more refined aspect of what we are to do with the child. First, we must understand the human being in an anthropological-anthroposophical manner. The most important educational deeds lie in the observation of everything that properly organizes the breathing process in relationship to the nerve-sense process. In a higher sense, children must learn to receive into their spirit what they are given by being born to breathe. This part of education will tend toward the spirit-soul. When we bring the breathing into harmony with the nerve-sense process, then we draw the spirit-soul into the child's physical life. Roughly stated, we can say that children cannot yet of themselves breathe properly, and that education consists in teaching proper breathing.

However, there is something else that children cannot yet properly do, and we must address this in order to create harmony between two parts of the human being, between the temporal body and the spirit-soul. The other thing children cannot yet properly do at the beginning of their earthly existence (you will notice that normally what we must spiritually emphasize appears to contradict external world experience) is to complete the transition between sleeping and waking in a way appropriate to human beings. At a superficial level we can, of course, say that children sleep quite well. They sleep much more than older people do. They even sleep into life. However, the child is not yet capable of the inner basis of sleeping and waking. Children experience all kinds of things in the physical plane. They use their limbs, they eat, drink and breathe. However, because they experience so much in the physical plane—what they see and hear, and what they do with their arms and legs—when they go from waking to sleeping they cannot take everything they have experienced physically into the spiritual world, process it there and then bring the results of this work back to the physical plane. Children's sleep differs from the sleep of an adult.[12] Normally, adults process their waking experiences during sleep.[13] Children cannot yet carry their waking experiences into sleep. Thus, in sleep they settle into the general cosmic order without taking their physical experience into the cosmic order. Through proper education, we must bring children to the point that they can carry their experience in the physical plane into what the soul-spirit does during sleep. As teachers, we cannot give children anything from the higher worlds. What human beings receive from the higher worlds comes to them during sleep. All we can do is to use the time children spend in the physical plane to help them gradually become able to take what we do with them into the spiritual world. Then, what they carry in can flow back into the physical world as strength, strength they can bring from the spiritual world to become real human beings in physical existence.

At first, we direct all teaching toward a very high realm, toward teaching proper breathing and the proper rhythm between sleeping and waking. Of course, we will become acquainted with behavioral measures that are not simply a training of breathing or a training of falling asleep and awakening. All that will only be in the background. What we will learn are concrete measures. However, we must be conscious down to the very foundation of what we do. We must be aware that when we teach children about this or that subject, we are actually working toward bringing the spirit-soul more into the temporal body and, at the same time in another direction, to bring temporality more into the spirit-soul.

Do not underestimate the importance of what I have just said, because you will not be good teachers if you focus only upon what you do and not upon what you are. Through anthroposophy, we need to understand the importance for human beings on earth to act not only through what they do, but, more importantly, through what they are. There can be a major difference between the way one teacher and another enters the classroom. There can be a great difference, and it does not depend simply upon whether one teacher is more clever than another in superficial pedagogical techniques. Rather, the main difference in the effectiveness of teaching comes from the thoughts the teacher has had during the entire time of his or her existence and brings into the classroom. A teacher concerned with developing humans affects the students quite differently from a teacher who never thinks about such things. What actually occurs at the moment you have such thoughts, that is, when you begin to understand the cosmic meaning of the breathing process and its transformation through education, or the cosmic meaning of the rhythm between sleeping and waking? At the moment you have such thoughts, something within you fights against everything that is merely personality. At this moment everything that forms the basis of your personality is dampened. Something of what predominates in people because they are physical human beings is quelled.

When you enter the classroom in this unpretentious state, then through inner powers a relationship is created between you and the students. In the beginning, it is possible that superficial occurrences contradict this. You go into the school, and you may have rascals before you who laugh at you. Through thoughts like those we wish to cultivate here, you must so strengthen yourself that you pay no attention to this laughing and accept it simply as a superficial occurrence in the same way you would regard being out without an umbrella when it suddenly begins to rain. This is certainly an unpleasant surprise. Normally people differentiate between being laughed at and being surprised by rain when they have no umbrella. However, no difference may be made. We must develop such strong thoughts that we will not differentiate between being laughed at and an unexpected rain shower. If we permeate ourselves with these thoughts and truly believe them, then perhaps in a week or two (or maybe even longer), regardless of how much the children laugh at us, we will be able to create the relationship to them that we desire. We must create this relationship, even in the face of resistance, from what we make of ourselves. Above all, we must be conscious of the primary pedagogical task, namely that we must first make something of ourselves so that a living inner spiritual relationship exists between the teacher and the children. We must enter the classroom in the awareness that this spiritual relationship exists, that it is not only the words and the reprimands we give the children or our capability to teach that exist. All these things are superficial, but things to which, of course, we must attend. However, we cannot properly attend to them when we do not create a basis, namely, the relationship between the thoughts that fill us and the facts that should enter into the bodies and souls of the children during instruction. Our attitude in teaching would be incomplete if we were not aware that human beings are born to have the possibility of doing what they cannot do in the spiritual world. We must teach in order to bring breathing into the proper harmony with the spiritual world. In the same way, human beings in the spiritual world cannot accomplish the rhythmical changes between sleeping and waking that they can accomplish in the physical world. Through education we must regulate this rhythm so that human beings properly integrate the temporal body into the soul-spirit. This is something that, of course, we should not view as an abstraction and use directly in teaching, but it must guide us as a thought concerning the essence of human beings.

Notes of Three Participants

Participants in the course: Berta Molt, Emil Molt, Caroline von Heydebrand, E. A. Karl Stockmeyer, Leonie von Mirbach, Elfriede Herrmann, Rudolf Treichler, Hertha Koegel, Paul Baumann, Rudolf Meyer, Johannes Geyer, Herbert Hahn, Friedrich Oehlschlegel, Marie Steiner, Elisabeth Dollfus-Baumann, Hannah Lang, Ludwig Noll, Mieta Waller-Pyle, Hermann Heisler.

Invited guests were: Andreas Körner, Luise Kieser, Walter Johannes Stein, Alexander Strakosch, Karl Emil Wolfer.

The invitation to participate as a guest was only given to those members of the Anthroposophical Society who had already indicated a desire to create a similar school in other locations. In addition, educators from the Ministry of Education were invited. K. E. Wolfer and A. Körner were invited for reasons of public relations.

Finally, Ida and Maria Uhland were invited. They were, however, unable to attend because they were unable to obtain leave from their school.

The spoken text was not retained stenographically at this point. Two participants in the seminar, Caroline von Heydebrand (1886-1938) and Herbert Hahn (1890-1970) have written from memory the content of Rudolf Steiner's spoken words. In addition to these notes, an entry exists from the diary of Walter Johannes Stein (1891-1957) who also participated in the course.

Notes from Caroline von Heydebrand:
"We want to form our thoughts so that we can be conscious of the following: Behind each of us stands our Angel gently laying hands upon our head. This Angel gives each of you the strength you need. Above your heads hovers a ring of Archangels. They convey from one to the other of you what each of you has to give to the other. They connect your souls. Thus you receive the courage you require. (From this courage, the Archangels form a vessel.) The Light of Wisdom is given to us by the Higher Beings of the Archai, who do not form themselves into a ring, but come from the beginning of time, reveal themselves and disappear into primordial distances. They project into this space only as a drop. (A drop of Time Light falls into the vessel of courage from the active Time Spirit.)"

Notes from Herbert Hahn:
"In that we actively turn to the pedagogy of this fifth cultural epoch, and in that we wish to be active as teachers, we may carry in consciousness the fact that the Beings of the Third Hierarchy are now moving to connect themselves with our work.

Behind each individual member of the now-forming faculty, we see an Angel standing. He lays both hands upon the head of the earthly being entrusted to him, and in this position and with this gesture allows *strength* to flow over to the human. It is the strength that provides the Imaginations necessary for the deed to be completed. Creatively Imagining, awakening powerful Imaginations, the Angel thus stands behind each individual.

Raising our view higher, we see hovering above the heads of this forming faculty a host of Archangels. Circling again and again, they carry from each of us to the other what results from our spiritual encounter with our own Angel. And they carry it, enriched by the strength of all the others, back to us. In this circle, which acts like an activity of spiritual formation, a vessel is formed above the heads of those united in this common striving. This vessel is formed from a specific substance— Courage. At the same time, these circling, connecting Archangels allow creatively Inspirational forces to enter into their movements. The Archangels open the source for those Inspirations necessary for our work.

Raising our view still higher, it rises up to the realm of the Archai. They are not represented in their entirety. However, from their realm, the Realm of Light, they let a drop descend into the vessel of Courage. We feel that this drop of Light is given to us from the good Spirit of our Time, who stands behind the Founder and the Founding of this new school. It is the creative forces of Intuition at work in this drop of Light. The Archai want to awaken the necessary Intuition in those now entering this new pedagogical work.

Giving Strength, Courage and Light, beings of the third Hierarchy take part in what is now being founded. Imaginatively, Inspiringly, Intuitively, they wish to connect with our earthly deeds."

From early, undated notes by Herbert Hahn:
"Imagine, how behind each of you stands your Angel. The Angel wishes to give Strength.

Circling above all of you, carrying the fruit of your work and your experiences from one to another, is a ring of Archangels.

From their circling and carrying, the Archangels form a vessel of Courage.

From the heights, the good Spirit of the Time, who is one of the Archai, allows a drop of Light to fall into the vessel. In this manner, the Archai give a drop of Light."

Diary entry from August 21, 1919 by Walter Johannes Stein:
"Beginning of the Course. Opened by Dr. Steiner at 9:00 A.M.

Strength	–	Angel
Courage	–	Archangel
Light	–	Archai

Thank the . . . [good Spirits] who gave Molt the idea. The Gods will work further with what our Deed will become."

2

In the future, all instruction must be built upon psychology developed from an anthroposophical understanding of the world. Everyone recognizes that instruction must be generally based upon psychology, and that in the past, for example, the widespread Herbartian pedagogy based its educational methods on Herbart's psychology.[1] In the last centuries up to the present, a certain factor inhibited the rise of a genuinely useful psychology. This can be traced to the fact that in our age, the Age of the Consciousness Soul, we have not achieved the spiritual deepening that could cultivate a real understanding of the human soul.[2] However, those psychological concepts formed from the knowledge of the fourth post-Atlantean period are today more or less without content and have become clichés in the realm of understanding the soul. If you look at a modern psychology book, or at anything to do with psychology, you will find it has no true content. You have the feeling that psychologists only play with concepts. For example, who forms clear concepts of thinking or willing today? You can find definition after definition of thinking or willing in various psychological and pedagogical works, but such definitions can give you no real picture of thinking or willing. Due to historical necessity, people have completely neglected to connect the soul of individual human beings to the cosmos. People are not in a position to understand how the human soul relates to the cosmos. You can get an idea of human nature only when you can see the relationship of the individual human being to the whole cosmos.

Let us look at what is normally called a thought.[3] We must certainly develop thinking, feeling and willing in the children.[4] Thus, we must first develop a clear concept of what thinking is. Those who objectively look at how thoughts live in human beings will immediately notice their pictorial character. Thoughts have a pictorial character.[5] Those who would seek something existential in thinking, who would seek real existence in a thought, fall prey to a great illusion. What would it mean if thoughts had their own existence? Without doubt, we do have existential aspects. Take, for example, the features of our physical body. (What I have to say here is only of a rough nature.) Take, for example, our eyes, nose or stomach, all of which are existential features. Although we live in these features, we cannot think with them. The essence of your own being is expressed in these features, you identify yourself with them. However, the fact that thoughts have a pictorial quality and are not so integrated with us that we are part of them, gives us the possibility of comprehending something. Our thoughts do not actually exist, they are only pictures. A great error was made at the end of the last human developmental period when existence was equated with thinking. "*Cogito ergo sum*" is the greatest error ever placed at the head of the modern world view.[6] In the full compass of *cogito* there is no *sum,* only *non sum.* This means, so far as my cognition is concerned, I do not exist, only a picture exists.

When you examine the pictorial character of thinking, you must focus upon it in a qualitative way. You need to see the mobility of thoughts. In a sense, you need to form an inadequate concept of activity which, nonetheless, somehow resonates with existence. However, we must recognize that in the activity of thinking we have only pictorial activity.[7] Thus, everything that evolves through thinking is the metamorphosis of pictures. However, pictures must be pictures of something; they cannot just be pictures. If you reflect upon the image in a mirror, you could say that the image appears in the mirror; however, what is in the image is not behind the mirror but exists elsewhere quite independently. It does not at all matter to the mirror what it reflects. All kinds of things can be reflected in the mirror. If we know that thinking is a pictorial activity exactly in this sense, then we must ask, what do our thoughts depict? Of course, conventional science can tell us nothing about this; only spiritual science can help. Thinking is a picturing of all our experiences before birth or before conception. You cannot come to a true understanding of thinking if you are not certain that you have lived before birth. In the same way that a mirror reflects spatial objects, your present life reflects your life between death and a new birth, and this reflection is your pictorial thinking.[8]

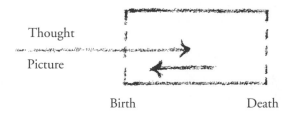

Thought

Picture

Birth   Death

Therefore, when you think of it pictorially, you must imagine the course of your life to be confined left and right between birth and death. Furthermore, you must imagine that thought images from before your birth continuously play into it and are reflected by human nature. In this manner, in that the activity you undertook in the spiritual world before birth is reflected by your physical body, you experience pictorial thinking. For those with sufficient insight, thinking itself is proof of pre-birth existence because it is a picture of this existence.

I first wanted to put this out as an idea (we will return to an actual explanation of these things later) to make you aware that in this way we can free ourselves of the definitions found in works on psychology and pedagogy. I also want to make you aware that we can come to a true comprehension of thinking when we know that thoughts reflect the activity of the soul in the pure spiritual world before birth. All other definitions of thinking are useless because they do not give us an idea of what thinking is.

Now we want to turn in the same way to the question of will.[9] For normal consciousness the will is extremely baffling. It is the nemesis of psychologists simply because they view the will as something very real, but basically without true content. If you look at the content psychologists ascribe to the will, you will find this content always derives from thinking. Considered alone, the will has no actual content. It is also the case that no definitions exist for willing; to define the will is even more difficult because it has no real content. But, what is will, really? It is nothing other than the seed within us of what our spirit-soul reality will become after death. That is, if you imagine what our spirit-soul reality will be after death, and if you picture it as a seed within us now, then you have the will. In our drawing, the course of life ends on the side with death, but the will goes beyond that.

| Thought | | Will |
| Picture | Birth | Death | Seed |

Thus, on the one side we need to see thinking, which we must comprehend as a picture of prenatal life, and on the other side, willing, which we must comprehend as a seed for something later.[10] Consider the difference between seed and picture. A seed is something super-real, a picture is something sub-real. A seed will only later become something real. It carries in it the characteristics of what will be real later. Thus, the will is, in fact, of a very spiritual nature. Schopenhauer felt that, but he was unable to recognize that the will is the seed of the spirit-soul that will develop in the spiritual world after death.[11]

You can see how soul life is, in a certain way, divided into pictorial thinking and seedlike willing. Between the picture and the seed lies a boundary. This boundary is the life of the physical human being, who reflects prenatal existence and thus creates pictorial thoughts, and who prevents the will from maturing, thus keeping it a seed always. We must, therefore, ask, what forces are active here?

Clearly, certain forces must exist in human beings that cause the reflecting of prenatal reality and inhibit the germination of postdeath reality. Here we come to the most important psychological concepts of my book *Theosophy*, namely the reflections of antipathy and sympathy.[12] We are in the physical world now because we could no longer remain in the spiritual world. (This is the connection with the first lecture.) To the extent we are in the physical world, we develop an antipathy against everything spiritual; thus, we reflect prenatal spiritual reality as an unconscious antipathy. We carry the force of antipathy in us, and through it transform prenatal experience into a mere mental picture. Sympathy is our connection to the reality of the will which radiates into our existence after death. We are not directly conscious of these two things, sympathy and antipathy, but they live in us unconsciously. They represent our feeling, which exists as a continuous rhythm of the interplay between sympathy and antipathy.[13]

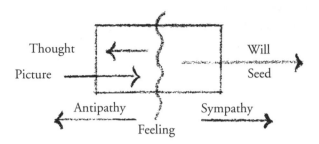

Our world of feeling develops in us as a continuous interplay—systole, diastole—between sympathy and antipathy. This interplay exists continuously in us. Antipathy, goes in one direction, continuously transforming our soul life into a life of ideas. Sympathy goes in the other, transforming our soul life into what we know as our deeds of will, into the seed of what is spiritual reality after death. Here we arrive at a real understanding of spirit-soul life: We create the germinal soul life as a rhythm between sympathy and antipathy.

What is it that you reflect in antipathy? You reflect the entire life, the entire world, that you lived through before birth. This primarily has a cognitive character. You therefore owe your cognition to your prenatal life shining in to your life after birth. The cognition that is present to a much higher degree as reality before birth is weakened to a picture through antipathy. Cognition comes into contact with antipathy and is thus weakened to a pictorial thought.

When antipathy is strong enough, something quite special occurs. In ordinary life after birth, we could not think pictorially if we did not use the force that remains with us from before birth. If today as a physical being you can present things to yourself in pictures, then you do so not with your own power, but with the force still active in you from the time before birth. You might think that this force ceases activity with conception; however, it remains active and we think pictorially by using this force that still radiates into us. You have in you on an ongoing basis the living experience from before birth, only you have the strength to reflect it. It encounters your antipathy.[14] If you now think pictorially, then every such picture encounters antipathy; and if the antipathy is strong enough, memory is created. Thus, memory is nothing other than the result of antipathy active in us.[15] Here you have the connection between undifferentiated reflection of emotional antipathy, and the concrete reflection, the pictorial reflection, carried out by the activity of perception in memory. Memory is only heightened antipathy. You cannot have memory if you have such great sympathy for your thoughts that you "swallow" them. You have memory only because you have a kind of disgust for these thoughts which prompts you to reflect them and bring them into consciousness. This is their reality.

When you have gone through this whole procedure, when you have pictured something, reflected it in memory and retained this picture, then the concept is created.[16] In this way, you have on the one side of soul activity, antipathy, which is connected with our prenatal life.

Now take the other side, willing, which is the seed within us of life after death. Willing lives in us because we have sympathy with it, because we have sympathy with this seed that develops only after death. Just as pictorial thinking is based upon antipathy, willing is based upon sympathy. If sympathy is strong enough, as when thoughts become memory through antipathy, then imagination is created through sympathy.[17] Exactly in the way that memory arises from antipathy, imagination arises from sympathy. If your imagination is strong enough (and in normal life this occurs only unconsciously), if it is so strong that it permeates your whole being right into the senses, then you have the normal pictures which enable you to think of external things. Just as concepts arise out of memory, the living pictures that provide sense perceptions of things arise from imagination.[18] They arise out of the will.

A major error perpetuated in psychology is the belief that we look at things, create abstractions from them and then arrive at a picture. This is not the case. That we perceive chalk as white, for instance, arises out of the use of the will, which through sympathy and imagination becomes a living picture.[19] In contrast, our forming of a concept has a quite different origin because the concept arises out of memory.

This describes the soul. You cannot grasp human nature if you do not grasp the difference between the sympathetic and antipathetic aspects of human beings. The sympathetic and antipathetic aspects as I have described them are expressed in the world of souls after death. There, sympathy and antipathy exist undisguised.

I have just described the human soul.[20] On the physical plane it is connected with the human body. Everything connected with the soul is revealed in the temporal body. On the one side, the body expresses antipathy, memory and concept through the nervous system. Prenatal life organizes the nervous system in the human body. The soul experiences prior to birth act upon the human body through antipathy, memory and concept to create the nerves. This is the proper understanding of the nerves. All talk about a differentiation into sensory and motor nerves is, as I have often mentioned, nonsense.[21]

In the same way, willing, sympathy, imagination and living pictures work in a certain relationship to the human being. This is connected with something seedlike that must remain seedlike and, thus, may never come to a real conclusion, but must disintegrate at the moment of creation. It must remain a germ and never go too far in development; thus, it must perish in the moment of creation. Here we come to something quite important in the human being. You must learn to understand the whole human: spirit, soul and body. Something is continuously formed in the human being that always has the tendency to become spiritual. But, because people egotistically love it so much, they want to hold it in the body, and it can never become spiritual; it dissolves into their living physical bodies. We have something in us that is material, but continuously has the tendency to slip out of the material state into a spiritual state. We do not allow it to become spiritual, and thus we destroy it the moment it desires to become spiritual. This is the blood, the counterpart to the nerves.

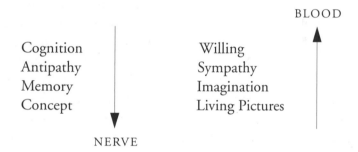

BLOOD

Cognition	Willing
Antipathy	Sympathy
Memory	Imagination
Concept	Living Pictures

NERVE

Blood is truly a "very special fluid." Were we able to remove it from the human body so that it would still remain blood and not be destroyed by other physical agents (which, of course, is not possible in earthly conditions), it would whirl up as a vortex of spirit. Blood must be destroyed so that we can hold it within us as long as we are on the Earth, until death, so that it does not spiral upward as spirit. We continuously create blood and destroy blood—create blood and destroy blood—through inhaling and exhaling.

We have a polaric process in us. We have those processes that run parallel to the blood, parallel to the bloodstream, and continuously tend to lead our existence out into the spiritual. To speak of motor nerves in the normal way is nonsense because motor nerves would actually be the bloodstream. In contrast to blood, all nerves are predisposed to continuously die and become physical. What lies along the nerve paths is actually excreted material. The nerve is actually an excretion. Blood always tends to become more spiritual and nerves always more material. This is the polarity.

We will take up these basic principles in later lectures and see how, when we follow them, they can help us shape instruction in a healthy way, so that we can educate children for soundness of body and soul rather than for decadence of spirit and soul. There is so much failure in education because so much is not recognized. Physiologists believe that they are on to something when they speak of sensory and motor nerves, but they are actually only playing with words.[22] They speak of motor nerves because people cannot walk when certain nerves are damaged, for instance those in the legs. They say someone cannot walk because the nerves that set the legs in motion, the motor nerves, are paralyzed. In truth, that person cannot walk because he or she really cannot perceive his or her own legs. Our age has of necessity become lost in a series of errors so that we can have the opportunity to work our way through these errors and become free human beings.

Now think about what I have just shown, that the essence of the human being can be understood only in connection with the cosmos. When we think, we have the cosmos in us. We were in the cosmos before we were born, and our experiences then reflect in us now. We will again be in the cosmos when we go through the gates of death, and our future life is expressed, seed-like, in what occurs in our will. What works in us unconsciously, works quite consciously in the cosmos as higher cognition.

We have a threefold expression of sympathy and antipathy in the bodily revelation. In a certain sense, we have three centers where sympathy and antipathy play into one another.[23] In the head, we have one such center where the interaction of blood and nerves (through which memory arises) occurs. Everywhere nerve activity is interrupted, everywhere there is a gap, a place exists where sympathy and antipathy interact. For example, another such gap is to be found in the spinal cord when one nerve goes toward the posterior horns and the other away from the anterior horns.[24] There is another such gap in the ganglia imbedded in the sympathetic nerves. We are not at all the uncomplicated beings we may seem. In three places in our organism, in the head, in the chest and in the lower body, there are boundaries where antipathy and sympathy encounter one another. In perception and willing it is not so that something is led from a sensory to a motor nerve, but, rather, a spark jumps from one nerve to another in the brain and spinal cord and thereby touches our souls. In these locations where the nerves are interrupted, we are connected with our sympathy and antipathy in our bodies.[25] We are also connected where the ganglia develop into the sympathetic nerve system.

We are connected with our experience in the cosmos. Just as we unfold activities that are to continue in the cosmos, the cosmos continuously unfolds in us the activities of antipathy and sympathy. When we reflect upon ourselves as human beings, we see that we ourselves are the result of cosmic sympathies and antipathies. Of ourselves, we develop antipathy, and the cosmos cultivates antipathy together with us. We develop sympathy, and the cosmos cultivates sympathy with us.

As we appear physically, we are clearly divided into the head system, the chest system and the abdominal system, including the limbs.[26] Please consider that this division into separate parts can be very easily attacked because of the modern fondness for systematizing; people want to neatly delineate each individual part. If you say that we differentiate between the human head, chest and abdomen-limbs, then people will be of the opinion that each of these must have its own well-defined boundary. People want to draw lines when they differentiate, but when we speak of reality, this is impossible. In our heads, we are mainly head, but we are head in our entire being, only the rest is not primarily head. In the same way that we have actual sense organs in our head, we have them all over our entire body; for example, the sense of touch and the sense of temperature. When we perceive temperature, we are all head. In our heads we are mainly head, elsewhere we are simply head "in passing." In this way the various parts intermingle, but it is not so easy with the limbs as pedantic people would like. Thus, the head is a continuum, only in the head it is particularly well-formed. It is the same with the chest. The chest is the actual chest, but only in the main since the whole human being is also chest. In the head, there is something like the chest and also something like the abdomen and limbs; the parts are intermingled. It is the same with the abdomen. Physiologists have also noticed that the head has qualities of the abdomen. The highly refined development of the head-nerve system is not found in the outer cortex we are so proud of, but under it. The beautiful structure of the outer cortex is, in a sense, a degeneration. It represents more of a digestive system in the outer portions of the brain. People need not be particularly proud of the mantle of the brain; it is more like a degeneration of the complicated brain into a more digestive brain. We have the mantle of the brain so that the nerves having to do with cognition can be properly nourished. The reason our brain is better developed than an animal brain is that we can feed the brain nerves better. Only in this way, namely, that we can feed the brain nerves better than animals can, do we have the possibility of more fully developing our higher cognition. However, the brain and nerve system have nothing at all to do with actual cognition; they are only the expression of cognition in the physical organism.

We may ask, ignoring the chest for now, why do we have the polarity between the head and the limbs-abdomen? We have it because at a particular point in time the head was "exhaled" by the cosmos. The human head was formed by cosmic antipathy. When the cosmos is so "repulsed" by what human beings have in them that the cosmos expels it, then this form is created. Human beings carry a representation of the cosmos in their head.[27] The roundly formed human head is such a picture. Cosmic antipathy creates a picture of the cosmos outside itself. That is our head. We can use our head as an organ for our freedom because this head was previously expelled from the cosmos. We do not properly understand the head if we think of it as being integrated into the cosmos in the same way as our limbs, which are connected with sexuality, are integrated. Our limbs are integrated into the cosmos, and the cosmos draws them in and has sympathy with them in the same way that it has antipathy for our heads. In the head our antipathy collides with that of the cosmos. Our perceptions arise in the collision of our antipathies with those of the cosmos. All inner life occurring on the other side of the human being arises from the loving, sympathetic embracing of our limb system by the cosmos.

Thus, the form of the human body is an expression of how the human soul is created from the cosmos and what is received from the cosmos following this separation. When you observe things in this way, you will more easily see that there is a tremendous difference between the development of will and that of thinking. If you particularly emphasize the development of thinking, you actually direct the entire human being back to prenatal life. You will injure children if you educate them rationally because you will then utilize their will in something they have already completed—namely, life before birth. You may not mix too many abstract concepts into the education you bring to children. You must bring in more pictures. Why? You can see the reason in our table [refer to table, page 57]. These pictures are living pictures that go through imagination and sympathy. Concepts are abstractions, and they go through memory and antipathy. They come from life before birth. If you use a lot of abstractions with children, you will stimulate them to concentrate particularly intensively upon the formation of carbonic acid in the blood and upon the crystallization process in the body, upon dying.[28] If you bring children as many living pictures as possible, if you educate them by speaking in pictures, then you sow the seed for a continuous retention of oxygen, for continuous development, because you direct the children toward the future, toward life after death. When we teach, in a certain sense we again take up the activities we experienced before birth. We must see that thinking is a pictorial activity which is based in what we experienced before birth. Spiritual forces acted upon us so that a pictorial activity was sown in us which continues after birth. When we present pictures to children in teaching, we begin to take up this cosmic activity again. We sow pictures in the children, which can become seeds because we cultivate them in bodily activity. As we as educators develop our capability to act through pictures, we must continuously have the feeling that we work upon the whole human being, that we create a resonance in the whole human being when we work through pictures.

To take this into our own feelings, namely, that education is a continuation of supersensible activity before birth, gives education the necessary consecration.[29] Without this we cannot educate at all.

Thus, we have learned two conceptual systems: cognition, antipathy, memory, concept—willing, sympathy, imagination, living pictures; two systems that, through their specialized use, can further our practice of education.

3

Behind everything they do in school, *the laws of the Cosmos* modern teachers must hold a comprehensive view of cosmic law. It is obvious that education, particularly in the lower grades, requires that the teacher's soul have a relationship to the highest ideals of humanity. One reason for the current illness in education is that we have held teachers of the lower grades in a kind of dependency: we have viewed their work as less valuable than that of teachers in the higher grades. It is not my intention to discuss the general question of the cultural activity of the social organism at this time.[1] However, we must note that in the future we must view all teachers as equal, and the public must feel that teachers of the lower grades are just as worthy as teachers of the higher grades, particularly regarding their spiritual character. Thus, it will come as no surprise today when we consider what even teachers of the lower grades must know without fail, although they cannot use it directly with the children. It must, however, stand behind all teaching that is to be fruitful.

In teaching, we bring the child the natural world, on the one side, and on the other, the spiritual world. As human beings, we have a relationship with the natural world, on the one hand, and the spiritual world on the other, insofar as we are earthly creatures and exist physically between birth and death.

Modern psychology is quite weakly developed. Psychology in particular suffers from the aftereffects of the Catholic dogma promulgated in 869,[2] which obscured an older insight based in instinctive knowledge—namely, the insight that human beings consist of body, soul, and spirit. From modern psychology you hear almost nothing but talk of a simple two-part human being. You hear that people consist only of body and soul (or flesh and spirit, depending upon what you want to call it). People regard flesh and body, or spirit and soul, as essentially the same thing. Nearly all psychological theories result from the error of the two-part nature of the human being. It is not possible to achieve real insight into human nature if we accept only these two parts as real. Thus, in principle, nearly everything that appears today in psychology is quite amateurish, often only a play on words.

All this is the result of that great error, which became so significant in the second half of the nineteenth century because people totally misunderstood a genuinely great achievement of physical science. You may be aware that the good citizens of Heilbronn have erected, in the middle of their city, a statue of a man who in his lifetime was locked in an insane asylum: Julius Robert Mayer.[3] Of course, you know that we associate this man, of whom the people of Heilbronn are quite proud today, with the so-called Law of Conservation of Energy. This law states that the amount of all energy or forces within the universe is a constant, and that these forces are only transformed, so that, for instance, a force appears at one time as heat, at another time as mechanical energy, and so forth. However, Mayer's law appears in this form only when it is fundamentally misunderstood! What was important for Mayer was the discovery of the metamorphosis of forces, not the creation of such an abstract law as the Law of Conservation of Energy.

When viewed broadly, what is the significance of the Law of Conservation of Energy for our civilization? It is the main hurdle to understanding the human being at all. When we believe that forces are never created, we can no longer achieve an understanding of true human nature. We can find the true essence of humanity in just the fact that through human beings new forces are continually created. In the world in which we live, human beings are the only beings in whom new forces and, as we will hear later, even new matter, are formed. However, because the current world view is incapable of accepting thoughts through which we can fully recognize the human being, people come along with this Law of Conservation of Energy. In a certain sense this law disturbs nothing if we look only at the other kingdoms of nature—the mineral, plant and animal kingdoms—but it immediately destroys all real understanding when we attempt to get close to human nature.

As teachers, you will need to make nature understandable to your pupils and, at the same time, guide them to a comprehension of spiritual life. Without being familiar, at least to a certain extent, with nature and without a relationship to spiritual life, people today cannot become part of social life. Let us now first turn our attention to nature.

Nature presents itself to us in such a way that we face it, on the one side, with our ideas and thoughts, which, as you know, are pictorial in character and are a kind of reflection of prenatal life. On the other side, we face nature with something that is of a will character and implies a germ of our life after death. It continuously directs us toward nature. That, of course, seems to indicate that nature exists in two parts, which has brought forth the erroneous view that human beings consist of only two parts. We will come back to this point shortly.

If we turn our thinking and ideas only toward nature, then we can comprehend only what is continuously dying there. This is a particularly important principle. You should be quite clear that when you learn those beautiful laws of nature that have been discovered with the help of reason and the power of reflective thinking, those laws always relate to what is in the process of dying.

When the germinal living will turns toward nature, it experiences something quite different from those natural laws based upon what is dead. Because you still carry many ideas that have arisen from the present time and the errors of modern conventional science, you will probably have difficulty in understanding that. What brings our senses (in the full spectrum of the twelve senses) into relationship with the outer world is not of a cognitive, but of a willing nature.[4] Modern people have completely lost that insight. When they read in Plato that the actual basis of seeing is the reaching out of a kind of tentacle to the things seen, they think it is something childish.[5] Of course, these tentacles are not perceptible with the normal senses, but Plato's awareness of their existence indicates he had penetrated the supersensible world. The way we see things is, in fact, nothing other than a more refined process similar to grasping things with our hands. For example, picking up a piece of chalk is a physical process very similar to the spiritual process that occurs when you radiate etheric forces from your eyes to grasp an object through seeing. If modern people could observe anything, they would be able to derive such facts from observations of nature. If, for example, you look at the eyes of a horse and the way they are directed outward, then you will feel that simply through the position of its eyes, the horse is in a different relationship to its surroundings than a human being is. We can best make the reason for the difference clear by the following hypothetical situation. Imagine that your arms were such that it was impossible for you to cross them in front of you. You would always remain at the eurythmy position of "Ah" and could never come to "O," because you could not bring your arms together in front of you. Concerning the supersensible "arms" of its eyes, the horse is in the same situation; the "arms" of its left eye can never touch those of its right eye. Human beings, due to the position of their eyes, are able to allow these supersensible arms to touch one another. That is the basis of the supersensible sense of the I. Were we never able to touch right and left, or were this touching to have the minimal importance it has with animals that cannot, for example, use their forefeet for prayer or other similar spiritual activity, we could never achieve a spiritual sense of our Self.[6]

What is important for the sensitivity in the eye and ear is not so much the passive element, but the active element that we extend to things through the will. Modern philosophy has often had a notion of something correct and has created all kinds of words that, in general, only prove how far it is from grasping what is correct. We find in the "attributes" of Lotze's[7] philosophy an indication of his recognition of the activity of the will-sense life. However, our sense organism is of a willing nature, particularly the senses of touch, taste and smell which are very clearly connected with the metabolism in a higher sense.[8]

Thus, we can say that when human beings intellectually confront nature and comprehend what is dead, then these dead laws become a part of them. However, people comprehend what raises nature above death and becomes the world's future by means of an apparently undefinable will that extends back into the senses.

Think about how alive your relationship to nature will be when you properly envision what I have just said. You will then say to yourself, "When I go out into nature, light and colors sparkle before me. As I absorb the light with its colors, I unite myself with that part of nature that it sends forth into the future. When I return to my study and think about nature and spin out laws about it, then I busy myself with that part of nature that continually dies." In nature, dying and becoming are continuously interwoven. We comprehend dying because we carry in us a reflection of our prenatal life, the world of intellect, the world of thought through which we can comprehend the dying that lies at the foundation of nature. We can understand that part of nature that will exist in the future because we can comprehend nature not only with our intellect and our life of thinking, but because we can grasp it with that part of ourselves that is will.

If human beings were unable to retain something from their pre-earthly life throughout their earthly life, if they were unable to save something from their pre-earthly life that then becomes the life of thinking, they could never achieve freedom. Human beings would have a relationship only to death, and when they would want to free what relates only to dead nature, they would want to free something dying. If they wanted to use what connects them with nature as willing beings, then they would fall into a stupor because everything that connects them with nature as willing beings is still a seed. They would be beings of nature, but not free beings.

Above these two activities, the comprehension through the intellect of what is dead and the comprehension through the will of what is living, is something that only human beings and no other earthly beings carry within themselves from birth until death. That is pure thinking, thinking unrelated to external nature, but related to the supersensible in human beings, to what makes human beings independent beings and to something that is above the sub-dead and super-living. If we wish to speak of human freedom, then we must respect this aspect of autonomy in human beings; we must look at the pure sense-free thinking in which the will always lives.[9]

However, if you look at nature from this point of view, then you will say, "I look at nature and the stream of dying is in me as is the stream of new becoming; dying and being reborn." Modern science understands very little about that relationship because, for science, nature forms a unity, and dying and becoming are continuously mixed together. Today, much that scientists say about nature and the essence of nature is very confused because dying and becoming are continuously mixed together. If you want to separate these two streams in a pure form, then you must ask yourself how nature would be if the human being did not exist.

Modern science and its underlying philosophy are in an awkward position when faced with that problem. Imagine, if you will, that you ask a modern scientist how nature and the essence of nature would be if there were no human beings? The natural scientist would, of course, at first be shocked, since the question is so unusual. However, he or she would consider scientific information to answer the question and would say that then there would be minerals, plants and animals on the Earth, but no people. The course of the Earth from the very beginning, when it was still in the Kant-Laplace nebulous state, would have continued on just as it did, only the process would not have included humans.[10] No other answer would be possible. The scientist could perhaps add that although people dig in the soil as farmers or construct machines to change the Earth's surface and thereby effect changes, such changes are not very important compared with the changes brought forth by nature itself. Thus, the scientist would, in principle, always say that minerals, plants and animals would develop without the existence of people.

This is incorrect. If the evolution of the Earth did not include human beings, then most animals would not exist. A major portion of the animals, particularly the higher animals, arose within earthly evolution only because human beings needed to use their elbows (of course, I speak here only pictorially). At a particular stage in their earthly development, human beings, to develop further, needed to rid their nature, which then was much different than it is now, of the higher animals. We can perhaps comprehend this cleansing if we imagine how, in a mixture in which something is dissolved, the dissolved substance precipitates and falls. In the same way, human beings in an earlier stage of development were one with the animal world, and then the animal world precipitated out.[11] In earthly development, animals would not have become what they are today had humanity not needed to become what it is now. Thus, without the inclusion of humanity in earthly development, animals and the Earth itself would look much different than they do today.

Let us now go on to the mineral and plant world. We must be quite clear that not only the lower animal forms, but also the plant and mineral world would have petrified long ago and ceased development were there no human beings on the Earth. Here again the modern world view, based upon a one-sided view of nature could only say that this is all well and good: people die and we cremate their bodies or bury them and thus give them over to the Earth; however, that has no real meaning for earthly development since if the Earth were not to take human bodies into itself, its development would continue exactly in the same way. This world view means, however, that people are totally unaware that the continuous giving over of human corpses to the Earth, regardless of whether it occurs through cremation or burial, is a real process with continuous consequences.[12]

Farm wives are much more aware than city women that yeast has a certain meaning in baking bread, even though only a small amount is added. They know that bread could not rise if they did not add yeast to the dough. In the same way, earthly development would have long ago reached its final stage were the Earth not continuously fed with the forces of human corpses, the forces released by the human spirit-soul at death. The forces that earthly development continuously receives through the acceptance of human corpses, that is, the forces contained in those corpses supports the evolution of the Earth. Without the support of such forces today, minerals could no longer unfold the forces of crystallization. The minerals would otherwise have crumbled and dissolved long ago. Through such forces, plants that no longer could grow are able to grow today. It is the same with the lower animals. It is human beings who, through their bodies, provide the leaven, similar to yeast, for the Earth's further development.

Whether humanity lives upon the Earth or not is not a question without meaning. It is simply not true that earthly development of the mineral, plant and animal kingdoms would progress if human beings did not exist! The process of nature is a unified and closed process in which the human being belongs. We can properly picture the human being only when we think of humanity as standing, even in death, within the cosmic process.

If you consider this, then it will be no surprise when I also say that the human being stepping down from the spiritual world into the physical is clothed with the physical body. Of course, the body is different when received as a child than when we lay it aside at some age through death. Something has happened with the body. What happens can only occur when human spiritual forces permeate this body. We all eat the same things animals eat; that is, we transform external material in the same way that animals transform it. However, we transform it under the influence of something animals do not have, something that comes down from the spiritual world to unite itself with the physical human body. Thus, we make something different than what plants or animals make with matter. The material in the human body that we give over to the Earth at death is transformed matter, and is something different than what the human received at birth. The matter and, also, the forces the human being receives at birth are renewed during life and returned to the Earth transformed. The matter and forces returned to the Earth at death are not the same as those received at birth. Thus, the human being returns to the Earth something that continuously flows from the supersensible world into the physical, sense-perceptible earthly process. Human beings bring something down from the supersensible world at birth that, together with the intake of matter and forces during their lifetime, joins with their body and is then given over to the Earth at death. Thus, the human provides a continuous trickle of the supersensible into the sensible and physical. You can easily understand that even if the supersensible constantly rained into the sensible, these drops would remain unfruitful for the Earth if human beings did not first receive them and then convey them to the Earth. These drops, which the human being begins to receive at birth and gives up at death, are a continuous fertilization of the Earth by supersensible powers. Through that fertilization, the supersensible powers sustain the Earth's evolutionary process. Without the human corpse, the Earth would be long dead.

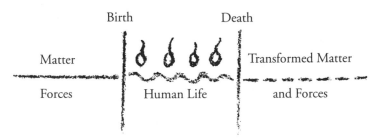

Having said that, we may now ask what the forces of death have to do with human nature. Of course, the death-bringing forces that are continuously active in nature act also upon human nature. If human beings did not continuously enliven it, nature would die. How do these death-bringing forces act upon human nature? They act to bring forth all the human attributes that range from the skeletal structure to the nervous system. What forms the bones and all things connected with them has quite a different nature from what forms the other systems. The death-bringing forces act upon us, and when we leave them as they are, we become human bone. The death-bringing forces act upon us, and when we weaken them, we become human nerve. What is a nerve?[13] A nerve is something that continuously desires to become bone and is hindered only by its connection to aspects of human nature that are part of neither the skeleton nor the nervous system. The nerve continuously attempts to harden and is continuously compelled to die in the sense that human bones are dead to a high degree. In animal bones, the situation is somewhat different in that they are much more alive than human bones. Thus, we can imagine one side of human nature as the activity of the death-bringing stream upon the skeleton and nerve system. That is one pole.

The other stream, the continuous life-giving forces, is active upon the muscles and blood and everything connected with them. The only reason the nerves do not become bones is that the forces active in the blood and muscles counteract this inclination. The nerve does not become bone because the blood and muscles oppose this and inhibit its calcification. Rickets, which is the hindrance of the proper dying of the bones by the blood and muscles, occurs when, during growth, an incorrect relationship exists between the bones on the one side and the blood and muscles on the other.[14] It is thus extremely important to develop the proper interaction between the muscles and blood on the one side and the skeleton and nerves on the other. The capability of the eye to connect the essence of willing living in the muscles and blood with the wisdom lying in the bones and nerves arises because of the way the bones and nerves are related to the eye. The bones withdraw and form a recess, leaving only their weakened form, the nerves,[15] in the eye. Here again we come to something that played a major role in older science, but that modern science laughs at as a childish idea. Nevertheless, modern science will again come back to it in a different form.

The ancients always felt a relationship between the substance of the nerves and the substance of bones, and they believed that people thought with their bones as well as with their nerves. This is also true. We can thank the capacity of our skeletal system for everything we have in abstract science. For example, why can human beings develop geometry? The higher animals have no geometry; we can see that in their way of living. It is pure nonsense to say that perhaps the higher animals have geometry, but we do not notice it. Human beings create geometry, but how does the human being create the idea of a triangle, for example? If we really consider that human beings developed the idea of a triangle, we will find something marvelous: out of their pure geometric imagination, human beings developed the triangle, which exists nowhere in concrete life. Much that is unknown about the heart of events in the world lies open to us. For example, assume you are standing in a particular place in this room. As a supersensible human being, at various times you make remarkable gestures of which you are normally unaware. For instance, you go a little to one side and then a little to the other, and then you come back to where you originally were. You unconsciously move along a line in space that, in reality, forms a triangle. Such movements exist even though you do not perceive them. However, because your backbone is vertical, you live in the plane in which these movements occur.

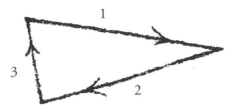

Animals do not live in this plane because their spinal cord lies differently, so that they do not carry out these movements. Because the human spinal cord is vertical, human beings live in the plane of this movement. Humans are not conscious of this; they do not say to themselves, "I continuously dance in a triangle." However, they draw a triangle and say, "This is a triangle!" In truth, it is only a cosmic movement performed unconsciously.

The movements you record in geometry when you draw geometrical figures are also performed by the Earth. The Earth has more movements than are ascribed to it by the Copernican point of view; it continuously performs other quite artistic movements. Still more complicated movements occur; for example, those of the geometric solids, the cube, the octahedron, the dodecahedron. These solids are not fantasies; they are real, but unconscious. In subconscious human knowledge, there are remarkable resonances with them and with other forms. Our skeleton has considerable knowledge, but because we cannot reach down into the skeleton with our consciousness, our awareness of that knowledge fades and is reflected only in the geometric pictures drawn by human beings. The human being is directly coupled to the cosmos, and with the development of geometry, something the human being does in the cosmos is modeled.

Here we see on the one side a world that surrounds us and is continuously dying. On the other side, we see something that enters into the forces of our blood and muscles and is in continuous movement, in continuous fluctuation, in continuous becoming and creation—something always an embryo, in which nothing is dead. We slow the process of dying within us, as only we human beings can slow it, and bring into it the process of creation. If human beings did not exist on Earth, then this dying would have long ago spread over the Earth, and the Earth would have become a great crystallized form. Individual crystals would no longer survive. We tear the individual crystals from the great process of crystallization and retain them so long as we need them for our human development. Thus, we also sustain activity in the life of the Earth. People sustain the life of the Earth, and thus they cannot be disconnected from the life of the Earth. Out of his pessimism, Eduard von Hartmann had a real thought that one day humanity would be so mature that all people would kill themselves.[16] We need not even add what Hartmann, due to the limitations of his scientific point of view, wanted. Because he was not satisfied with all people killing themselves, he also wanted to blow up the Earth. He did not need to add this. He needed only to designate the day of the great suicide, and the Earth would have slowly destroyed itself! earthly development cannot continue without what human beings implant in the Earth. We must allow this knowledge to permeate our feeling. We must understand these things now.

Perhaps you recall that in my earliest writings a recurring thought was that I wanted to base knowledge upon something other than the current thinking.[17] In Anglo-American philosophy, the human being is only an observer of the world. Humans with their inner soul process are simply observers of the world. In that line of thinking, if human beings did not exist and if their souls did not relive what occurs in the outside world, everything would still be as it is. People thought that point of view was as valid for the natural scientific developments I have just discussed as it was for philosophy. Modern philosophers are quite comfortable as world observers, that is, quite comfortable in the dying element of cognition. I wanted to guide cognition out of this dying element. Therefore, I have always repeated that the human being is not simply an observer of the world. Rather the human being is the world stage upon which the great cosmic events play again and again. I have always said that human beings with their soul life are the stage upon which world events play. That is one way we can express this view in a philosophical, abstract form. In the final chapter of my book *Truth and Knowledge,* I emphasize that we cannot find an equivalent in the remainder of nature for what occurs in human beings.[18] The remainder of nature, which is at the same time a cosmic process, enters the human being. The human soul is a stage upon which not simply a human, but a cosmic process plays out. Today, that is difficult for many people to understand. However, unless you penetrate such views, it is impossible to be a good teacher.

What really happens in human beings? On the one hand we have the skeletal-nerve activity and on the other, the blood-muscle activity. The interaction of these two continuously creates matter and energy anew. The Earth is saved from death because human beings create matter and energy. Now you can connect what I just said, namely, that the blood, through its connection with the nerves, acts to create matter and energy, with what I said in the last lecture, that the blood is continuously on the path toward spirituality and meets resistance there. We will further connect these two thoughts and build upon them. However, you can already see how erroneous the commonly held idea of the conservation of energy and matter is, since what occurs within human nature refutes it. As normally presented, it is only an obstacle for a real understanding of the human being. Something fertile for science can be achieved only when people replace their thoughts on the conservation of energy and matter with the synthetic thought that, although nothing can come from nothing, something can be so transformed that it ceases to exist and something else arises.

You see how much of our thinking goes in the wrong direction. We formulate, for example, something like the Law of Conservation of Energy and Matter, and proclaim it as a law of nature. This is the result of a certain tendency in our ideas, or, more generally, in our soul life, toward a one-sided description of things, whereas we should only postulate from our developed ideas, rather than proclaim laws. Thus, you can find, for example, in physics books, the Law of Impermeability: At a point in space where one body exists, another cannot exist at the same time. This is stated as a general characteristic of bodies. However, what we should say is that those bodies or beings are impermeable whose nature is such that where they are in space, no other being of the same nature can be at the same time. We should use concepts only to separate one area from another. We should only set up postulates and not give definitions that claim to be universal. Thus, we should not form a Law of Conservation of Energy and Matter, but rather seek the beings for which this law has meaning. In the nineteenth century, there was a particular striving to create laws and then claim them to be valid for everything, instead of using the life of the soul to approach and observe things as we experience them.

4

If you recall what I said yesterday in my semipublic lecture, you will understand that in the future teachers must place special value upon forming will and feeling.[1,2] I said yesterday that even those who do not think in terms of a renewal of education also stress the importance of developing will and feeling. However, in spite of all their goodwill, those people accomplish little that develops will and feeling. Will and feeling are left more and more to chance because there is no insight into the true nature of willing.

To begin with, I would like to note that only when we really understand the will can we understand even a part of the feelings that move us. Thus, we can ask ourselves, "What is a feeling, really?" A feeling is closely related to will. Will is only feeling made active and feeling is repressed will. That part of will that we do not completely express and that remains in the soul is feeling; feeling is blunted will. Thus, we can first understand the nature of feeling only when we have penetrated the nature of willing.

You can see from my explanation up to this point that during life between birth and death, we do not completely form everything that lives in the will. When we carry out a deed of will, there always remains something that is not expended in life before dying. Something of every willed decision and every willed deed remains in the human being and lives on through death. We must take this remainder into account throughout life, particularly in childhood.

We know that when we look at the complete human being, we see the human body, soul and spirit. The body, at least in its coarser constituents, is born.[3] You can find more details concerning this in my book *Theosophy*.[4] The body is part of the stream of genetic heredity; it carries inherited traits and so forth. The soul is that part of prenatal existence most closely connected to the body. However, what is spiritual in modern human beings exists only as a tendency. (In human beings in a distant future, it will be different.) So here, where we wish to lay the foundation for a good pedagogy, we must take into account what is present only as a spiritual tendency in human beings of the present developmental era. We should be very clear about which human tendencies are present for a distant human future.

What we call Spirit Self is present only as tendency.[5] We cannot immediately include Spirit Self as a part of human nature when we speak of modern human beings. Nevertheless, a clear awareness of Spirit Self is present in people capable of seeing what is spiritual. They know that the entire oriental consciousness (insofar as it is a developed consciousness) calls Spirit Self manas, and that in oriental culture, manas is spoken of as something living within human beings. Also, occidental peoples, who have not been completely "educated" have a clear awareness of Spirit Self. I can say without reserve that a clear awareness is present because common people, at least before they came completely under the control of a materialistic attitude, called what remained of a human being after death, the "manes."[6] People say that what remains after death is the "manes": manas equals manes. As I said, common people have a clear consciousness of this, because in this case they use the plural: the "manes." Since, in anthroposophy, we connect Spirit Self more closely with the human being before death, we use the singular: Spirit Self. Common people, since they speak more out of reality and more out of a naive understanding of Spirit Self, use the plural in speaking of the manes, because at the moment a person goes through the gates of death, a number of spiritual beings receive him or her. I have already mentioned in another context that we each have our personal spiritual guide who is a member of the hierarchy of Angels, and that standing above that are the spirits of the Archangelic hierarchy who become active when we go through the gates of death. Thus, we immediately have an existence in relationship to many, because many of the Archangels are active in our existence. Common people feel this quite clearly because they know that the human being, in contrast to the apparently individual existence here on Earth, can then be perceived as a plurality. Thus, the "manes" is something that lives in the naive collective consciousness about the plurality of Spirit Self, of manas.

Then there is a second higher aspect of the human being that we call Life Spirit. The Life Spirit is barely perceptible in modern human beings. It is something very spiritual that will develop in the distant future. The highest part of the human being is something that presently exists only as a barely perceptible tendency, the actual Spirit Human.

Even though these three higher parts of human nature exist only as tendencies in modern human life between birth and death, they undergo an important development between death and rebirth, of course under the protection of higher spiritual beings. When a human being dies and again becomes accustomed to life in the spiritual world, these three aspects develop quite clearly in a manner that points to a future human existence. Just as the human being develops the spirit-soul during life between birth and death, in the same manner there is a clear development after death, only then the human being is connected to spiritual beings of the higher hierarchies by something akin to an umbilical cord.[7]

Let us now add to those barely perceptible higher portions of human nature what we can already perceive, namely, what the Consciousness Soul, the Comprehension Soul and the Sentient Soul express. These are the actual components of the human soul. Today, if we wish to speak about the human soul and how it lives in the body, we must speak about these three aspects. If we wish to speak about the human body, we must speak of the sentient body (the least perceptible body, which we also call the astral body), the etheric body and the coarse physical body, which we can see with our eyes and which conventional science dissects. Thus, we have before us the complete human being.

Now you know that we bear a physical body in common with the animals. Only when we compare the nine aspects of the human being with the animal world do we arrive at a feeling and an idea of the relationship of people to animals useful for comprehending the will. That is, we are able to comprehend the will only when we know that just as the human soul is clothed with a physical body, animals are also clothed with a physical body. However, in many respects, the physical body of animals is formed differently from that of the human being. The human physical body is not nearer perfection than is that of the animal. Consider, for example, the beaver and how it forms its lodge. Humans cannot do that if they have not studied, if, in fact, they have not gone through a very complicated schooling and learned architecture and so forth. The beaver builds its lodge out of the function of its body. Its physical body is formed to fit into the physical world such that the beaver can use what lives in the form of this body to create its lodge. In this connection, the beaver's physical body is its schoolmaster. We can also find in the form of the physical bodies of wasps, bees and other lower animals something that is not present in the human physical body to so great an extent or with such strength. All this is what we encompass with the concept of instinct. We can only study instinct when we see it in relation to the form of the physical body. If we study the entire animal world and how it spreads itself before us, everywhere we will find a guide for the study of the various kinds of instinct in the physical forms of animals. If we wish to study the will, we must seek it first in the realm of instinct, and we must be conscious that we will find instinct in the various animal forms. If we were to look at and sketch the major forms of individual animals, we would be able to sketch the different areas of instinct. The physical bodies of different animals form a picture of what exists as instinct in the will. When we accept this point of view, we can make some sense of the world. We can look at the forms of the animal bodies and see in them symbols created by nature of the instincts it desires to be real and living.

The etheric body lives in our physical body, completely forming and permeating it. However, it is beyond imperceptible to the external senses. When we look at the nature of will, we see that the etheric body takes hold of what is physically expressed as instincts in the same way that it permeates the physical body. Instinct then becomes a drive. Will is instinct in the physical body, but when the etheric body begins to control instinct, will becomes a drive.[8] It is quite interesting to see how instinct that is concretely visible in external forms becomes more inward and more unified when we consider it to be a drive. We always speak of instinct, whether we find it in animals or in a weakened form in human beings, as something forced upon the being from outside. When we think of drives, we must remember that because the supersensible etheric body has taken control of instinct, their expression comes more from within. Instinct thus becomes a drive.[9]

The human being also has a sentient body that lies deeper still. When it takes hold of a drive, not only does the drive becomes internal, but instinct and drive are raised to consciousness, resulting in desire. Just as we find drives in animals, we also find desires because animals have all three of these bodies, the physical, the etheric and the sentient or astral. However, when you speak of a desire, you will quite instinctively view desire as something inner. When you speak of a drive, you speak of something expressed uniformly during the entire time from birth until old age. When you speak of desire, you speak of something created by the soul, a momentary creation. A desire need not be a characteristic, it need not adhere to the soul; rather it arises then fades away. Thus, we can see desires as something more closely connected with the soul than simple drives.

Now we may ask what occurs when a human being draws what lives in the temporal body as instinct, drive and desire into his or her I, that is, into the Sentient Soul, the Comprehension Soul and the Consciousness Soul. (This is something that cannot occur in animals.) Here we cannot differentiate quite so clearly as we were able to do in the temporal body, because in the soul of modern human beings everything is all mixed up. The problem in modern psychology is that psychologists do not know whether they should strictly separate the aspects of the soul, or whether they should allow them to flow into one another. The old, strict differentiation between will, feeling and thinking plays a role in certain schools of psychology. In some, for example those tending toward the Herbartian view, everything tends more toward the direction of thinking;[10] and in others, such as the Wundtian school, more toward the will.[11] There is no firm idea about what we can do

with the various soul aspects because in practical life the I permeates all aspects of the soul in modern human beings so that
the three aspects of the soul are not readily apparent. Thus,
there are no words to differentiate between what exists when
will is taken over by the soul, by the I, and aspects of will that
exist as instinct, drive and desire. Generally speaking, however,
we refer to instinct, drive and desire when influenced by the I
as "motive," so, when we speak of the will impulses in the soul
and in the I, we speak of motives and know that, although animals can have desires, they can have no motives.[12] In human
beings a desire first arises by being brought into the soul, creating a strong incentive to inwardly understand a motive. Only
in human beings do desires become motives of will. Human
beings have instincts, drives and desires in common with the
animal world, but only humans can raise these to a motive.
Thus we have what is present as will in modern human beings.
It quite clearly exists, and anyone who observes human beings
at all will say concerning the nature of human will, that to
understand someone is to know what motivates that person.
But not quite! Something quite subtle occurs when someone
develops motives, and we must carefully and with all acumen
take this subtlety into account.

You need to differentiate clearly what I mean by this
subtlety in the will impulse from what is more a thought. I do
not mean what is thought-like in the will impulse. You can,
for example, think, "What I wanted or did was good," or you
could have some other idea. I do not mean that. What I mean
is something that touches the will quite subtly. Even if we have
motives, there is something that still acts upon the will,
namely, the wish. I do not mean the strongly formed wishes
from which we form desires, but those subtle wishes that
accompany all of our motives. They are always present. We are
particularly aware of these wishes when we do something that

arises out of a motive in our will, and then think about it and say to ourselves, "What you have just done, you could have done much better." However, is there anything in life of which we could not say that we could have done it better? It would be sad if there were anything with which we could be completely satisfied, because there is nothing we could not do better. The difference between a person standing higher and one standing lower in life is precisely that the latter always desires to be satisfied with himself. The person standing higher in life is never completely satisfied because the subtle wish to do better, even to do things differently, always exists as a motive. This is an area that is often misunderstood. People see something great when they regret a deed. However, that is not the best we can do with a deed because we often base our regret in egotism; namely, people desire to have done the deed better to be better people. That is egotistical. Our striving will be without egotism only when we cease to desire to have done a completed deed better and instead place greater value in doing the same deed better the next time. The intent and the effort to do something better the next time is higher than regret. The wish echoes in this intent so that we may ask what it is that resounds as a wish. For those who can truly observe the soul, what resounds is the first intimation of everything that remains after death. What we feel is something of this remainder—namely, that we should have done better, that we wish we had done better.[13] This form of a wish as I have just described it belongs to Spirit Self.

A wish can become clearer and more concrete. It then becomes similar to intent. We can form a kind of idea of how we could do the deed better, should we need to do it again. However, I do not value such pictures very highly, but rather what lies in the realm of feeling and willing that accompanies every motive to do better the next time in a similar situation.

Here the so-called human subconscious comes strongly to the fore. In your normal consciousness you will not always be able to create a picture of how you could do a similar deed better the next time you act out of your will. The other person who lives in you, the second person, always develops a clear picture (not as an idea, but according to will) of how to carry out an action should you again be in the same situation. Do not underestimate this fact! Do not underestimate the second person who lives in you.

Today, there is much drivel about this second person by the so-called science that calls itself analytic psychology, or psychoanalysis.[14] Psychoanalysis introduces itself with some textbook example.[15] I have already mentioned this example; however, we would do well to recall it again. It is the following:

A man gives a party in his home, and he has planned that immediately after the party, his wife will leave for a resort. Numerous people attend the party, among them a particular woman. He gives the party and takes his wife to the train. The party guests, among them the woman, leave to go home. On their way, the guests with the woman are surprised by a carriage rounding the corner of a crossroads just as all the guests arrive there. What do the guests do? Everyone except the woman moves to the side of the road to allow the carriage to pass. She runs as fast as she can down the middle of the street in front of the horses. The carriage driver does not stop, and the other guests are very startled. However, the woman runs so quickly that the others cannot follow her, and she continues running until she comes to a bridge. It still does not occur to her to move to one side. She falls in the water, is rescued and brought back to the home of the host. She can now spend the night there.

You can find this event given as an example in many psycho-analysis textbooks. However, there is something in it that is widely misinterpreted. We must ask ourselves, "What is the basis of this whole episode?" The basis is the willing of the woman. What did she really want? She wanted to return to the host's home after his wife had left because she was in love with him. However, the desire was not a conscious one, but something lying in the subconscious. The subconscious second person living within someone is often more clever than the person. The subconscious was so clever in this particular case that the woman set up the whole process up to the moment she fell into the water in order to return to the host's home. She could even prophetically see that she would be saved. Psychoanalysis attempts to understand these hidden powers of the soul, but speaks only vaguely about a second person. However, we can know that what is active in the subconscious powers of the soul and often expressed very cleverly, in fact, more cleverly than the normal characteristics of the soul, exists in every person.

Deep in every person sits another person. In that other person a better person also lives, a person who always promises to do a completed deed better the next time. Thus, with each deed there is also a subtle and unconscious, a subconscious, intent to do the deed better in the next similar situation.

When we free the soul from the body, intent becomes decision. The intent lies like a seed in the soul; the decision comes later. Decision occurs in Spirit Human just as intent exists in Life Spirit and the pure wish in Spirit Self. If you look at the human as a willing being, you will find all of these elements: instinct, drive, desire and motive, and also, more subtly, what lives in Spirit Self, Life Spirit and Spirit Human as wish, intent and decision.

This has tremendous importance for human development. What lives quietly while preserving itself for the time after death is expressed pictorially by people between birth and death. We refer to it with the same words. In our thinking we also experience wish, intent and decision. However, we can experience wish, intent and decision in a way befitting us as human beings only when these things are properly developed in us. What wish, intent and decision really are in the depths of human nature are not outwardly expressed between birth and death. The pictures occur only in our thoughts. If you only develop the usual kind of consciousness you cannot at all know what a wish is. You have only thought about the wish. For this reason, Herbart believes that striving is already present in the idea of the wish. It is the same with intent; here also you have only the thought. You want to do such and such that is something real playing out in the depths of your soul, but you do not know the reason. Now we come to decision! Who knows anything about this? Psychology normally speaks only about some general desire. In spite of all this, the teacher must touch all three of these forces of the soul to regulate and order them. We must work with just what occurs in the depths of human nature when we wish to work in education.

Spirit Human	Decision
Life Spirit	Intent
Spirit Self	Wish
Consciousness Soul	
Comprehension Soul }	Motive
Sentient Soul	
Sentient/Astral Body	Desire
Ether Body	Drive
Physical Body	Instinct

It is particularly important that as teachers we are aware that it is insufficient to form education according to common practice; we must form education based upon a true understanding of the inner human being.

Popular socialism makes exactly this mistake, namely, of attempting to form education according to common practice. Think for a moment about how it would be if we based future education on the usual ideals of the Marxist socialists. This has already occurred in Russia, and because of that the Lunatcharski school reform is something terrible.[16] It is the death of all civilization! Though many horrible things result from Bolshevism, the worst of these will be the Bolshevik teaching method! If it were victorious, then it would destroy everything that has come into civilization from earlier times. This would not happen immediately with the first generation, but certainly with the coming generations, and thus, all civilization would soon disappear from the face of the Earth.[17] Some people must have already seen this. Recall that we now live under the dilettantish demands of moderate socialism. Socialism already tends toward this upside-down view. It mixes the good together with the bad. In this very room, you have already heard people singing the praises of Bolshevism who have absolutely no idea that, through Bolshevism, the devil rides straight into socialism.

We must be particularly careful here. We need people who know that social progress requires that teachers have an intimate understanding of the human being. We must know that future teachers need a deep inner comprehension of human nature, that they must live with an inner connection to human nature, and that, in teaching, they may not use the practices common among adults. What do most Marxists desire? They want to create socialist schools, they want to dismantle the principal's office without replacing it and they want to teach as many children as possible. Only something terrible can result!

I was once in a country boarding school and, wanting to observe the teaching of the most high-minded class, the religion class, I entered the classroom.[18] One rascal lay on the window sill, dangling his feet out the window; a second sat on the floor; a third lay somewhere on his stomach with his head raised. This is how the children were in the room. Then the so-called religion teacher came and with no particular introduction read a short story by Gottfried Keller. The children accompanied his reading with various noises and distractions. When he was finished, the religion class was over, and everyone went outside. During this experience a picture arose in me that next to this boarding school there was a large sheep pen, and that these children lived only a few steps away. We should not criticize such things too sharply. They arise out of much goodwill, but are a complete misunderstanding of what civilization needs for the future.

What do modern people want to achieve with the so-called socialist program? People want to deal with children the same way adults deal with one another. However, that is the worst thing we can do in education. We must be conscious that the child needs to develop quite different strengths in both body and soul than adults need to develop in their relations with one another. Education must work with what lies deep in the soul, otherwise we will not progress. We must, therefore, ask how education affects the nature of human will. We must seriously address this question.

If you recall what I said yesterday, you will remember that I mentioned that all intellectual things are will grown old.[19] They are the will in old age. Thus, all normal, rationally motivated instruction, all normal reprimands and all concepts used in teaching have absolutely no effect upon the school-age child. In short, we may say that feeling is developing, that is, not yet existent, will. However, the whole person lives in the will, so that we must take into account the child's unconscious decisions. We must guard against the belief that all those things we believe we have thought out well have any influence upon the child's will. We must ask ourselves how we can influence the child's feeling in a good way. We can do that only when we have repetitive activity. You cannot have the proper effect upon the child's will when you tell the child just once what is right, but only when you allow the child to do something today, tomorrow and the next day. The proper action does not at all lie in reprimanding the child or giving the child rules of morality, but in guiding the child to something that you believe will awaken a feeling for what is right and allowing the child to repeat this. You must raise such deeds to habit. The more things remain as unconscious habit, the better it is for the development of feeling. The more the child becomes aware of the need to do deeds out of devotion to repetition, because they should and must be done, the more you elevate these to true will impulses. Thus, unconscious repetition cultivates feeling; fully conscious repetition cultivates the will impulse because through it the power of decision increases. Having the child consciously repeat things spurs on the power to decide that would otherwise remain only in the subconscious. In connection with cultivating the will, we may not take into account what is particularly important in intellectual life. In intellectual life we tend to emphasize that the better the child understands something, the better our teaching is. We lay particular value upon immediate understanding, upon immediate retention. However, what the child immediately understands and retains does not act upon the feeling and will. Only what the child does repeatedly and sees as the proper thing to do under the given circumstances acts upon feeling and will.

Earlier, more patriarchal education used this fact. Things became simply a matter of habit. In all such things done in this manner lies something quite good pedagogically. For instance, why did people say the Lord's Prayer every day? Were people today asked to read the same story every day, they would refuse because it would be much too boring. Modern people have been trained for one-time experiences. Earlier people not only prayed the same prayer every day, but they also had a storybook that they read at least once every week. Thus, they also had much stronger wills than those people who undergo modern education. Cultivation of the will is based in unconscious and conscious repetition. We must take that into account. It is insufficient to say abstractly that we should cultivate the will. When that occurs, people may believe that if they have a good idea about developing the will and, through some subtle method, bring this idea to the child, they have done something to develop the child's will. In reality, this is useless. The only result is weak and nervous people in continual need of reprimands. People will have inner strength when we, for example, tell the children to do this and that today and tomorrow and the next day. They will do it out of respect for authority, because they know that in school someone must command. Thus, to give each child some task to do every day, possibly for the whole school year, is something that strongly acts to develop the will. It creates contact between the children, strengthens the authority of the teacher and brings the children to a repetitive activity that strongly affects the will.

Why do artistic activities affect the formation of the will particularly strongly? Because first, practice is based upon repetition, and second, what people receive through artistic activity always gives them joy. People enjoy art again and again, not just the first time. Art has a quality that can excite people not just once, but can time and again directly give them joy. For this reason, we directly connect the artistic element with what we want to achieve in teaching. I want to speak more about that tomorrow. Today, I wanted to show how we must form the will quite differently than we develop the intellect.

5

STUTTGART / AUGUST 26, 1919

Yesterday we spoke about how the will is integrated into the human organism. We now want to use what we have learned about the relationship of will to the human being to obtain a view of the rest of human nature.

You will have noticed that until now my discussions of the human being have been mainly concerned with intellectual and cognitive activities on the one hand and with the activity of the will on the other. I have shown how thinking relates to the human nervous system and how strength of will relates to the activity of the blood. When you think about what we have already discussed, you may ask yourself what the situation is with the third capacity of the soul, with the activity of feeling. We have not yet taken this into account. However, as we focus today more upon the activity of feeling, we will be able to penetrate the other two sides of human nature, the cognition and the will, more intensely.

Nevertheless, we must be clear about one thing that I have also mentioned in various other connections, namely that we cannot pedantically separate the capacities of the soul—thinking, feeling, willing—because in the living soul one activity always involves others.

Let us first look at the will. You will surely be aware that you cannot want something that you have not yet penetrated through thinking, that is, through a cognitive activity. Attempt to concentrate, if only superficially, upon your willing. You will find that in the act of willing there is always some kind of thinking. If thinking were omitted from a deed of will, you would not even be human. If you did not integrate the deeds that well forth out of your will with thinking, you would just do every willed deed dumbly and instinctively.

In the same way that all willing contains thinking, all thinking contains the will. Even a superficial observation of yourself will reveal that when you think, you always allow the will to flow into the formation of thoughts. A subtle will activity permeates how you form thoughts, how you connect thoughts with one another and how you proceed to judgment and decision.

We can only say that willing is mainly will activity and contains an undercurrent of thinking; thinking is mainly thought activity and has an undercurrent of will. Thus, it is not possible to pedantically segregate individual soul activities for observation because one flows into the other.

What you can recognize as the soul, the intertwining of soul activities, you see expressed in the body that reveals the soul activity. Take the human eye, for example. When we observe it in its totality, the nerves continue into the eye. However, the same is true of the blood vessels. In that the nerves continue into the eye, thinking and cognitive activity flow into the eye, and where the blood vessels continue into the eye, the activity of the will also flows into it. In this way, will and cognition are connected even to the periphery of the body's sense activities. The cognitive element enters our will and movements through the nerve pathways, and the will element enters through the blood vessels. This is true for all the senses, as well as for all limbs that serve the will.

Now we must also learn about the particularities of cognitive activity. I have already mentioned them, but we need to be fully aware of everything that lies in the direction of cognition and thinking throughout the whole complex of human activity. I have already said that antipathy lives in cognition and thinking. As strange as it may seem, antipathy permeates everything that tends toward thinking. You might say, "When I look at something, I am certainly not being antipathetic!" Nevertheless, you are. You exercise antipathy when you look at an object. If there were only nerve activity in your eye, then every object you look at would be repulsive and antipathetic to you. The feeling of antipathy in seeing is quelled in your consciousness since will activity, sympathy, enters into every activity of the eye because the blood vessels stretch into your physical eye. Through a balance between sympathy and antipathy, an objective act of seeing occurs. It occurs because sympathy and antipathy come into balance, but we are not at all conscious of this interplay.

If, as I have already mentioned in this connection, you study Goethe's *Theory of Color*, namely, the physiological-didactic portion, then you will see that since Goethe encompasses the deeper aspect of sight, he can observe sympathy and antipathy in the nuances of color.[1] You need only penetrate the activity of a sense organ a little to immediately see how sympathy and antipathy arise in sensing. Antipathy originates in the cognitive aspect, in the conceptual aspect, in the nerves; sympathy originates in the will aspect, in the blood.[2]

In my general anthroposophical lectures, I have often emphasized the important difference between the eyes of animals and the eyes of human beings. Animals characteristically have more blood activity in the eye than does the human being. In some animals you will even find organs that serve this activity of the blood such as the falciform process and the pleated pecten.[3] From that you can see that animals have more blood activity in the eye than human beings. This is also true for the other sense organs, which means that in their senses, animals develop much more sympathy, instinctive sympathy, with their surroundings than human beings do. In reality, human beings, although they are normally not conscious of it, have more antipathy with their surroundings than animals do. People become conscious of this antipathy only when they react with disgust to an intensified impression of their surroundings. When people are disgusted by their perceptions, their disgust is only an intensification of normal sense perception. If you go somewhere that smells bad, and the bad smell disgusts you, your feeling of disgust is nothing other than an increase of what occurs in all sensing, only the disgust that accompanies perception normally remains subconscious. If we human beings had no more antipathy to our surroundings than animals do, then we would not separate ourselves so strongly from our surroundings as we, in fact, do. Animals have much more sympathy with their surroundings and are more integrated into them and therefore are more dependent upon climate and season and so forth than human beings. People have a personality because they have more antipathy toward their surroundings. That we can separate ourselves from our surroundings through unconscious antipathy gives us an awareness of our individual personality.

Here we have an indication of something important in comprehending the human being. We have seen how thinking and willing or, expressed physically, the activity of the nerves and the blood, flow together in cognitive or reflective activity.

In the same way, thinking and willing come together in the active will. Whenever we want something we always develop sympathy with what is wanted. However, it would always remain an instinctive desire if we could not bring into this sympathy the antipathy that provides a separation between the personality and what is wanted. The problem is that the sympathy with what is wanted dominates, and we can create balance only when we bring in antipathy. Nevertheless, sympathy remains unconscious, and only a little of it penetrates what is wanted. For those few things into which we bring real enthusiasm, devotion, and love, and not simply rationality, sympathy dominates so strongly in willing that it rises into our consciousness, saturating our will with sympathy; otherwise the will remains as an objective connection with our surroundings.[4] Just as our antipathy to our surroundings can become conscious only in exceptional cases of cognition, our always present sympathy to our surroundings can become conscious only in exceptional cases, in cases of enthusiasm and devotion. Otherwise, we would always do everything instinctively. We would never be able to relate to what the world objectively demands of us, say in social life. We must penetrate what is wanted with thinking so that what is wanted integrates us into the human totality and cosmic process.[5]

If you consider what normal life would be like if the whole process I have just described were conscious, you can perhaps clearly see what would occur, what confusion would result in the human soul. If this process in the human soul were always conscious in normal life, then we would generally be conscious of the antipathy that accompanies all our deeds. That would be terrible! People would go through the world always feeling themselves to be in an atmosphere of antipathy. The world has been wisely created such that, even though antipathy is necessary as a force in our deeds, we are not conscious of it, and it remains subconsciousness.

We are now looking at a curious mystery of human nature, a mystery that every decent person feels, but one of which the teacher should be fully conscious. As children, we act almost exclusively from sympathy. As strange as it may sound, everything that children do, they do out of sympathy toward the

child does out of love + sympathy

deed. When sympathy is born into the world it is strong love and willing. However, it cannot remain so; we must permeate it with thinking and in a sense continuously illuminate it with thinking. This occurs comprehensively when we integrate moral ideals into our simple instincts. Now you may be better able to comprehend what antipathy means in this area. If the instinctive impulses[6] that we find in small children were to remain only sympathetic throughout life, we would develop only animalistically under the influence of instincts. We must become antipathetic to these instincts; that is, we must pour antipathy into them. When we pour antipathy into them through our moral ideals, which are antipathetic to instincts, then we put antipathy into childlike sympathy or instincts, into our life between birth and death. Thus, moral development is always something ascetic, only we must understand this asceticism in the proper sense. We always practice it in combating animalism.

From what I have just said, we should learn not only to what high degree willing is willing in the practical activities of human beings, but also to what extent thinking and cognitive activity thoroughly permeate willing.

Human feeling stands right in the middle between thinking cognition and willing. If you imagine willing and thinking as I have just developed them, then you will see that everything that is sympathy, namely willing, flows to one side from a point in the middle. You will also see that everything that is antipathy, or thinking, flows to the other side. However, the sympathy of willing interacts with thinking and the antipathy of thinking interacts with willing. Thus, humans become complete when something developed primarily in one direction also interacts with what develops in the other direction. Feeling lies in the middle between thinking and willing, so that feeling connects with thinking in one direction, and willing in the other. Just as you cannot easily separate thinking and willing within the human soul, you can even less easily separate the aspects of thinking and willing in feeling. The aspects of thinking and willing are very closely interconnected with feeling.

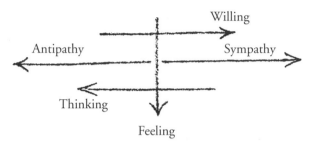

Simple self-observation, even if superficial, can convince you of the correctness of what I have just said. What I have already said will lead to your seeing this correctness since normally we raise objective willing to activity by enthusiasm or love. Here you can see clearly how willing required by the external circumstances of life is filled with feeling. If you do something out of enthusiasm or love, you act by allowing the will to be permeated with subjective feeling. When you look more closely, for instance in Goethe's color theory, you will see how feeling mixes into sensing. When sensing increases to disgust, or, on the other hand, to the pleasant feeling of inhaling the scent of a flower, you can clearly see how feeling enters into sensing.

However, feeling also enters into thinking. At one time there was a remarkable philosophical debate in Heidelberg between the psychologist Franz Brentano[7] and the logician Sigwart.[8] These two men argued about the nature of human judgment. Sigwart thought that when people made a judgment, for instance, "Human beings should be good," such a judgment always contained feeling; in other words, feeling made the decision. Brentano thought that judgment and feeling, that is, emotion, were so different that we could not even comprehend judging if feeling played a role. He thought that subjectivity would then enter into judgment, whereas our judgments want objectivity.

Such arguments only show that neither psychologists nor logicians have correctly identified the central fact, namely, the interaction of soul activities. Recall what must be considered here. On the one hand, we have the capacity of judgment that, of course, must decide about something objective. Whether or not people must be good cannot depend upon our subjective feelings, and thus the content of the judgment must be objective. However, we must also consider something quite different when we judge. Things that are objectively correct are for that very reason not conscious in our souls. We must first receive them consciously into our souls. But, we cannot have any conscious judgment in our souls without interacting with feeling. Thus, Brentano and Sigwart could have agreed with each other if they had both said that the objective content of a judgment lies outside feeling. However, for the subjective human soul to be convinced of the correctness of a judgment, feeling must develop.

You can see how difficult it is to arrive at any exact concepts with the inexact philosophical methods currently in use. To arrive at exact concepts, we must first develop ourselves. Today, however, only spiritual science provides the schooling needed to reach exact concepts. Conventional science thinks that it has exact concepts and mocks what anthroposophy gives. Science has no idea that the concepts derived from anthroposophy are more exact than those in normal usage because they derive from reality and not from simple word play.

When you follow feeling toward thinking and, in the other direction, toward will, you will realize that feeling stands between cognition and willing in the center of soul activity and radiates its essence in both directions. At the same time, feeling is incomplete cognition and incomplete will; it is restrained cognition and restrained will. Thus, feeling is composed of the sympathy and the antipathy that are, as you have seen, hidden in both cognition and willing. Both sympathy and antipathy are present, but hidden in cognition and willing because they interact in the bodily activities of the nerves and blood. In feeling, they are evident.

What then are the physical expressions of feeling? Everywhere in the human body you will find that the blood vessels and the nerve paths touch each other in various ways. Everywhere blood vessels and nerve paths touch, real feeling is created. However, in the senses, for example, the nerves and blood are so subtle that we no longer notice the feeling. Subtle feeling permeates our seeing and hearing, but we do not perceive it. The more separate the sense organ is from the remainder of the body, the less we can perceive the feeling. In seeing, we hardly notice the sympathizing and antipathizing because the eye is imbedded in a bony socket that is almost completely separated from the remainder of the body. Also, the nerves and blood vessels going into the eye are extremely fine. The sensation of feeling in the eye is extremely suppressed. In hearing, feeling is much less suppressed. Hearing is much more closely integrated into the overall activity of the body than is seeing. Since the structures of the numerous organs in the ear are quite different from the structures of the organs of the eye, the ear is, in many respects, a much truer reflection of what occurs in the entire body. Thus, what occurs as sensing in the ear is more strongly accompanied by feeling. Even people who have very acute hearing will have difficulty being clear about what in hearing, particularly artistic hearing, is simply cognition and what is feeling. This touches upon something interesting that plays a direct role in modern artistic productions.

You certainly all know the figure Beckmesser in Richard Wagner's *Meistersinger*.[9] What is Beckmesser really supposed to represent? He represents someone who understands music, but who completely forgets that human feeling interacts with rational hearing. Wagner, who presented his own opinion in the role of Walter, was, on the other hand, one-sidedly convinced that feeling is mainly what lives in music. In contrast to the correct view of the interaction of feeling and cognition in musical hearing, the misunderstandings represented by Walter and Beckmesser were expressed in a historical event. As Wagner's opera became well known, an opponent of his view was found in the person of Eduard Hanslick in Vienna.[10] Hanslick regarded everything expressed from the realm of feeling in Wagner's music as unmusical. Perhaps no more psychologically interesting writings about art exist than *Vom Musikalisch-Schönen* [Concerning what is musically beautiful] by Eduard Hanslick. The main theme of this book is that those who emphasize feeling in music are not real musicians and have no true sense of music. True musicians are only those who see the objective connecting of tone to tone as the true center of music, the arabesque devoid of feeling, joining only tone upon tone. With wonderful purity, Hanslick insists that the highest in music occurs only in tone pictures, and he mocks everything connected with Wagner's central view, namely, the creation of music from feeling. That such an argument between Hanslick and Wagner could even occur in the field of music shows that modern psychological ideas about soul activity were completely unclear; otherwise, a one-sided tendency like Hanslick's could not arise. However, if we can see through the one-sidedness and focus upon the philosophical strength of Hanslick's discussions, then we might say that this book is quite insightful.

Thus you can see that, to a greater or lesser extent, the senses cognitively permeate the periphery of the whole human being who now lives as a being of feeling.

This will and must make you take notice of a pedagogical insight that has caused great confusion in modern scientific thought. If we had not spoken here in preparation for what shall guide you into a reforming activity, then you would have had to assemble all the present pedagogies, psychologies and logics, as well as teaching methods, and take from them what you wish to practice in your teaching. You would have had to bring into your teaching what has become common. However, what is common today suffers from a great psychological error. In every psychology you will find a so-called sensory theory. When people investigate the basis of sense activity, they derive how the eyes, the ears, the nose and so forth sense. They then bring all this together in the major abstraction "sensory activity." This is a great mistake, an enormous error. If you take only the senses known to today's physiologists or psychologists, if you look only at the physical body, you observe that the nature of the sense of vision is something quite different from that of the sense of hearing. The eye and the ear have two very different natures. Then we have the sense of touch, which has barely been researched, not even in an unsatisfactory manner as is the case with the eye and the ear! However, let us remain with the eye and the ear. Seeing and hearing are so different that to combine these two activities into a "general sensory activity" results in nebulous theory. If we wanted to be really accurate, we would have to speak only of the activity of the eye or of the ear, or of the organs of smell and so forth. In them, we would find such great differences that we would soon lose all desire to create a general sensory physiology in the way done by modern psychologists.

We can have insight into the human soul only when we remain in the area I attempted to delineate in my discussions in *Truth and Science* and in *Intuitive Thinking as a Spiritual Path: A Philosophy of Freedom*. Then, we can speak of a unified soul without falling into abstractions. Then, we stand on firm ground because we assume that the human being lives into the world and is not the totality of reality. The human being does not have the totality of reality from the beginning. The human being continues to develop, and in this further development, what previously was not reality becomes, through the interaction of thinking and perceiving, true reality. The human being must "conquer" reality. In this regard, the Kantianism that has eaten into everything has created terrible confusion. What does Kantianism do? From the beginning it dogmatically states that we are to look at the world surrounding us, but that only the reflection of this world lives in us. Kant derives all his other deductions from this. He is not at all clear about what exists in the perceptible human surroundings.[11] Reality is not in the surroundings, nor in appearance, but first arises through our "conquering" reality, so the last thing we arrive at is reality. In principle, true reality is what human beings see at the moment they can no longer speak, namely, in that moment when they go through the gates of death.

Many false assumptions have entered modern culture, and these act most disastrously in education. We must strive to replace false concepts with correct ones. We will then be able to correctly carry out what we must do in teaching.

6

Until now, we have attempted to comprehend the human being from the perspective of the soul to the extent necessary for educating children. To have a complete picture, we will need to keep the spiritual, soul and physical aspects separate, and consider the human being from each of these points of view. We will first complete our consideration of the soul, since the soul lies closest to normal life. You will have noticed that we have already focused on the soul by using antipathy and sympathy as the main concepts for understanding the human being. It would not be appropriate to go directly from a consideration of the soul to a consideration of the physical body, since we know from spiritual scientific contemplation that we can understand the physical body only when it is approached as a revelation of the spirit and soul. Thus, to our general picture of the soul, we will now add a consideration of the human being from the perspective of the spirit. Only later will we discuss human nature in the way done by anthropology, namely, how the human being appears in the physical world.

Whenever you want to suitably consider the human being from any particular standpoint, you must always return to the three parts of the human soul—that is, to cognition that occurs in thinking, to feeling, and to willing. Until now, we have brought thinking or cognition, feeling and willing into relationship with antipathy and sympathy. We now wish to consider willing, feeling and cognition from the perspective of the spirit.

From the spiritual point of view, you will also find a difference between willing, feeling and thinking cognition. Consider the following: When you perceive cognitively, you must feel (I wish to express myself pictorially here because a picture will help us understand) that, in a sense, you live in light. You recognize and experience that your I is completely immersed in cognitive activity. In a sense, all the activity you call cognition is in everything your I does. At the same time, what your I does is contained in cognitive activity. You are completely in the light and live in fully conscious activity. It would be horrible if you were not fully conscious in your cognition. Think about how it would be if you felt that when you are making a decision, something unconscious happens to your I, and the result of this process is your decision! Suppose you would make a judgment, for example, "That person is a good person." You should be aware that what you need to be able to make this judgment—the subject "person" and the predicate "is a good" —is part of a process that for you is very present and is completely permeated by the light of consciousness. If you had to assume that while you were making the judgment, some demon or a natural cause tossed "person" together with "being good," then you would not be completely conscious in this thought, and your judgments would always contain something unconscious. The important point in thinking cognition is that you are completely conscious in the whole web of cognitive activity.

This is not true with willing. You know quite well that when you develop the simplest form of willing, for instance, walking, you live with full consciousness only in the idea of walking. You know nothing of what occurs with your muscles as you move one leg in front of the other or of what occurs in the mechanism and organism of your body. Imagine all you would need to learn about the world if you wanted to go consciously through the process necessary in willing to walk. You would have to know exactly what nutrients your leg muscles and other parts of your body require when you walk. You have never calculated how much nutrition you need, but you know quite well that all this occurs very unconsciously in your body. When we will, we always mix something unconscious into our activity. However, the situation is not quite the same when we consider the nature of willing within our organism. Also, we do not completely comprehend with the light of consciousness what we do when we extend our willing to the external world.

Suppose you have two vertical blocks and you decide to lay a third block across them. You need to differentiate precisely what lives in everything that you do in a fully conscious cognitive activity from what lives in your fully conscious activity when you make the judgment that someone is good, where your cognition is fully included.

You need to differentiate what lives as cognitive activity from what you know nothing about even though you do it with your full will. Why do the two columns support the beam lying upon them? Modern physics has only hypotheses about this.

When people believe they know why the two columns support the beam, they are only fooling themselves. Everything people have created as concepts of cohesion, adhesion, the force of gravity and so forth are, in principle, only hypotheses for external knowledge. We count upon these hypotheses when we act. We count upon the fact that the two columns that are to carry the beam will not crumple if they have a certain thickness. Nevertheless, we can as little penetrate this entire event as we can penetrate the movement of our legs when we want to move forward. An element that does not reach our consciousness is mingled with our willing. In its broadest sense, willing has an element of unconsciousness in it.

Feeling stands midway between willing and thinking. Feeling is permeated partially by consciousness and partially by unconsciousness. In this way, feeling partakes of the characteristics of cognitive thinking and of felt willing. What do we actually have before us from the spiritual point of view?

You can come to grips with this from the perspective of the spirit only if you comprehend the facts I have just described in the following way. In normal life we speak of a wakeful, conscious state. However, this state of consciousness exists only in the activity of cognitive thinking. If you wish to speak precisely about the extent to which people are awake, you must say that people are awake only when and if they perceive something through cognitive thinking.

Now, how is it with willing? You all know the state of consciousness of sleep (you may also call it the state of unconsciousness). You know that we are not conscious of our experiences during sleep. It is the same with everything that enters our willing. As people, if we are willing beings, we sleep even when we are awake. We always have within us a sleeping person, namely, the willing person, and accompany that person with the wakeful, the thinking cognitive person; when we are willing beings, we also sleep from the moment of waking until going to sleep. There is always something sleeping in us, namely, the inner essence of willing. We are no more conscious of this than of the processes that occur during sleep. We cannot completely comprehend the human being if we do not know that sleep plays into wakefulness when the human being is a being of will.

Feeling exists in the middle, so we may now ask, "How conscious is feeling?" Feeling is midway between waking and sleeping. You experience feelings in your soul in the same way that you experience dreams, except that you remember dreams and you directly experience feelings. However, the inner mood of soul you have and know through your feelings is the same as the one you have through your dreams. When you are awake, you not only are awake when you are thinking and asleep when you are willing, you also dream when you are feeling. There are, in fact, three states of consciousness during the time we are awake—that is, waking in cognitive thinking, dreaming in feeling and sleeping in willing. Normal dreamless sleep is, from the perspective of the spirit, nothing other than the complete devotion of the human soul to what it is devoted to in daytime willing.[1] The only difference is that in actual sleep, we sleep with our entire soul, and in waking we sleep only with our willing. Concerning what we normally call dreaming, during sleep we are devoted with our entire soul to what we call a dream; while awake we are devoted to this dreamy state of soul only as feeling human beings.

If you consider this pedagogically, the fact that children are different regarding the wakefulness of their consciousness will not surprise you. You will find that children who tend toward an excessive feeling life are dreamy children, so that children whose thinking is not yet fully awake become easily devoted to dreaming. You can be effective with such children through strong feelings. You can hope that these strong feelings will awaken the light of cognition in these children, since sleeping has a rhythm that tends to awaken after some time. If we approach a child who dreamily broods in his or her feeling with strong feelings, then the strong feelings we implant in that child will themselves awaken as thoughts after a time.

Children who brood even more, who may even be numb to the life of feeling, have a tendency to be particularly strong willed. If you consider this, you will see that you can unravel many puzzles in children's lives. You may have a child in class who appears to be completely stupid. You might judge that child as mentally retarded or slow. You might examine him or her psychologically, using memory tests and other such things done by educational psychologists. Then you might say that the child is retarded or slow and belongs in a school for mentally retarded children, or, what is now popularly called a school for the developmentally disabled. Were you to make such a judgment, you would not come close to the nature of the child. Perhaps that child tends to be particularly strong in the will. Perhaps he or she is one of those children who later in life, out of choleric temperament, become especially active. But for now the will is sleeping. If the thinking cognition of those children is destined to awaken only later, then the teacher must handle them in an appropriate manner so that later in life they can be called to significant activity. At first, such children appear to be quite dumb, but may not be. You must have an eye for such children to awaken their will. That is, you must act upon their drowsiness so that, by and by, later in life they can awaken their sleeping will since all sleep has the tendency to awaken. Their will may be very strong, but now it only sleeps and is concealed by this sleeping. You must handle such children so that you count upon their capacity to understand and comprehend as little as possible. You must use things that in a sense hammer strongly upon the will of those children, for instance, when they are speaking, you also have them walk. Take such children (you will not have many of them) out of the class and, while they are speaking, have them walk. For other children, this would be exciting, but for those children it is developmental. For instance, "the" (step) "man" (step) "is" (step) "good" (step). In this way, you connect the entire will with what is purely intellectual thinking, and slowly you will succeed in awakening the will to think in such children. Only the insight that in the waking human there are different states of consciousness, waking, dreaming and sleeping can bring us to a true understanding of our task regarding the developing human being.

We can now ask something else: What is the relationship of the actual center of the human being, the I, to these different states? You will most easily comprehend this if you assume something that is undeniable, namely, that what we call the world or the cosmos consists of activities. For us as human beings, these activities are expressed in various ways throughout life. We know that forces are at work in life. For example, life energy is active all around us. Interwoven between the basic forces and life energy is everything that acts, for example, as heat and fire. Just think to what extent we exist in an environment where fire affects so much.

In certain parts of the Earth, for example in southern Italy, you need only ignite a piece of paper, and at the same moment a great deal of smoke begins to come out of the ground.[2] Why is this? This happens because when you ignite a piece of paper, the resulting heat thins the surrounding air and the rising smoke draws up the forces that are otherwise under the Earth's surface. By the time you drop the burning paper onto the ground, you stand in a cloud of smoke. This is an experiment any tourist in Naples can conduct. I give this as an example of why, if we do not consider the world superficially, we must admit that we live in an environment everywhere permeated by forces.

There are also forces higher than heat that exist in our surroundings. We are always moving through them as we go through the physical world. Although we are normally unaware of it, our physical body is so constituted that we can do this. In this way, we walk through the world with our physical body.

We could not move through those forces with our I, the most recent development in our evolution, if our I needed to focus on them. The I cannot concentrate on everything in its environment. The I must still be protected from entering into all world forces. Someday it will develop sufficiently to be able to integrate into those world forces, but it cannot do so yet. Because the I is completely awake, it is essential that we are not placed in the real world, that is, our surroundings, but only in a picture of the world. In our thinking cognition we therefore have only the pictures of the world we already discussed from the perspective of the soul.

Let us now consider this from the perspective of the spirit. In thinking cognition we live in pictures. At the present stage of human development, between birth and death we can live with our completely awake I only in pictures of the cosmos, not yet in the real cosmos. Thus, when awake, our body must first present us the pictures of the cosmos, and then our I lives in these pictures.

Psychologists give considerable effort to determining the relationship between body and soul. They speak of an interaction between body and soul, of psycho-physical parallelism and other such things. In principle, all these things are just childish concepts. The true process is that in the morning when the I enters the waking state, it enters the body, not the physical processes of the body, but the world of pictures created at the innermost level of the body by external processes. In this manner the I is given thinking cognition.

It is different with feeling. Here, the I permeates the real physical body, not just pictures. If, in this permeation, the I were completely conscious, then it would (understand this from the point of view of the soul) literally burn up. If the same thing happened with feeling that happens with thinking, when you permeate the pictures created by your body with your I, then your soul would burn up. You could not bear it. You can only experience the permeation of feeling in a dreamy, reduced state of consciousness. Only in dreams can you endure what actually occurs in your body as feeling.

You can endure what occurs as willing only when you sleep. If you had to experience everything that occurs when you will in normal life, your experience would be horrible. You would be gripped by terrible pain if, for example, you really had to experience how the strength brought to your organism by food was used by your legs to walk. You are lucky you do not experience that, or rather, that you experience it only in sleep. To experience it wakefully would mean the worst pain thinkable, a terrible pain. We might even say that were we to become awake in willing, the pain that is otherwise latent and numbed by the sleepiness of the will would be conscious.[3]

Now you can understand my description of the life of the I during the time we normally call being awake, which includes fully awake, dreamily awake and sleepily awake, that is, my description of what the I as it lives in the body in its normal state of wakefulness actually experiences. The I lives in thinking cognition when it is awake in the body; there it is completely awake. However, it lives there only in pictures so that human beings, if they do not do the exercises in my book *How to Know Higher Worlds,* live between birth and death only in pictures through their thinking cognition.

Then the I enters partially awake into the processes that cause feeling. In feeling, we are not fully awake, only dreamily awake. How do we experience what we go through in feeling in this dreamy state of wakefulness? We experience it in what has always been called inspiration, inspired imagination, unconscious inspired imagination. It is the source of everything that rises to wakeful consciousness from the artist's feelings. Only there is it experienced. There, everything that often rises as a sudden inspiration into wakeful human consciousness and then becomes pictures is experienced. In my book *How to Know Higher Worlds*, what I call Inspiration is only the unconscious inspiration of feeling that everyone has, raised to the light of fully conscious experience.

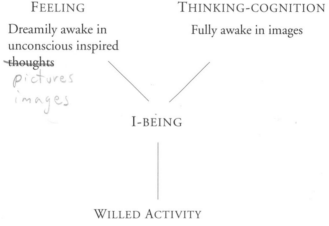

FEELING   THINKING-COGNITION

Dreamily awake in   Fully awake in images
unconscious inspired
thoughts

I-BEING

WILLED ACTIVITY

Sleepily unconscious in intuitions

When people with particular abilities speak of their inspirations, what they actually speak of is what the world lays into their feeling and what, due to their personal capacities, they allow to rise into their fully awake consciousness. It is just as much a part of reality as the content of thoughts. However, between birth and death, these unconscious inspirations reflect those cosmic processes that we can only experience dreamily, lest our I burn up or suffocate in them. Such suffocation often begins with people in abnormal states. Remember what happens when you have a nightmare.[4] Then there is an attempt to change the relationship between you and the air into an abnormal one, similar to what exists when this relationship is not healthy. Since this change wants to enter into your I consciousness, you will not be conscious of it as something normal, but rather as something tormenting you, namely, as a nightmare. All breathing, every breath, would be just as tormenting as the abnormal breathing of a nightmare if you had to experience it with full consciousness. You would experience it in your feeling, but it would be very painful for you. For this reason, it is numbed, and thus we do not experience it as a physical process, but only as a dreamlike feeling.

The processes that play out in willing would be terribly painful! Therefore, we may say, as a third thing, that the I sleeps in willed activity. What we experience, we experience only in sharply reduced consciousness, in sleeping consciousness, in unconscious intuition. People continually have unconscious intuitions, but these live in willing. People sleep in their willing and are therefore unable to bring it up into normal life. Unconscious intuitions come into life only under the most favorable circumstances, and then people dully experience the spiritual world.

There is something peculiar in normal human life. We all know the complete consciousness in the wakefulness of thinking cognition. There we are, so to speak, in the light of consciousness; we all experience it. Often when people begin to think about the world, they say that they have intuitions. Undefinable feelings come from these intuitions. What people say can often be very confusing, or it can be ordered unconsciously. When a poet speaks of intuitions, it is quite proper that they are not derived from the source lying closest at hand, namely from the inspiration of the feeling life, but rather that they are brought from the unconscious intuitions arising in the region of the sleeping will.

Those who have insight into these things can see the underlying principles in even the most superficial coincidences in life. You may, for example, read the second part of Goethe's *Faust* and want to thoroughly understand how the unusual construction of these verses came about. Goethe was quite old at the time when he wrote the second part of *Faust*, at least most of it. He wrote it by dictating to his secretary, John. Had Goethe actually written, he would probably not have created such curiously devised verses. While he dictated, Goethe continuously paced up and down in his small study in Weimar, and this pacing back and forth is part of the conception of the second part of *Faust*. In that Goethe developed an unconscious willing deed in his pacing, something arose out of his intuition, and what he had someone else write down on paper was visible in his external activity.

Say that you wanted to make a table of the life of the I in the body, and you made it in the following manner:

> I. Waking   —   Pictorial Cognition
>
> II. Dreaming —   Inspired Feeling
>
> III. Sleeping   —   Intuitive Willing

Then you would not be able to understand why the intuition people instinctively speak of arises more easily in the pictorial recognition of everyday life than in inspired feeling, which is closer. However, if you correctly draw this (the table above is incorrect), if you draw it in the following way, then you will more easily understand these things.

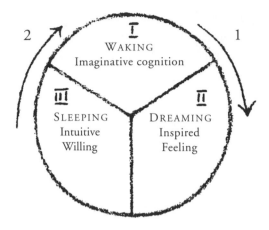

You would then realize that pictorial cognition enters inspirations in the direction of Arrow 1, and arises again from intuition (Arrow 2). However, the cognition indicated by Arrow 1 is the entering into the body. Now observe yourselves: right now you are sitting or standing quietly and are involved in thoughtful cognition and observation of the outer world. You are living in pictures. What the I otherwise experiences in world processes enters the body first through feeling, then through willing. You pay no attention to what is in feeling nor, at first, to what is in willing. Only when you begin to walk, when you begin to act, do you first become aware of willing, not feeling. In the process of entering into the body and then again of rising in the direction indicated by Arrow 2, intuitive willing comes closer to pictorial consciousness than does dreamy inspired feeling. Thus, you will find that people often say that they have a vague feeling. What I have described in my book *How to Know Higher Worlds* as Intuition is then confused with the superficial intuition of normal consciousness.

Now you can understand the form of the human body. For a moment, think of yourself walking and observing the world. Imagine that it is not your lower body that walks, but that your head has legs and could walk. Then, your observation of the world and your will would be completely intertwined, resulting in your being able to walk only when asleep. However, because your head sits upon your shoulders and upon the remainder of your body, it rests upon the body. It rests, and you carry your head because you move only the remainder of your body. However, the head must be able to rest upon the body, otherwise it could not be the organ of thinking cognition. The sleeping will must be removed from it because, if you could set it into motion, removing it from its relatively motionless state and giving it its own movement, then the head would sleep. The head allows the body to accomplish actual willing and lives in this body as in a carriage, allowing itself to be moved about in this manner. It is possible for human beings to be wakefully active only because the head allows itself to be moved about by the body as if in a carriage and during this movement the resting head is at the same time active. You can truly grasp the form of the human body only if you comprehend things this way.

Love of heart reach out to love of soul
Love warmth ray out to spirit-light
So we would draw near to you
Thinking with you thoughts of spirits
Feeling in you love of worlds
Spiritually willing by you
Live to be one being weaving

(only verbs)
So spiritual being can hear you

7

It is important for you to have insight into what the essence of the human being actually is. In our survey of general pedagogy, we have attempted to understand the human being, first from the point of view of the soul and then from the standpoint of the spirit. Today, we want to continue the latter. Of course, we will have to continually refer to pedagogical concepts, and to commonplace modern ideas about the soul and psychology since you will later want to study pedagogical and psychological literature.

When we look at the human being from the perspective of the soul, our emphasis is on discovering the role of antipathies and sympathies. However, when we look at the human being from the spiritual standpoint, we must focus upon discovering states of consciousness. Yesterday, we discussed the three states of consciousness active within the human being, waking, dreaming, and sleeping, and we showed that waking is really present only in thinking cognition, while dreaming prevails in feeling and sleep in willing.

All comprehension is only the act of relating one thing to another. In the world, we cannot comprehend other than by relating one thing to another. That is the method. When we cognitively relate ourselves to the world, we first observe.

Either we observe with our senses, as we normally do, or we develop ourselves further and observe with the soul and the spirit, as we do with Imagination, Inspiration and Intuition. However, spiritual observation is still only observation, and we must complete it through comprehension. We can understand only when we relate one thing to another in our surroundings and in the cosmos. You can create good concepts of body, soul and spirit when you take into account the complete human life-span.[1] However, you must remember that in relationships like those I will mention in a moment, we have only the very first steps of comprehension. You must further develop these concepts.

If you observe a newborn child and look at its form, its movements, how it expresses itself in crying and babbling and so forth, you will get a picture of the human body. However, you will have a complete picture of the human body only when you relate it to human middle age and old age. In middle age, the human is more connected with the soul and in old age, more with the spirit. It would be easily possible to contradict this last observation. Many people might, of course, say that in old age people again become feebleminded. This objection is raised particularly by materialism about the soul-spirit, namely, that in old age people become mentally weak. Materialists contend that even such a great person as Kant became feebleminded in old age. That is true. The objection raised by materialists is true, but it does not prove what they want it to prove. Kant, as he stood before the gates of death, was wiser than he was in his childhood, but in his childhood his body was capable of absorbing all his wisdom.[2] In this way, his wisdom could become conscious in the physical body. However, in old age his body was incapable of absorbing what the spirit gave him. His body was no longer a good tool of the spirit. Thus, in the physical plane Kant was no longer able to become conscious of what lived in his spirit. In spite of the apparent validity of the objection just described, we must nevertheless be clear that in old age people become wise and astute, and that they approach the spiritual world. Thus, we will need to recognize the beginnings of spiritual characteristics in older people who have maintained an elasticity and life force for their spirit. There are such possibilities.

In Berlin there were once two professors. The one, Michelet, was a Hegelian and was over ninety.[3] Since he was rather astute, he was given an emeritus professorship, however, even though he was old, he still held his lectures. Then there was another professor, Zeller, a historian of Greek philosophy.[4] In comparison to Michelet, Zeller was a youngster since he was only seventy. Yet you could hear everywhere that he felt the burden of age, and that he could no longer hold his lectures. To this, Michelet always said, "I do not understand Zeller. I could give lectures all day long, but Zeller in his youthfulness continually says that that would be too difficult for him!"

We may find only a few instances where the spirit is visible in the physical existence of old age. Nevertheless, it is possible.

In contrast, if we look at how human beings express themselves in middle age, we can find the basis for observing the soul. People in middle age can more easily deny the soul. They can appear either without a soul or extremely inspired since the soul exists in human freedom, which includes education. That many middle-aged people appear to have no soul proves nothing in regard to the fact that middle age is actually the age of the soul. If you compare the child's wiggly, unconscious physical nature with the contemplative, quiet nature of older people, you have, on the one side, the child's body that particularly emphasizes itself, and, on the other, the body of an older person that allows itself to recede, that, in a certain sense, denies itself as a body.

If we apply this view more to the soul, then we would say that people carry within themselves thinking cognition, feeling and willing. If we look at a child, we see in the picture of the child's soul a close connection between willing and feeling. We could say that in the child, willing and feeling are grown together. When children kick or wiggle, they make exactly those movements that reflect their feelings at that moment. The child is unable to separate movement from feeling.

With elderly people, it is different. There the situation is just the opposite, namely, thinking cognition and feeling are grown together, and the will presents itself independently. The course that human life follows is such that feeling, which is at first connected to willing, slowly separates itself from willing during the passage of life. In education we are quite often concerned with the question of separating feeling from willing. When freed from willing, feeling then connects itself with thinking cognition and is concerned with it in later life. We properly prepare children for later life only when we enable them to successfully separate feeling from willing. Later, as men or women, they can connect their free feeling with thinking cognition, and, thus, fully meet life. Why do we listen to older people when they tell us about their life experiences? Because during their lives, they have connected their personal feeling with their concepts and ideas. They do not tell us about theories, they tell us about the feelings they have joined to ideas and concepts. From elderly people who have really connected their feeling with thinking cognition, concepts and ideas sound warm, they sound saturated with reality, they are concrete, personal. With people who have not progressed as adults, concepts and ideas sound theoretical, abstract and sterile. It is a part of human life that the capacities of the human soul develop along a certain path; the feeling will of the child develops into the feeling thinking of an older person, and between these two lies human life. We can properly prepare children for this human life only if we can examine education psychologically.

In observing the world, we must consider something that occurs first and that all psychological theories describe as occurring first, namely, sensation. We have sensation when any of our senses encounters our surroundings.[5] We sense colors, tones, heat and cold. This is the way our senses communicate with our surroundings.

You cannot get an accurate picture of what sensation really is from the way sensing is normally described in psychology. When psychologists speak of sensation, they say that a physical process occurs, such as the vibrations of light or waves in the air that stream to our sense organs and stimulate them. Psychologists talk about stimulation, elevate it to a specialized term, but have no desire to fully understand it. Through the sense organ, stimulation creates a feeling in our soul, a qualitative feeling arising from a physical process, for example, hearing, which results from the vibrations of waves in the air. This is what psychologists usually say. Modern scientific psychology is totally unable to give any information about how this actually occurs.

You will come closer to an understanding of such things when, instead of looking to psychological considerations, you use your insight into the nature of sensation to answer the question as to which soul force is most closely connected with sensation. Psychologists simplify such things by simply make sensing part of cognition. They say that first we sense, then we perceive, then we make ourselves a picture, form concepts and so forth. At first, this appears to be the process, but they pay no attention to the actual nature of sensation.

If, through sufficient self-observation, we really see what sensing is, we will recognize that sensing has the nature of will with a tendency toward feeling. At first, it is not connected with thinking cognition, but with feeling will. I do not know how many psychological theories have recognized anything of the relationship of sensing to feeling will (of course, we cannot know all the countless modern scientific theories). To say that sensing is related to will would not be quite correct, because it is related to feeling will. That it is related to feeling was recognized by at least one psychologist, who has particularly well-developed powers of observation, namely, Moriz Benedikt in Vienna.[6]

Of course, psychologists hardly notice this psychological theory. There is something unusual about it. First, Moriz Benedikt is, by training, a criminal anthropologist, but he writes about psychological theories. Second, he is a natural scientist, but he writes about the importance of poetry in education and even analyzes such works to show how we can use them. This is something horrible: the man claims to be a scientist but believes psychologists can learn something from poets! Finally, a third thing: this man is a Jewish natural scientist who has written a psychological text and dedicated it to no less than a Catholic priest then on the theological faculty of the University of Vienna, Laurenz Müllner.[7] These three terrible things make it impossible for "real" psychologists to take this person seriously. Nevertheless, they would take him seriously if they read his psychological text. They would find so many really striking perceptions in it that they would gain much, even though they would have to reject the conclusions of his psychological theory, anchored as they are in Benedikt's materialistic way of thinking. Psychologists would not gain anything from the totality of Benedikt's book, but would gain much from his specific observations. This is a case where we must seek the best in the world where it occurs. If someone is a good observer in specific instances but has a repulsive general tendency, as is the case with Benedikt, then we need not reject that person's good specific observations.

Sensations as they occur in human beings are feeling will. We must, therefore, say that where human senses are externally active (we carry the senses on the surface of our body, if I may express this coarsely), feeling will exists in a certain sense. If we draw a sketch of the human being, we could say that on the surface (remember this is all only schematic) we have the sphere of the senses, and it is there that feeling will exists (see sketch, page 129). What is it that we do on this surface where feeling will exists insofar as the surface of the body is the area of sensing? We practice an activity that is half sleep and half dream; we could call it a dreamy sleep or a sleepy dream. We sleep not only at night, but continuously at our periphery, on the outer surface of our bodies, and as people we are unable to completely comprehend our sensations because, in the area where these sensations occur, we only sleepily dream. Psychologists have no idea that what keeps us from comprehending sensations is identical to what hinders us from bringing our dreams into clear consciousness when we wake up in the morning. The concepts of sleep and dream have another meaning much different from those we normally use. In normal life we only know that when we go to bed at night, we sleep. We do not realize that sleep is something much more widespread that occurs continuously on the surface of our body. Dreams continuously mix with sleep on our bodily surface. These "dreams" are sensations before the intellect and thinking cognition comprehends them.

You must also seek children's will and feeling in their senses. For this reason we emphasize so strongly that we must continuously act upon the children's will when we educate them intellectually. Into everything children see, into everything they perceive, we must also incorporate will and feeling, otherwise we will deny the children's sensations. We can only speak to elderly people, to those in the twilight of life, when we understand that their sensations are already metamorphosed. In elderly people, sensations have already moved from feeling will to feeling thinking. In such people, sensations are something different and are more like thought and less like the restlessness of will. That is, they have greater quietude. Only in elderly people are sensations more like concepts and ideas.

Usually psychologists do not make these fine distinctions about sensations. For them, the sensations of elderly people are the same as those of children because sensation is simply sensation. This is the same kind of logic as saying a butter knife is a type of knife, and therefore we could use it to carve meat because a knife is a knife. In such cases, people form the concept from the word; however, we should never do that. Instead, we should form the concept from the facts. We find that sensations live and that they go through a certain process during life, that they are more like will in children and more like the intellect in elderly people. Of course, it is easier for people simply to derive concepts from words, which is why we have so many people who explain the meaning of words. But, that can have a very negative effect upon us.

I once met with a former schoolmate.[8] We had both attended the same elementary school, and then I went to high school, and he went to a teacher training school, which, in addition, was Hungarian. In those days, in the 1870s, that really meant something.[9] After several years we met again and talked about light. I had learned what was taught in regular physics, namely that light had something to do with waves and ether and so forth. This was, at least, something that could be seen as the basis of light. My former schoolmate said that he had also learned about light, namely that light is the reason we see![10] This was simply playing with words! In this way, concepts become simple explanations of words. You can imagine what kind of education the children who were taught by this man received. We must pry ourselves away from words and come to the spirit of things. When we want to understand something, we must not always think immediately about the word, but instead seek out the real relationships. If we look up the origins of the word "spirit" in Mauthner's etymology and ask how the word first arises, we will find that it is connected with "foam or froth, spray" and with "gas."[11,12] This relationship exists, but it would not lead to anything useful. Unfortunately, this method often appears in a concealed form in Bible research, and thus the Bible is the book most people, particularly modern theologians, least understand.

Our goal must be to proceed everywhere in an objective manner; for instance, we do not attempt to form a concept of spirit through etymological research, but rather compare the child's physical activity with that of an older person. By relating facts with one another, we can arrive at true concepts. We can have a real concept of sensation only when we know that it originates as feeling will in the child's physical periphery because, in comparison with the child's inner being, the physical periphery sleeps and dreams. You are fully awake in thinking cognition, but you are also fully awake only inside your body. On the periphery, on the surface of the body, you continue to sleep. Furthermore, what occurs in the surroundings of the body or, better said, on the surface of the body, occurs in a similar way in the head and occurs most strongly the deeper we go into the human being, in muscles and blood. There again, the human being sleeps and dreams. People sleep and dream on the surface, and again, more inwardly, they also sleep and dream. Our feeling that is more soul-will, our feeling will, our life of desire, remains more within us and thus is also in a dreaming sleep. Where, then, are we completely awake? In the area between, during our waking hours.

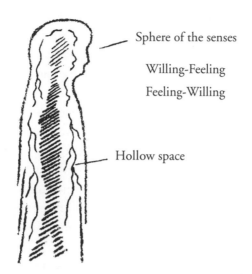

Our spatial application of wakefulness and sleep to the human being is from a spiritual standpoint connected with the human form. From the spiritual perspective, we can see the human being as sleeping on the surface and deep within, and, during life between birth and death, able to be fully awake only in the space between. Which organs are most fully developed in this middle region? They are those organs, particularly in the head, that we call the nerves, namely the nervous system. The nervous system sends its runners both to the furthest extent of the surface and also deep inside. The nerves go to all these areas and, in addition, to areas of the middle zone such as the brain, particularly the spinal cord, and, also, the vagus nerve in front. There we have the opportunity to be completely awake. Where the nerves are most completely developed is also where we can be most awake. However, the nervous system has an unusual relationship to the spirit. It is an organ that, due to the functions of the body, always tends to decay and become mineralized. If, in a living human, you could separate the nervous system from the remaining elements of gland-muscle-blood and from the bone element (you could, though, leave the bone system together with the nervous system), you would already have a corpse in a living human being. Dying occurs continuously in the human nervous system. The nervous system is the only system that has no direct connection to the spirit-soul. Blood, muscles and so forth always have some direct connection to the spirit-soul; however, the nervous system never has a direct connection. That it has any connection to the spirit-soul is only because it continuously shuts itself off from human functioning; it is not present because it continuously decays. The other elements live, and therefore form direct connections to the spirit-soul. The nervous system is in a continuous state of dying. It is always saying to the human being, "You can develop because I present you with no hindrance, because I make sure that I am not there with my life!" That is what is so peculiar. In psychology and physiology you will find the nervous system presented as the organ from which we receive sensations, thinking and the spirit-soul in general. However, how is it that this organ is the intermediary? It is possible only because the nervous system removes itself from life and thereby presents no hindrance to thinking and sensing; it, in fact, has absolutely no connection to thinking and feeling, and, where it exists, it allows the human being to be empty in relationship to the spirit-soul. Where the nerves exist, the spirit-soul meets only spaces, gaps; and, where these gaps exist, the spirit-soul can enter. We must be thankful to the nervous system that it is not concerned with the spirit-soul and that it, in fact, does not do any of the things physiologists and psychologists say it does. If, for only five minutes, the nerves did what physiologists and psychologists say nerves do, in those five minutes we would be unable to know anything of the world—we would sleep. The nerves do the same thing that all other organs do that mediate sleep, that mediate the feeling will.

It is difficult for us when we confront what physiology and psychology say is the truth because people say we turn the world upside down. The truth is that it is already standing on its head, and that we need to set it on its legs through spiritual science. Physiologists say that nerves, particularly the brain, are the organs of thinking. The truth is that the brain and nervous system are connected with thinking cognition only because they always shut themselves off from human functioning, thereby allowing thinking cognition to unfold.

Let us now focus quite exactly upon something. In the sense sphere surrounding the human being, real processes occur which are always entering world events. For example, light acts upon the human being through the eye. In the eye, that is, in the sense sphere, real processes occur, namely a physical-chemical process. It continues into the depths of the human body and eventually comes to that inner region (the dark shaded area of the sketch, page 129) where such physical-chemical processes again occur. Now imagine that you are standing in front of a lit surface, and that light rays from this lit surface fall upon your eyes. There physical-chemical processes occur and continue on into the muscle and blood within you. In between is an empty zone. In this vacant zone, which exists due to the emptiness of the nerves, such processes as occur in the eye or deeper within you do not develop. What exists in this middle zone is a continuation of what exists outside, namely the nature of light, the nature of colors themselves and so forth. Therefore, on the surface of our body where the senses are, we have real processes that are dependent on the eye, the ear, organs for sensing heat and so forth. Similar processes also exist deep within us. However, in between, where the nerves spread out and make free space, we can live with what exists outside. The eye changes light and color. However, where you have nerves, you are, regarding life, empty; here, light and color do not

change, and thus you live with light and color. You are separated from the outer world only concerning the sense sphere;
but within, you live with these outer processes as though from
inside a shell. There, you yourself become light; there, you
yourself become tone; there, the processes spread out because
the nerves present none of the hindrances of blood and muscle.

Now, we can have a feeling for the importance of this. In the
empty space present within us, we are awake in relation to life
while, on our outermost surface and at our innermost core, we
sleepily dream and dreamily sleep. We are completely awake
only in a region lying between our outermost periphery and
innermost depths. All this is said in relationship to spatiality.

When we observe the human being from the viewpoint of
the spirit, we must also connect the temporal with waking,
sleeping and dreaming.

You learn something. You learn it such that it enters your
consciousness. During the time you are concerned with it and
when you think about it, it is in your consciousness. Then,
your life goes on to something else. Something else gains your
interest and takes your attention. What happens now to what
you learned before, to the object of your previous concern? It
begins to go to sleep, and when you again recall it, it awakens.
You can understand these things only when you replace all
that playing with psychological words such as remembering
and forgetting with real concepts. What is remembering? It is
the awakening of an integrated group of pictures. And what is
forgetting? That is the going to sleep of an integrated group of
pictures. In this way, you can compare reality with things
really experienced and not simply have word definitions. If
you think about waking and sleeping, if you experience yourself going to sleep or see others going to sleep, you have there a
real process. You can relate forgetting, an inner activity of the
soul, to a real process, not to some word, and you can say that

forgetting is only another kind of sleeping and remembering only an awakening.

You can come to a spiritual comprehension of the world only when you compare things that are real. To connect the body and spirit, at least in a rudimentary manner, by comparing the stage of life during childhood with that of old age, you must compare remembering and forgetting by relating them to something real, to going to sleep and awakening.[13]

What will be so very necessary for the future of humanity is that people accustom themselves to delving into reality. Today, people think almost only in words; they do not think in terms of reality. How could people today gain a sense for what is real and for what we can have when we speak of remembering and awakening? In the broad spectrum of connotations of these words, people will hear everything possible in order to define memory, but they will not think to look at reality, at the facts themselves, in order to understand memory.

It is therefore understandable that when we speak to people about something like the threefold social organism, which derives completely out of reality and not out of abstract concepts, they at first do not understand this because they are unaccustomed to deriving things from reality.[14] They do not associate any concepts with things derived out of reality. In their theories, socialist leaders, for example, have not the least idea of deriving things out of reality. They represent the final stage, the final level of decadence, with their explanation of words. These people believe they understand something of reality better than anyone else; however, when they begin to speak, they can use only the most meaningless words. The above is only a parenthetical remark but it is connected with our modern stream of thinking. However, educators must understand the times in which they live because they must also understand the children of those times.

8

Yesterday we saw that we can understand something like memory and remembering only when we relate it to processes more easily observed, namely to sleeping and waking. From this you can see that our pedagogical goal must be to bring the unknown closer and closer to the known. This is also true regarding the formation of spiritual ideas.

You might say that sleeping and waking are more obscure than remembering and forgetting, and that, for this reason, an understanding of sleeping and waking will not contribute much to a discussion of remembering and forgetting. Nevertheless, if we carefully observe what people lose through restless sleep, we can infer something about how the failure to bring forgetting into a proper relationship with remembering disturbs all of human soul life. We know from experience that a reasonable amount of sleep is necessary to keep our consciousness from becoming weaker and weaker, to keep it from taking on the characteristic described by saying that, due to disturbed sleep, all kinds of things in our surroundings impress our I too strongly. Even with a relatively small disturbance during sleep, for example, insomnia, you can see that this is the case. Suppose that during the night you did not sleep well. (I am assuming that the reason you did not sleep is not because you were particularly active and used the night to work. In such a case, the situation is somewhat different.) Suppose some physical condition, or perhaps mosquitoes, in other words, something external, disturbs your sleep. You may notice on the next day that things disturb you more than usual. In a sense, your I is more sensitive.

It is much the same when forgetting and remembering play improperly into human soul life. When does that occur? It occurs when we are unable to use our will to regulate our forgetting and remembering. Many people daydream through life, and we can already see this tendency in early childhood. Something in their surroundings makes an impression upon them and gains their attention, but they do not properly follow this impression. Instead, they let it whoosh by. In a sense, they do not properly connect their I with the impression. Since they are not really interested in their surroundings, they also daydream in randomly occurring images. They do not purposely seek to increase the store of thoughts necessary to understand something well at any given occasion. Instead, they allow the images that arise within to come up by themselves. One image appears and then soon another, and the free will has no particular influence upon the process. In many respects, this is the state of soul for many people, but it arises especially during childhood.

We can help bring remembering and forgetting increasingly into the realm of the will if we know that sleeping and waking play a role in remembering and forgetting during our waking hours. We can ask, where does remembering come from? It comes about because the will, in which we are asleep, takes an image from deep in the unconscious and brings it into consciousness. The strength of the sleeping will causes the process of remembering in the same way that the human I and the astral body gather strength in the spiritual world between sleeping and awakening to refresh the physical and the etheric bodies. However, the will is sleeping, and, therefore, you cannot directly make children learn to use their will. Wanting to make children use their will is the same thing as telling people to be well behaved during sleep so that they can bring this good behavior into their lives when they awaken in the morning. We cannot, therefore, expect the sleeping will to pull itself together to directly control the process of remembering. What can we do? We cannot, of course, expect children to pull themselves together in specific instances to control the process of remembering, but we can raise children so that they develop habits of soul, body and spirit that lead to this kind of focusing of the will. Let us look at this in more detail.

Suppose, for example, that through a particular method you awaken in the children a lively interest in the animal kingdom. Of course, you cannot develop it in a single day. You will have to arrange the instruction so that an interest in the animal kingdom gradually develops and awakens. When children undergo such instruction, the more lively their awakened interest is, the more the instruction affects their will. If, in the normal course of life, they need to remember ideas about animals, the will is then able to bring these up from the subconscious and out of forgetfulness. Only when you affect what is habitual in people can you bring order into their will, and thus into their power of remembering. In other words, you must see why everything that awakens intense interest in children also helps strengthen their memory. We must increase the power to remember through the feeling and will and not through simple intellectual memory exercises.

You can thus see how the world, particularly the human world, in a sense consists of separate parts and how those separate parts work together. We cannot understand the human soul if we do not separate the soul into its thinking, or thinking cognition, feeling and willing parts. However, thinking cognition, feeling and willing are not present in a pure form anywhere. The three things work together and are interwoven into a unity. That is also true of human nature in its entirety, right into the physical.

I have already mentioned to you that the human being is primarily head in his or her head, but that, in fact, the head aspect exists everywhere in the human body. As a chest being, humans are mostly chest, but they are actually a chest being everywhere because the head also has something of a chest nature, as do the limbs. As a being of limbs, the human being is primarily limb, but actually the whole human being is a limb being since the characteristic of the limbs exists in the head as well as the chest. For example, the limbs are involved with breathing through the skin and so forth.

If we want to come closer to reality, particularly the reality of human nature, then we must clearly take all separation in the context of unity. If we only focused upon abstract unity, we could not understand anything. If we never separated things, the world would remain vague, as when all cats in the night seem gray. People who want to understand everything in abstractions see the world as only gray. If we only divide and separate and keep things apart, we never come to a real understanding, because we then comprehend only differences, and understanding is absent.

The nature of everything that constitutes a human being is partly cognitive, partly feeling and partly willing. What is cognitive is mainly cognitive, but also has aspects of feeling and willing. What is feeling is mainly feeling, but also has cognitive and willing aspects. It is the same with willing. We can now apply that to what I described yesterday as the sense realm. If you really want to understand what I now want to present, you must rid yourselves of all pedantry; otherwise you may find the crassest contradiction to what I said in yesterday's lecture.

However, reality consists of contradictions. We do not comprehend reality if we do not look at the contradictions of the
world.

Altogether the human being has twelve senses.[1] The reason
normal science recognizes only five, six or seven senses is that
these senses are particularly obvious and the remainder are less
obvious. I have often mentioned the twelve human senses, but
today we want to recall them again in our souls. Usually people
speak of the senses of hearing, temperature, sight, taste, smell
and touch. Sometimes the senses of temperature and touch are
combined, which is like saying smoke and dust are the same
because their appearance is similar. Actually, it should no
longer be necessary to mention that the senses of temperature
and touch are two very different human characteristics and are
two different ways that human beings relate to the world. At
best, modern psychologists differentiate these two senses and,
perhaps, add the sense of balance. Some people add one more
sense.[2] However, it is not included in sense physiology or sense
psychology because people simply do not see that human
beings, when perceiving the I of other human beings, have a
similar relationship to the world similar to the one they have
when perceiving color with their sense of sight.

Today, people tend to mix everything together. When people
think about the idea of the I, they first think of the nature of
their own soul and are then satisfied. Psychologists do something similar. They do not consider that if I collect all my experiences and call the sum of these experiences "I," it is very
different from what I refer to when I meet someone and relate
to another person such that I also refer to that person as an "I."
These are two very different activities of the spirit-soul. When I
summarize my life's activities with the comprehensive term "I,"
I have something purely within me. When I meet another person and through my relationship to that person express that he

or she has something like my I, I engage in the interplay that flows between me and the other person. I must, therefore, say that the perception of my own I within me is something different from recognizing the I of another person. The perception of the other person's I is founded in the I-sense in the same way that the perception of color is based upon the sense of sight, or tone upon the sense of hearing. Nature does not make the organ for "I-ing" as easy for people to recognize as the organ for seeing. However, we could well use the word "I-ing" for the perceiving of another's I, just as we use the word "seeing" for perceiving colors. The organ in human beings for perceiving colors is on the surface, but the organ for perceiving the I spreads over the entire human being and consists of a very subtle substance. For that reason, people do not speak of an organ for perceiving another's I. This "I-ing" organ is different from what enables me to experience my own I. There is, in fact, a tremendous difference between experiencing my own I and perceiving the I of another person. Perceiving of someone else's I is primarily a cognitive process, or at least a process similar to cognition, but experiencing my own I is a will process.

We now have something to which a pedant could easily object, saying that in the last lecture I said all sense activity is primarily will activity, but now I have just created an I-sense and say it is primarily a cognitive sense. However, if you characterize the I-sense in the way I have attempted in my recent edition of *Intuitive Thinking as a Spiritual Path: A Philosophy of Freedom,* you would realize that this I-sense works in a very complicated way.[3] What is the basis of actually perceiving the I of another human being? Modern abstractionists say quite peculiar things. They say that actually we see people's form, hear their tones and then know we look just as human as they do and have within ourselves a being that thinks, feels and wills, and is therefore also a human being in a soul-spiritual sense. Thus, through analogy, I conclude that just as I am a thinking, feeling and willing being, it is the same with others. I make a conclusion about others through analogy with myself. This conclusion is nothing more than folly. The interrelationship between one person and another involves something quite different. If you meet another person, the following occurs: For a short period you perceive a person, and he or she makes an impression upon you. That impression disturbs you inwardly; you feel that the person, a being comparable to yourself, makes an impression upon you like an attack. The result is that you defend yourself inwardly, you resist this attack and become inwardly aggressive toward the person. In this aggression you become crippled, and the aggression ceases. Then the other person can again make an impression upon you, and after you thus have time to regain your aggressive strength, you carry out another act of aggression. Again, you become numb, and the other person again makes an impression upon you, and so forth. This is the relationship that exists when one person meets another and perceives the other I—that is, devotion to the other–inner resistance; sympathy–antipathy. I am not speaking now of feeling, but just the perception of meeting. The soul vibrates; it vibrates sympathy–antipathy, sympathy–antipathy, sympathy–antipathy. You can read about this in the new edition of *Intuitive Thinking as a Spiritual Path*.

However, there is still something else. As sympathy develops, you go to sleep in the other person; as antipathy develops, you wake up, and so forth. In the vibrations of meeting another person, there is a rapid alternation between waking and sleeping. We have to thank the organ of the I-sense that this can occur. This organ of I-sensing is so formed that it explores the I of another person, not wakefully but in its sleeping will, and then quickly delivers the results of this sleepy exploration to cognition, that is, to the nervous system. If we look at these things properly, the main thing in perceiving another person is the will, but the will as developed not in wakefulness, but in sleep. We continually include sleeping moments in the act of perceiving the I of another, and what lies in between is cognition. This moves quickly into the area where the nervous system lives, such that I can indeed call the perceiving of another person a cognitive process. However, I must realize that this cognitive process is only a metamorphosis of a sleeping will process. Thus, this sense process is a will process, only we do not recognize it as such. We are not conscious in the cognition we experience in sleep.

The next sense we have to consider is separate from the I-sense and all the other senses. I call it the sense of thought. The sense of thought is not a sense for perceiving our own thoughts, but for perceiving the thoughts of other people. Psychologists have developed grotesque ideas about it. As a whole, people are so impressed by the connection between speech and thinking that they believe we apprehend thoughts with speech. That is ridiculous, since through your sense of thought you can perceive thoughts in gestures just as you can perceive them in speech. Speech only transmits thoughts. You must perceive thoughts through your sense of thought. When we have finally created all the sounds of speech as movement forms in eurythmy, then someone would need only to perform them eurhythmically and out of these movements you could read the thoughts just as you can hear them through speech.[4] In short, the sense of thought is something different from what is active in the sense of speech. There we have the specific sense of speech.

We then have the senses of hearing, temperature, sight, taste, and smell. Next, we have a sense of balance. We have a sense-like consciousness that we are in balance.[5] We have such an awareness. Through a specific inner sense perception, we know how to orient ourselves left and right, front and back. We know how to maintain our balance so that we do not fall. If the organ of our sense of balance were destroyed, we would fall. We could not maintain our balance just as we could not relate to colors if the eye were destroyed. In the same way that we have a sense for perceiving our balance, we also have a sense of our own movement through which we can differentiate whether we are still or moving and whether we are flexing our muscles. Thus, along with a sense of balance, we also have a sense of movement. Besides that, we also have a sense for perceiving the condition of our body in the broadest sense, the sense of life. Many people are very dependent upon this sense of life. They perceive whether they have eaten too much or too little, or whether they are tired or not, or whether they feel comfortable or uncomfortable. In short, the states of our own bodies are reflected in the sense of life. Thus, we have a total of twelve senses. Human beings have, in truth, twelve such senses.

By recognizing that our understanding of the senses is based upon will, we have eliminated possible pedantic objections to their existence. We can now further divide the senses. First, we have the four senses of touch, life, movement and balance. These senses are primarily permeated by will. Will acts through these senses in perception. Feel, for example, how will acts in perceiving movement, even if you move while standing still. The resting will also acts in the perception of balance. Will is very active in the sense of life, and it is active when you explore your surroundings through touch because touching something is basically a negotiation between your will and the surroundings. In short, we can say that the senses of balance, movement, life and touch are will-senses in the narrower sense. For example, your hand moves when you examine something by touch, so it is obvious that the sense of touch exists. The existence of the senses of life, movement and balance is not so obvious. However, because these are will-senses in a special sense, and the will sleeps, people sleep through these senses. In most psychological theories you will not find these senses even mentioned because regarding many things science comfortably sleeps the sleep of the human being.

The next group of senses, namely smell, taste, sight and temperature, are primarily senses of feeling. The naive consciousness particularly feels the relationship of smelling and tasting to feeling. There are particular reasons why people do not feel that relationship with sight and temperature. Because sense of temperature is thrown together with the sense of touch, people do not notice that it is closely related to feeling. Things are at once incorrectly combined and incorrectly differentiated. The sense of touch is, in truth, much more will-oriented, whereas the sense of temperature is oriented only toward feeling. People do not realize that the sense of sight is also a feeling-sense because they do not observe such things as are found in Goethe's color theory. There Goethe clearly sets forth the relationship of color to feeling and how it finally leads to will impulses. However, why do people so little notice that, in the sense of sight, feeling predominates?

We nearly always see things so that when they give the colors to us, they also show us the boundaries of colors, namely, lines and forms. We are not normally aware of how we perceive when we perceive color and form at the same time. Someone who perceives a colored circle might say, "I see the color, and I see the roundness of the circle or the circular form." However, here two very different things are confused. At first you see only the color through the specific activity of the eye. You see the circular form when you subconsciously use the sense of movement and unconsciously make a circular movement in the etheric or astral body, thus raising it into cognition. When the circle you have apprehended through your sense of movement rises to cognition, it is then joined with the perceived color. You take the form out of your entire body when you appeal to the sense of movement spread out over your entire body. You clothe yourself in something that I previously discussed when I said that human beings actually perform geometric forms in the cosmos and then raise them into cognition.[6]

Today, official science is not at all interested in such a refined way of observation, so it does not distinguish between seeing color and perceiving form with the help of the sense of movement, but mixes everything together. In the future, however, we will not be able to educate with such confusion. How will it be possible to educate human seeing if we do not know that the whole human being participates in seeing through the sense of movement? Now, something else arises. You think about seeing when you perceive colored forms. Seeing, the perceiving of colored forms, is a complicated activity. Because you are a whole human being, you can inwardly reunite the two things you perceive through sight and the sense of movement. You would numbly gaze at a red circle if you did not perceive the color red and the circular form through quite different means. However, you do not gaze numbly because you perceive things from two sides, namely, color through the eye and form with the help of the sense of movement; in life you must again integrate these two things. Then you form a judgment, and thus you can now comprehend judging as a living bodily process that arises because your senses present you with the world analyzed into parts. The world you experience comes to you in twelve different ways, and you reunite things through your judging, because individual things do not want to remain individual. The circular form does not accept being simply a circular form as presented through the sense of movement. Color does not accept being simply color as perceived by the eye. Things force you to reunite them, and you declare yourself inwardly ready to forge the connection. Here the act of judgment becomes an expression of your entire human being.

Now you can see the deeper meaning of our relationship to the world. If we did not have twelve senses, we would look at our surroundings like idiots and could not experience inner judgment. However, because we do have twelve senses, we have a large number of possible ways to reunite what has been separated. What the sense of I experiences, we can connect with the other eleven senses, and the same is true for each sense. In this way we have a large number of combined relationships between the senses. Besides that, we also have a large number of possibilities when, for example, we connect the sense of I with both the senses of thought and speech. In this way, we can see the mysterious way human beings are connected with the world. The twelve senses separate things into their basic elements, and the human being must be able to put them back together again. In this way, people participate in the inner life of things. You can, therefore, understand how immensely important it is that we educate children and develop each of the senses in balance, since we can then systematically and consciously seek the relationships between the senses and perceptions.

I need to add that the sense of I and the senses of thought, hearing and speech are more cognitive senses, because the will in them is more the sleeping will, the really sleeping will that vibrates in cognitive activity. Thus, will, feeling and cognition live in the I region of human beings with the help of waking and sleeping.

We need to be clear that, when we look at the spirit, we can understand human beings only when we view them from three standpoints. However, it is not sufficient to always say spirit, spirit, spirit! Most people continually talk about spirit but do not know what to do with what spirit gives. We only properly take care of what is spirit-given when we work with states of consciousness. We must affect the spirit through states of consciousness such as waking, sleeping and dreaming. The soul is affected through sympathy and antipathy, that is, through the conditions met in life. The soul is affected continuously in the subconscious. The soul exists in the astral body and life in the etheric body. Between them is a continuous inner communication such that the soul automatically participates in the living conditions of the etheric body. The physical body is perceived through its forms. Yesterday, I used the sphere for the head, the crescent moon for the chest and lines for the limbs, but we still need to speak about the actual morphology of the human body.[7] We do not correctly speak about the spirit if we do not describe its existence in states of consciousness. We do not correctly speak about the soul if we do not reveal its life between sympathy and antipathy. We do not correctly speak about the physical body if we do not comprehend its true forms. We will speak more of this tomorrow.

9

If you fill your deep understanding of the developing human being with will and feeling, then you will teach well. A pedagogical instinct will awaken in you that will enable you to apply what comes from your will-permeated knowledge of child development. However, that knowledge must be real— that is, it must be based on a true understanding of the actual world.

To reach a real knowledge of the human being, we have attempted to visualize the human being, first from the viewpoint of the soul and then from that of the spirit. We want to recall that a spiritual comprehension of the human being requires that we reflect upon the various levels of consciousness. We need to realize that, at least at first, our spiritual life takes place in waking, dreaming and sleeping, and that we may view individual events in life as occurring in fully awake, dreaming or sleeping states. Now we will try to slowly shift our attention from the spirit down through the soul to the physical body, so that we can have the whole human being before us. Finally, we can finish our discussions with what is health-giving to children.

You know that the stage of life under consideration for teaching as a whole is the first two decades. You also know that the entire life of children in these first two decades is divided into three parts. Until the time of the change of teeth, children have a certain character that they express in their desire to be imitative beings. Children try to imitate everything they see. From the age of seven until puberty, everything the child wants to know, feel and do is based upon a desire to receive it from authorities. Only after puberty do children begin to want to relate to their environment through their own judgment. We must therefore take into account that when we have elementary school age children before us, we must develop human beings whose innermost essence strives toward authority. If we are not able to teach out of authority during this stage of life, we will be poor teachers.

Nevertheless, we now want to acquire an overview of the spiritual characteristics of human life. As we have already described from the most varied points of view, the full activity of human life encompasses cognitive thinking on the one side, willing on the other and feeling in the middle. Between birth and death, earthly human beings depend upon slowly imbuing cognitive thinking with logic and with everything that enables them to think logically. However, as teachers, you will have to keep what you know about logic in the background, since logic is something very academic. You should teach it to the children only through your bearing; however, as teachers, you must carry the most important elements of logic within you.

When we act logically, that is, when we act in a thinking, cognitive manner, this activity always exists in three parts.[1] First, in our thinking cognition we always have what we call conclusions. Normally, we express thinking in speech. If you look at the structure of speech, you will find that when you speak, you continually create conclusions. In human beings, the most conscious activity is that of forming conclusions.

People could not express themselves through language if they did not continually speak of conclusions, and they could not understand others if they did not continually receive conclusions. Theoretical logic usually dissects conclusions and thereby falsifies the conclusions that occur in normal life.[2] Theoretical logic does not take into account that we draw a conclusion when we look at something. Imagine going into a zoo and seeing a lion. What is the first thing you do when you perceive the lion? First, you become conscious of what you see as a lion; only through becoming conscious do you come to terms with your perception of the lion. Before going to the zoo, you already learned that things that look like the lion you are looking at are "animals." What you learned in life, you bring to the zoo. Then, you look at the lion and realize that it does what you have learned animals do. You connect this with what you already learned in life and then form the judgment that the lion is an animal. Only when you have formed this judgment do you understand the specific concept "lion." First, you form a conclusion, second, you make a judgment and, finally, you arrive at a concept. Of course, you do not know that you continually practice this; however, if you did not, you could not lead a conscious life that enables you to communicate with other humans through language. People normally believe that humans arrive first at concepts. That is not true. In life, the conclusion is first. If we do not arrive at the zoo with a concept of "lion," but instead add our new perception of the lion to our other experiences, then the first thing we do at the zoo is to draw a conclusion. We must be clear that when we go to the zoo and see a lion, this is only a single deed in the context of the remainder of life. We do not begin life when we go to the zoo and look at a lion. We connect that act to everything previous in life and everything previous in life plays a role. On the other hand, what we experience in the zoo, we take into the remainder of life. If we now consider the entire process, what is the lion first? First, it is a conclusion. A little later, the lion is a judgment. Finally, somewhat later, the lion is a concept.

If you open textbooks on logic, particularly older ones, you will normally find among the conclusions described one that is particularly well known: All people are mortal; John is a person; therefore, John is mortal. John is certainly the most famous person in logic. This separation of the three judgments "All people are mortal," "John is a person," "therefore, John is mortal," in fact, occurs only in the teaching of logic. In life, these three judgments are interwoven and are one, because life progresses in a thinking-cognitive way. You always make all three of these judgments simultaneously when you meet John. You include all three judgments in what you think about him. Thus, the conclusion exists first, then you form a judgment stated in the formal "conclusion," "Therefore, John is mortal." The last thing that you have is the specific concept of "the mortal John."

These three things—conclusion, judgment, concept—exist in cognition, that is, in the living human spirit.[3] How do they behave in the living human spirit?

Conclusions can live and be healthy only in the living human spirit. That is, the conclusion is healthy only when it exists in completely conscious life. That is very important, as we will see later.

For that reason, you ruin children's souls if you have the children memorize finished conclusions. What I now have to say about teaching is of fundamental importance when we have to act in a given instance. In the Waldorf School, you will have children of all ages with the results of their previous education. Other teachers have worked with these children, and you will find the results in conclusion, judgment and concept. You will need to have the children recall what they know, since you cannot begin with each child anew. We have the peculiar circumstance that we cannot build the school from the bottom up, but instead must immediately begin with eight grades. You will find before you the souls of children taught by others, and you must be careful in the beginning to avoid forcing the children to retrieve finished conclusions from their memory.[4] If those finished conclusions have been laid too strongly in their souls, then it is better to let them lie and now try to allow the children to focus upon concluding.

Judgments first develop, of course, in fully awake life. However, judgments can descend into the human soul, where the soul dreams. Conclusions should never trickle down into the dreaming soul, only judgments. But, everything we make in the way of judgments about the world trickles down into the dreaming soul.

What is this dreaming soul, really? As we have learned, it is more feeling oriented. When we form a judgment and then go on with our lives, we carry our judgments with us through the world. However, we carry them in the feeling, and that means judging is a kind of habit. You form children's soul habits through the way you teach them to judge. You must be completely conscious of this. Sentences are the expressions of judgment, and with each sentence you say to the children, you add one more building block to the habit life of the children's souls. Therefore, a teacher with real authority should be conscious that what he or she says clings to the habit life of the children's souls.

If we now go from judgment to concept, we must admit that what we develop as concepts descends into the deepest depths of human nature and, considered spiritually, descends into the sleeping soul. Concepts descend into the sleeping soul, and this is the soul that works on the body. The wakeful soul does not work on the body; the dreaming soul does to a limited extent, creating what is expressed in habitual gestures. However, the sleeping soul is active right into the form of the body. When you create concepts, that is, when you provide the results of judgments, you act upon the sleeping soul right into the children's bodies. The human body is all but completed when a person is born. The soul can at most refine what inheritance has already provided. Nevertheless, it does refine it. We go through the world and look at people. We see that people have distinct facial features. What do these facial features embody? Among other things, they carry the results of all the concepts taught them in childhood. All the concepts poured into the child's soul shine back at us from the face of the mature person, because, among other things, the sleeping soul has formed the adult's facial features in conformity with the concepts retained by the soul. Here we can see the consequence of our teaching. Through the formation of concepts, our teaching leaves its imprint on the person, right down into the body.

An observable modern phenomenon is people with decidedly bland faces. Hermann Bahr once expressed that in a Berlin lecture about his experiences.[5] He said that during the 1890s, if you were to walk through the streets in the Rhein or around Essen and meet people coming from the factories, you would get the vague feeling that there were no differences between the people you met. You would feel as if you only met copies of one person; that it was actually not possible to distinguish between people. That is an important observation, and Bahr made another observation that is also quite important. He said that if you were invited to supper in Berlin in the 1890s and were seated between two women, you could actually not distinguish between them, but you at least had one difference, namely, the one would be to the left, the other to the right. If you were then invited somewhere else, it could occur that you could not tell if a woman there was the woman from yesterday, or the one from the day before!

In other words, there is a certain uniformity among people. That is a sure sign that people were not properly raised. From such things, we must learn what is necessary to transform the educational system, because education goes so deeply into civilization. Concepts live unconsciously in people when they go through life without being confronted by a single fact.

Concepts can live in the unconscious. Judgments can live only as habits in semi-conscious dreaming, and conclusions should actually be present only in the fully conscious waking life. This means that while we must be very careful to speak with children about everything connected with conclusions, we should not provide them with finished conclusions, but only allow them to retain what will ripen into a concept with maturity. What do we need for this?

Imagine you form concepts, and these concepts are dead. Then, you inoculate children with conceptual corpses. If you inoculate children with dead concepts, you inject the corpses of concepts right into their physical bodies. What does a concept need to be like when we teach it to children? It must be living if children are to live with it. Children must live, and, therefore, concepts must also live. If you inoculate nine- or ten-year-old children with concepts that will remain the same when those children are thirty or forty years old, then you inoculate them with the corpses of concepts, because the concept cannot evolve as the children develop. You must teach the children concepts that can evolve throughout their lives. The teacher must be mindful to give children the kinds of concepts that can evolve in life. When the children are older, those concepts will not be the same as when they were received them. When you do this, you inoculate children with living concepts. When do you inoculate them with dead concepts? When you continually give them definitions, when you say, "A lion is . . . ," and have them memorize this, then you inoculate children with dead concepts. You assume that when the children are thirty years old, they will have exactly the same concepts you now teach. This means that continual defining is the death of living instruction. Then, what must we do? In teaching, we should not define, we should attempt to characterize. We characterize when we look at things from as many points of view as possible. If we teach children conventional natural history, for example, then we only define animals. We must try to portray animals from different standpoints in the various areas of instruction, for example, from the standpoint of how people came to understand an animal, how people use the animal's work and so forth. Rationally formed instruction can characterize if you do not simply describe a squid and then again later, a mouse, and again later, human beings (during the corresponding blocks of instruction), but rather place the squid, mouse and human being next to each other and relate them to one another.[6] In this case, these relationships are so manifold that no single definition emerges, but rather a portrayal. From the very beginning, appropriate instruction works not toward definitions, but toward characterization.

It is particularly important that we always be aware not to kill anything in children, but to teach them so that they remain lively and do not dry out and become stiff. When you teach children, you must carefully differentiate between concepts that are flexible and those (and they do exist) that do not need to change.[7] The latter concepts can give children a kind of framework in their souls. Of course, in this case you must remember to give children something that can remain for the rest of life. You may not give children dead, unchanging concepts about the details of life. You must give them living concepts about the specifics of life and the world, concepts that develop organically with the children. However, you must relate everything to the human being. In the end, everything in the children's comprehension must stream together into their concept of the human being. The concept of the human being may remain. Everything you provide children when you tell them a story and relate it to humans—when you relate the squid and the mouse to humans in natural history, when you excite a feeling of wonder for the telegraph that is completed by the ground wire—all of these are things that connect the whole world in its details to the human being.[8] This is something that can remain. We form the concept of human being only slowly, we cannot teach children a finished concept of human beings. However, when it is completed, it may remain. It is, indeed, the most beautiful thing a child can take from school into later life, namely the concept, the most multifaceted, most comprehensive concept of the human being.

What lives in human beings tends toward metamorphosis. If you can bring it about that the children have concepts of respect and honoring, concepts of all that we can call, in an all-encompassing sense, a prayerful attitude, then such thoughts will be living in children permeated with a prayerful attitude, and will remain into old age. In old age, these concepts will be transformed into a capacity to bless and to give others the results of a prayerful attitude. I once said that no elderly person who did not properly pray as a child would really be able to bless in old age. Older people can only properly bless, that is, with the greatest strength, if they properly prayed as children.

To teach concepts that are intimately connected with human nature means to give children living concepts. These living concepts undergo metamorphosis, transforming themselves throughout people's lives.

Now, let us look at the threefold nature of youthful life from a somewhat different standpoint. Until the time of the change of teeth, children want to imitate. Until the time of puberty, they want to stand under authority, and then they want to use their judgment in the world.

We can express this somewhat differently. What do human beings actually desire when they arrive from the spirit-soul world and clothe themselves with bodies? Human beings want to bring what they previously lived through in the spiritual world to the reality of the physical world. Before the change of teeth, human beings are, in a sense, focused upon the past. Human beings are still filled with the devotion developed in the spiritual world. For this reason they focus upon their surroundings by imitating people. What, then, is the basic impulse, the still completely unconscious tenor of children before the change of teeth? This attitude is something very beautiful that we must nurture. It is something that arises from an unconscious belief, namely that the world is moral. This is not completely true of modern souls; however, when people enter the world, because they are physical beings, there is a tendency to begin with an unconscious belief, namely, the world is moral. Until the change of teeth, and to an extent, beyond, it is good for education that we take this unconscious belief into account. I took this into account when I presented two readings, and showed that the preparation for them lives completely in the assumption of morality.[9] In the piece about the shepherd's dog, the butcher's dog, and the lap dog, human morals are reflected in the animal world. For Hoffmann von Fallersleben's poem about the violet, I attempted to bring morality without pedantry to children over seven by taking into account the supposition that the world is moral.[10] That children are a human race who still believes in the morality of the world and, therefore, believes they may imitate the world is precisely what is so uplifting and wonderful about them. Children live so much in the past and, in many respects, reveal, not the physical, but the prenatal, the spirit-soul past.

After human beings have gone through the change of teeth, they actually live constantly in the present, and until puberty are interested in things of the present. In teaching, we must always take into account that elementary school children always want to live in the present. How do people live in the present, then? We live in the present when we enjoy the world in a human, as opposed to an animalistic, way. It is quite true that elementary school children want to enjoy the world in school also. We should not miss the opportunity to teach in such a way that the education is something that is rather enjoyable for children, not animalistically enjoyable, but enjoyable in a higher human sense, and not something that evokes antipathy and repulsion. Pedagogy has made all kinds of good attempts in this area; however, there is also something dangerous here. The danger is that when we try to use the idea that teaching should be a source of joy, it can easily be distorted into something mundane, and that should not occur. We can only avoid that when, as teachers, we always want to raise ourselves above the mundane, the pedantic, the narrow-minded. We can accomplish this only if we maintain a living relationship to art. We make a particular assumption if we wish to enjoy the world humanly, and not animalistically, namely, that the world is beautiful. From the time of the change of teeth until puberty, children also unconsciously assume that they may find the world to be beautiful. We do not, in truth, take into account this unconscious assumption of children that the world is beautiful, and that, therefore, education must be beautiful, if we think we may teach in a banal fashion, from the sole standpoint of utility, and make up rules for teaching through demonstration. Instead, we must attempt to delve into artistic experience so that we permeate education, particularly in this time, with the artistic. We can certainly become sad when we read modern instruction manuals and see how the good intentions people have to make education a source of joy do not come to fruition when what the teachers say to the children makes such an unaesthetic and mundane impression. Today, people love to practice illustrative teaching according to the Socratic method.[11] However, the questions that are put to the children have the character of superficial utilitarianism and not the character of something living in beauty. Here, all the examples in the world are useless. It is useless to tell teachers that they should choose their examples through this or that method. Examples are useful only when teachers draw upon their own relationship to art in selecting tasteful things to speak about to the children.

Before the change of teeth, children's lives take place with the unconscious belief that the world is moral. The second period from the change of teeth until puberty occurs with the unconscious presumption that the world is beautiful. It is only at puberty that a tendency begins to develop to find the world true. Only then can instruction take on a "systematized" quality. Before puberty it is not wise to offer systematized instruction because children have a correct inner concept of truth only following puberty.

In this manner you will come to the insight that the developing child brings the past from the higher worlds into this physical world, and that following the change of teeth, the present comes alive in the elementary school child. You will realize that people then enter a stage of life when impulses for the future take root in their souls. Past, present and future, and the life in them: this is what exists in the growing human being.

We want to stop here now and in two days continue with this discussion that will more and more enter into practical teaching.

10

We have already discussed the nature of the human being from the viewpoints of the soul and of the spirit. We have at least shed some light on how to consider the human being from the standpoints of the spirit and of the soul. We need to supplement these considerations, first, by connecting the spiritual, soul and bodily viewpoints to achieve a complete survey of the human being, and then continuing on to an understanding of external physicality.

First, we want to recall something that must have already struck us in various ways, namely, that the three aspects of the human being have different forms.[1] We have already noted that the form of the head is spherical and that the physical nature of the human head lies in this form. We then took note that the human chest is a fragment of a sphere, so that schematically, where the head is a sphere and the chest a crescent moon, clearly this crescent is part of a sphere.[2] We can thus complete the moon form of the human chest. You can correctly envision this middle portion of the human whole only if you consider it a sphere, but a sphere with only a portion, the crescent moon, visible and the other portion invisible (see sketch on following page).[3] You may recognize that when ancient people, who had the capacity to see forms more clearly than we can now, spoke of the head as consonant with the sun and the chest with the moon, they were not incorrect. Just as you can see only a portion of the sphere when the moon is not full, in the same way, we can see only a fragment of the middle human aspect in the form of the chest. You can see that the form of the human head in the physical world is relatively complete. The head shows itself physically as something completed. In a certain sense, it is what it appears to be and hides the least of itself.

The human chest hides quite a bit of itself, leaving a portion of its nature invisible. To understand human nature, it is very important to recognize that a major portion of the chest is invisible. The chest reveals its physicality only on one side, that is, toward the rear; toward the front it blends into the soul state. The head is only body; the human chest is body toward the rear and soul toward the front. We carry a real body only in our head as it rests upon our shoulders. We have body and soul by separating the physical chest from the remainder of the chest aspect and allowing it to be acted upon by the soul.

I   II

The third aspect of the human being is the limbs. From the standpoint of external observation, the limbs are set into the other two aspects, particularly into the torso. How can we understand the nature of the human limbs? We can understand the nature of the human limbs only when we imagine that parts that differ from those remaining in the chest are left over from the spherical form. A portion of the periphery remains in the chest. What remain for the limbs are more from the inside of the sphere, the radii; the core of the sphere is attached as limbs.

As I have often said, simply inserting one thing into another schematically will not achieve much. You must always intertwine things because that is what enlivens them. We have the limb nature of the human being embodied in the limbs. But, you see, the head also has "limbs." If you really look at the skull, for example, you will find that the upper and lower jawbones[4] are set onto the skull (see sketch on previous page). They are really attached like limbs. The skull has its own limbs, the upper and lower jawbones, and they are attached to the skull like limbs, but they are stunted and are really only bony structures. There is yet another difference. If you look at the limbs of the skull, that is, the upper and lower jawbones, you will notice that what are important are the bones themselves. If you look at the limbs attached to the entire body, at the real nature of the human limbs, you will find their essence in their clothing of muscles and blood vessels. In a sense, the bones of the arms and legs, hands and feet are only inserted into the muscles and blood vessels. The muscles and blood vessels in the upper and lower jaws, the limbs of the head, are stunted. What does this mean? As we have already heard, the organ of will lies in the blood and muscles. Therefore, the arms and legs, hands and feet, are developed for the will. What primarily serve the will, namely blood and muscles, are to a certain extent removed from the limbs of the head because what should develop tend toward the intellect and thinking cognition. Thus, if you want to study the expression of the will in physical forms, you will study the arms and legs, hands and feet. If you want to study how intelligence is revealed to the world, then you will study the head as a skull, as a bony structure, and how limb-like structures, like the upper and lower jawbones, are connected with the head. You can always see external forms as revelations of inner things, and you can understand them only when you see them as revelations of inner things.

I have found that most people have great difficulty comprehending the relationship between the tubular arm and leg bones and the bowl-like bones of the head. It is good in this regard for teachers to learn a concept that lies far from normal life. Thus, we come to something very difficult, perhaps the most difficult thing we need to imagine, and something that we must get past in these pedagogical lectures.

You know that Goethe first turned his attention to the so-called vertebral theory of the skull.[5] What does that mean? It means he used metamorphic thinking in connection with the human being and its form. If you consider the human backbone, you will see that one vertebra sits upon the other. We can remove one vertebra with its horns and passage for the spinal cord [Dr. Steiner made a sketch].[6]

From his observation of a sheep's skull in Venice, Goethe perceived that all the bones of the head were transformed vertebrae.[7] That means that if you think of a vertebra and push it and pull it various ways, you will create the bowl-like form of the skull. This insight made a great impression upon Goethe and was very important for him because he had to conclude that the skull is a transformed, a more developed, spinal column.

You can relatively easily see that the skull arises out of a metamorphosis of the backbone. However, it is relatively difficult to comprehend the limb bones, even the limb bones of the head, that is, the upper and lower jaw, as a transformation of the vertebrae, or skull. (Goethe attempted this, but in a still superficial way.) Why is that? It is because a tubular bone is also a metamorphosis or a transformation of the skull, but in a quite particular way. You can relatively easily picture a vertebra transformed into a skull in that you think of the individual parts enlarged or reduced. However, it is not so easy to get the shape of tubular arm or leg bones from the bowl-shaped skull. You must use a certain procedure to achieve that. You must use the same procedure with tubular arm or leg bones that you would use when you put on a sock or a glove and first turn it inside out. It is relatively easy to imagine how a glove or a sock looks when turned inside out, but tubular bones are not uniform. They are not so thin walled as to be uniform inside and out. They are made differently on the inside and outside. If you made a sock in the same way and then made it elastic so that you could artistically form it with all kinds of bumps and dents, and then turned it inside out, you would no longer have the same form on the outside as the inside. It is the same with tubular bones. You must turn the inside toward the outside and the outside toward the inside. What results is the form of the skull. The human limbs are not only a transformation of the skull, they are, in addition, a skull turned inside out. Why is that so? It is so because the head has its center somewhere inside; it is concentric. The chest does not have its midpoint in the middle of the crescent; the midpoint of the chest lies very far away.[8] The sketch only partially indicates this since it would be very large if it were completely drawn. The chest has its center very far away.

Where does the midpoint of the limb system lie? Now we come to the second difficulty. The midpoint of the limbs lies in the complete circumference.[9] The middle point of the limbs is actually a sphere, the opposite of a point. It is a spherical surface. The middle is actually everywhere, and this is the reason that you can turn in every direction and that the radii enter from every direction. They are united with you.

What is in the head arises out of the head, but what occurs in the limbs unites itself with you. For this reason I said in another lecture that you must think of the limbs as being set into you.[10] We are really a whole universe, only what wants to enter us is concentrated at its end and becomes visible.

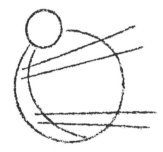

A very small portion of what we are becomes visible in our limbs, enough for the limbs to be something corporeal, but actually only a scintilla of what exists in the human limb system, namely the spirit. The body, soul and spirit exist in the human limb system. The body is only hinted at in the limbs; however, they also contain the soul as well as the spirit, which in principle encompasses the entire universe.

We can also make another sketch of the human being. We can view the human being as a gigantic sphere that encompasses the entire universe, then a smaller sphere and then a still smaller sphere. Only the smallest sphere is completely visible; the somewhat larger sphere is only partially visible; the largest sphere is visible only at the end of its radii and the remainder is invisible. In this way the form of the human being is created out of the universe.

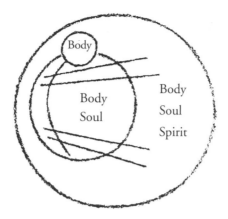

In the central system, in the chest, we have the head united with the limbs. If you look at the backbone and the connections to the ribs, you will see that toward the front there is an attempt at closure. In the back everything is closed; however, toward the front there is only an attempt at closure. The closer the ribs are to the head, the better they achieve closure, and the lower they lie, the more they fail at this. The last ribs do not come together at all because the outside forces that enter the limbs act against it.

The Greeks were still quite conscious that the human being is connected with the entirety of the macrocosm. The Egyptians also knew this very well, only they knew it abstractly. When you look at Egyptian sculpture, or at old statues in general, you can see the expression of this cosmic thought. You cannot understand what people in ancient times did if you do not know that their actions were consistent with their beliefs, namely, that the head is a small sphere, a miniaturized heavenly body, and that the limbs are a radial piece of the entire cosmos entering the human form. The Greeks had a beautiful and harmonious picture of this, which is why they were good sculptors. Today, you cannot really understand human sculpture unless you are aware of the connection of the human being with the cosmos. Otherwise, you only fumble around with external natural forms.

From what I just said, you will recognize that the limbs incline more toward the cosmos and the head more toward the individual human being. However, toward what do the limbs tend? They tend toward the cosmos in which the human being moves and continually changes position. They have a relationship to cosmic movement. You must understand that the limbs have a relationship to cosmic movement.

When we move around in the cosmos and perform deeds, we are limb human beings. What does cosmic movement have to do with our head? I already mentioned that, from another perspective, the head rests upon the shoulders. The head has the task of stilling the continuous movement of the cosmos. You can imagine yourself in your head by picturing yourself sitting in a train. The train moves forward and you sit quietly within it. In the same way your soul sits in your head as it allows the limbs to move it about and brings an inner stillness to this movement. Just as you can stretch out and rest in the train (if you have sufficient room, perhaps even a sleeping car)—despite the fact that this rest is not true rest since you are moving rapidly through the world, nevertheless, you have a feeling of resting—in the same way, the head calms what the limbs accomplish as cosmic movement. The chest is in the middle and mediates movement in the external world with what the head brings to rest.

Now imagine we human beings want to imitate cosmic movement with our limbs. What do we do then? We dance. In reality, we dance. What we commonly call dancing is only a fragmentary kind of dancing. All dancing arises out of the human limbs' imitation of the movements of the planets and other heavenly bodies, including the Earth itself.

However, what do the head and chest do when we imitate cosmic movements through dancing? In the head and chest it is as if we stifled our movements in the world. They cannot continue through the chest into the head because this fellow is sitting on our shoulders and does not allow movements to continue on into the soul. The soul has to participate in movement from a state of rest because the head rests upon the shoulders. What does the soul do then? It begins to reflect upon the dancing of the limbs. It starts to growl when the limbs perform irregular movements; it begins to murmur when the limbs move rhythmically, and it even begins to sing when the limbs move in harmony with the cosmic movements of the universe. In this way, dancing is transformed outwardly into song and inwardly into music.[11]

Unless sense physiology accepts the cosmic nature of the human being, it will never comprehend perception. It will never know how the movements in the air are connected with music. It will always maintain that movements are out there in the air and that people perceive music inwardly. That is what physiology and psychology texts state, the only difference being that one does so at the end and the other at the beginning.

Where does this come from? It arises out of the fact that people who practice psychology or physiology do not know that what people outwardly express in movement they inwardly bring to rest in the soul and thus begin to transform into tones. It is the same with other sense perceptions. Because the organs in the head do not participate in external movement, they reflect these movements back into the chest and transform them into tones, into other sense perceptions. This is the origin of all feeling and is also the connection with the arts.[12] The musical arts arise from the sculptural and architectural arts because the sculptural and architectural arts are outwardly what the musical arts are inwardly. The musical arts are the reflection of the world from within outwards. This is how people exist amid the cosmos. Feel a color as a movement that has come to rest. Just as when you stretch out in a train and have the illusion that you are at rest, you do not externally perceive the movement. You allow the train to move along. Through fine imperceptible movements of the limbs, you allow your body to participate in the outer world while inwardly, you perceive only colors and tones. You owe this to the fact that your head as a form is carried in rest by the limbs.

As I already said, what I have to tell you here is rather difficult. It is particularly difficult because absolutely nothing is done in our time to comprehend these things. Everything we currently understand as education is done so that people remain unknowledgable about these things. What actually occurs through our modern education? People cannot fully understand a sock or glove without turning it inside out because they will not know what touches their skin in the sock or glove. They will know only what is on the outside. In the same way modern education teaches people to know only what is turned toward the outside, and they have a concept for only half a human being. They cannot comprehend even the limbs because the limbs are the spirit turned inside out.

What we have presented today, we can also characterize in a different way. If we look at the whole human being standing before us in the world, first as a limb being, we find ourselves presented with spirit, soul and body. If we look at the human being as a chest being, we are presented with soul and body. The large sphere (see the sketch above): spirit, body, soul; the smaller sphere: body, soul; the smallest sphere: body only. At the Council of 869, the Bishops of the Catholic Church forbade humanity to know anything about the large sphere.[13] At that time they declared it a dogma of the Catholic Church that only the middle-sized and smallest spheres existed, that human beings consisted only of body and soul, and that the soul merely contained something spiritual. According to this view, the soul is also spirit-like. Since 869, spirit ceased to exist for the occidental culture arising from Catholicism. However, by removing the relationship to the spirit, the relationship of the human being to the cosmos was also severed. The human being was driven more and more into egotism. Therefore, religion itself became increasingly egotistical, and we now live in a time when we must again, through spiritual observation, encounter the relationship of human beings to the spirit and, thus, to the cosmos.

Who is actually responsible for the present scientific materialism? Since the Catholic Church banished the spirit at the Council of Constantinople in 869, it carries the primary responsibility for our scientific materialism. What actually occurred then? Look at the human head. It has so developed in the course of world events that it is today the oldest aspect of the human being. The head arose out of the higher and, going still further back, out of the lower, animals.[14] Regarding our head, we are descendants of the animal world. There is nothing more to say—the head is simply a more developed animal. We return to the world of the lower animals if we want to seek the predecessors of our heads. The chest was added to the head later and is not as animalistic. We received the chest only later. As human beings, we acquired the limbs as the latest organs, and they are the most human. They are not transformed animal organs, but were added later. The animalistic organs were formed independently from the cosmos to the animals, and the human organs were later added independently to the chest. However, because the Catholic Church wanted to hide the relationship of the human being to the cosmos, that is, the true nature of the human limbs, it carried only a small amount of the chest and more of the head, or skull, into the following ages. Thus, materialism came to the idea that the skull descended from the animals and now speaks of the idea that the entire human being descended from animals, whereas the chest and limb organs developed only later. Particularly because the Catholic Church wanted to hide the nature of the human limbs and their connection to the cosmos, it induced a later materialistic time to fall into the idea that only the head has any meaning and that it represents the entire human being. In truth, the Catholic Church is the creator of materialism in the study of evolution. It is particularly important that modern teachers know such things because they should connect their interests with what has occurred in the world. They should know the foundations of things that have occurred in the world.

Today, we have attempted to clarify how our era became materialistic by beginning with something quite different, namely with the sphere, the crescent and the radial form of the limbs. That is, we began with something apparently at the opposite pole in order to clarify a large, overpowering historical fact. This is necessary so that particularly the teacher, who otherwise can accomplish nothing with the growing child, is able to grasp cultural facts by the roots. Teachers can then take up something necessary to proper teaching through their unconscious and subconscious relationships to children. Teachers can then properly respect the human form and see it everywhere in relationship to the cosmos. They can approach the human form differently than when they see it only as a better-formed animal body. Today, teachers, even though they often give in to illusions when in their studies, basically stand before the children with a clear awareness that the growing child is a young calf or small animal, and that they are to develop this little animal a little further than nature has done. Teachers will feel differently when they say to themselves that here is a human being from whom relationships extend out to the entire cosmos and that when I do my work with every one of these growing children, I do something that has meaning for the entire universe. We are in the classroom, and within every child lies a center of the universe. The classroom is a center, yes, even many centers for the macrocosm. Think to yourselves how alive this feels and what it means! Think about how the idea of the cosmos and its connection to the human being becomes a feeling that makes each act of teaching holy. If we do not have such feelings about human beings and the cosmos, we cannot seriously and properly teach. At the moment when we have such feelings, they are carried through subearthly bonds to the children. In another regard, I mentioned that it is a thing filled with wonder to see that the Earth conducts electricity without wires when wires are attached to copper plates in the Earth.[15] If you go to school with only egotistical human feelings, then you will need all sorts of wires—words—to communicate with the children. If you have the great cosmic feelings that unfold such ideas as we have just developed, then a subearthly conductor goes to the child. Then you are one with the children. This is part of the mysterious relationship between you and all school children. We must base what we call pedagogy upon such feelings. Pedagogy may not be a system, it must be an art. Where is an art we can learn without continuously living in feeling? However, the feelings in which we must live in order to practice that great art of life that is pedagogy, the feelings that we must have for pedagogy, are brought to life only through an observation of the cosmos and its connection with the human being.

11

If you think about the spirit and soul nature of the human body as presented in yesterday's lecture, you will be able to quickly integrate everything necessary to comprehend the structure and development of the human body. Before we go on to describe the human body in the remaining lectures, we will first continue to illuminate the spirit-soul perspective.

Yesterday, you saw that the human being is comprised of three aspects—that is, the head, the torso, and the limbs. You also saw that each of these three aspects has a different relationship to the world of soul and spirit.

Let us first consider the form of the human head. Yesterday we said that the head is primarily physical. We saw that the chest has physical and soul characteristics, and the limbs physical, soul and spiritual characteristics. Of course, we have not completely described the nature of the head by saying that the head is primarily physical. In reality things are not so sharply separated from one another. We could just as well say that the head has soul and spiritual characteristics, only in a different way than the chest and limbs. When a human being is born, the head is primarily physical, that is, the form of the physical head expresses what, in a certain sense, constitutes the head. That is why the head looks as it does (it is also the first thing formed in human embryonic development); the general human spirit-soul characteristic first appears in the head. What is the relationship of the physical head to the spirit and soul? The head is the most completely formed part of the body. Because everything necessary for its formation has in earlier stages of development already passed from the animal-like stages up to the human being, it can physically be the most completely formed. The soul is connected with the head at birth and during the child's first years of life; everything connected with the soul dreams in the head. Also, the spirit sleeps in the head.

In the human head, we find an unusual integration of body, soul, and spirit. We have an extremely well developed body in the head. In it, we have a dreaming soul, a soul that clearly dreams, and a spirit that still sleeps. Our task is to see how to harmonize these facts with the development of the whole human being. This development is such that until the change of teeth, the human being is primarily an imitative being. Children imitate what they see in their surroundings. They can do that because the spirit aspect of their heads sleeps. Therefore, they can spend time with the spirit aspect of the head outside the bodily aspect, that is, spend time with it in their surroundings. When you sleep, you exist with your spirit-soul outside your body. Children exist outside their heads with their spirit-soul, with their sleeping spirit and dreaming soul; they live in their surroundings. This is the reason children are beings that imitate. It is also why a love of the surroundings, in particular, a love for the parents, develops in children's dreaming souls. However, when children acquire their second set of teeth, when their change of teeth is complete, it reflects the conclusion of the development of the head. Even though the head is complete when we are born, it still goes through a final stage of development during the first seven years of life. The conclusion of this development occurs with the change of teeth.

What is actually concluded? The development of the form is concluded. At this time, human beings have taken what hardens and gives form into their physical bodies. When we see the second set of teeth breaking through in a child, we can say that the child has finished the first confrontation with the world. That is, the child has done what is necessary to provide form. During the period when the child completes the formation of the head, something else occurs in the human chest.

In the chest, things are very different than in the head. From birth, from the very beginning, the chest has physical and soul characteristics. Unlike the head, the chest does not simply have physical characteristics. The chest has physical and soul characteristics, and only the spirit exists in a dreaming state outside it. When we observe children during the first years of life, we must focus upon the greater awareness, the greater liveliness, of the chest aspect compared with the head aspect. It would be completely incorrect if we were to view human beings as single entities chaotically thrown together.

The limbs are again different. Here, from the first moment of life, spirit, soul, and body are intimately connected and permeate each other. Here a child is first completely awake, as those who are to raise this kicking and wiggling child notice. Everything is awake, only undeveloped. The secret of human beings is that at birth the spirit aspect of the head is very well developed but sleeping, and the soul aspect of the head is well developed, but dreaming. They must slowly awaken. At birth, the limb aspect of the human being, although very much awake, is unformed and undeveloped.

Actually, we only need to develop the human limb aspect and part of the chest aspect. Here you have the first real attribute of education: the human limbs and chest have the task of awakening the head. You develop the limb aspect and a part of the chest aspect and allow them to awaken the other parts of the human chest and head. From this you can see that children present you with something substantial to work with. Children offer you complete spirits and relatively complete souls, which they brought into life at birth. You only need to develop the child's immature spirit and their even more immature soul.

If this were not the case, education and teaching would be impossible. If you imagine that we want to teach all of the spirit that a human being brings into the world, then, as teachers, we would need to be perfectly aware of what this person could become. In this case you might quickly give up teaching because you could only teach children to be as intelligent and genial as yourself. Of course, you would then be in the position of having to teach children who are in some ways more intelligent and more genial than you are. That is possible only because in teaching we are concerned with only part of the human being—that is, the part we can teach even though we are not as intelligent, as genial, or perhaps even as good as the student. The best we can do is to educate the will and part of the feeling soul. What we can educate through the will—that is, through the limbs, and through feeling, through part of the human chest—we can bring to the level of perfection we ourselves have reached. Just as a servant can awaken someone who is much more intelligent than he or she, so we can teach someone who may be more genial, or even better than we, something beyond what we ourselves are. Of course, we must be clear that, regarding intellectual things, we certainly do not need to be at the same level as a developing child. However, because so much depends upon the development of will, we must strive to be as good as possible. The children can become better than we are, but probably will not unless our teaching is supplemented by something from the world or other people.

In these lectures I have mentioned that a certain genius lives in language. The genius of language is, as I have said, ingenious. It is more clever than we are. We can learn much from the way language fits together and carries its spirit.

However, there is genius in more things in our surroundings than language. Think for a moment about what we have just learned, namely, that regarding the head, humans enter the world with a sleeping spirit and a dreaming soul. Recall that it is necessary from the very beginning, from birth, to educate children through the will because unless we act upon them through the will, we cannot reach the spirit sleeping in their heads. We would create a major gap in human development if we could not in some way reach the spirit aspect in the heads of people. When human beings are born the spirit in the heads is asleep. We cannot get a child with kicking legs to do gymnastics or eurythmy. This is impossible. We also cannot get a child when it is still kicking its legs and, at best, crying, to take up musical instruction. We cannot yet reach the child through art. We cannot yet find a clearly defined bridge from the will to the child's sleeping spirit. Later, when we can somehow reach the child's will, we can act upon the child's sleeping spirit if we can only get the child to say those first words, since a confronting of the will already exists there. Then the willed activity we can coax from the vocal organs through these first words acts on the spirit sleeping in the head and begins to awaken it. In the very beginning, however, we do not have any real bridge. There is no stream flowing from the limbs in which the will and spirit are awake to the sleeping spirit of the head. Some other means is required. In the first period of human life, we cannot accomplish much as teachers.

Something else exists that is also genius, that is spirit outside us. Language has its genius, but in the first stage of child development we are unable to appeal to the spirit of language. However, nature itself has its own genius and spirit. If this were not so, as human beings we would wither away because of the developmental gap at the beginning of our childhood. The genius of nature creates something that can form the bridge. From the development of the limbs, that is, from the limb-human, a substance is created that is directly connected to and contains something of this limb-human; and that substance is milk. Women create milk in direct connection to the upper limbs—that is, the arms. The milk-producing organs are an inner continuation of the limbs. In the animal and human kingdoms, milk is the only substance that has an inner kinship to the nature of the limbs. In a certain sense, milk is born out of the nature of the limbs, and therefore, has the power of the limbs' essence still in it. When the mother gives a child her milk, the milk acts as the only substance, or at least the main substance, to awaken the sleeping spirit that exists in all matter and manifests itself where it should. Milk carries its own spirit, and this spirit has the task of awakening the child's sleeping spirit. This is not simply a picture; it is a well-founded scientific fact that the genius of nature that creates milk out of the secret essence of nature, is the awakener of the child's sleeping human spirit. We must gain insight into such secret relationships in world existence. Only then can we grasp the wonderful regularities the world holds. We slowly understand that we are painfully ignorant when we create theories about material substances as if these substances were only an insignificant expanse to be divided into atoms and molecules. That is not what matter is. Matter is something like milk that is created with an inner need to awaken the sleeping human spirit. Just as we can speak of the needs of human beings and animals, that is, speak of strength based in will, in the same way, we can speak generally of the "needs" of matter. We can look at milk in a comprehensive way only if we say that as it is created, milk desires to be the awakener of the child's human spirit. If we properly look at things in this way, everything in our surroundings becomes alive. We can, therefore, never be free of the relationships between human beings and everything else that exists in the world.

You can see, from what I have just said, that the genius of nature attends to human development during the first stage of life. In a certain sense, we take up the work of the genius of nature when we further develop and educate the child. Through our language and deeds, which the child imitates and which affect the child through the will, we continue that activity we have seen the genius of nature effecting through milk, only we use humans as a means of providing this nutrition. We also see that nature teaches since the nutrition received through milk is the first means of education. Nature teaches naturally. We begin to teach the soul through our language and deeds, which act upon the child educationally. That is why it is so important to be conscious that as teachers we cannot do very much with the head. When it is born into the world, the head already presents us with what it will become. We can awaken what is in the head, but, we have no possibility of putting more there.

Here we need to become clear that birth can bring only certain things into earthly physical existence. The things that have arisen through superficial convention during the course of cultural development are totally unimportant for the spiritual world. For instance, our conventional means of reading or writing are, of course, not brought by the child (I have already discussed this from another point of view).[1] Spirits do not write, nor do they read. They do not read in books nor write with a pen. It is only a creation of spiritualists to think that spirits work with human language, or even write. What speech, or even writing contains is simply convention living upon the Earth. We do something good for the child only when we do not teach these conventions of reading and writing intellectually, but instead implant reading and writing into the child through the chest and limbs.

Of course, we have not simply left the children in their cradles before they are seven years old and begin elementary school. They have done things and through imitating adults have helped themselves along so that, in a certain sense, their head-spirit has awakened. When children begin elementary school, we can use what they have already awakened in their head-spirit to teach reading and writing in the conventional way. But, then we begin to damage this head-spirit through our influence. For this reason, I have said that, to be good, the instruction of reading and writing must be based in art. We must first introduce elements of drawing and painting and music, because these affect the human limb and chest aspects, and affect only indirectly the head. However, they do awaken what is in the head. You do not torture the head aspect in the way we do if we simply teach reading and writing in the intellectual, conventional way. If we first allow children to draw and then develop letters from their drawings, we teach the children from the limbs to the head. We show them an *f*, for example. If we make children look at the *f* and copy it, we act upon intellect, and then the intellect trains the will. This is the wrong way. The proper way is to do as much as possible through the will to awaken the intellect. We can do this only if we begin with the artistic and then go on to forming the intellect. During the first years of teaching, when we first receive the children, we must teach them reading and writing in an artistic way.

You must realize that while you are teaching children, they have things to do other than what you are doing with them. Children have all kinds of things to do which belong only indirectly to your domain. Children must grow. They must grow, and you need to be clear that while you are teaching, children must grow properly. What does that mean? It means that you should not disturb growth through your teaching; you should not engage children in anything that would disturb their growth. Your teaching must work in parallel with the needs of growth. What I have to say here is particularly important for the elementary school years. In the same way that what arises from the head before the change of teeth is connected with the *creation of form*, what occurs during the period of elementary schooling is the *development of life*, that is, growth and everything connected with it until puberty. The development of life arising out of the chest activity concludes only at puberty. Thus, during the development in elementary school, your primary concern is with the human chest aspect. You cannot be successful unless you realize that while you are teaching children, they develop through the chest organism. In a certain sense, you must be a comrade of nature, since nature develops children through the chest, that is, through breathing, nutrition, movement and so forth.

You must be a good friend of natural development. However, if you have no understanding of natural development, how can you possibly be a good friend to it? If, for example, you do not know how to teach through the soul in order to slow down or accelerate growth, how can you teach well? The way you affect the soul to a certain extent gives you the possibility of disturbing the growth forces in the developing children so that they may grow tall and lanky, which can be damaging under certain circumstances. To a certain extent you can unhealthfully retard the children's growth so that they remain short and stocky.[2] Of course, only to a certain degree, but you can do this. Therefore, you need insight into the relationships of human growth. You must have this insight from the point of view of both the soul and the physical body.

From the perspective of the soul, how can we gain in-sight about growth? Here we must turn to something better than conventional psychology. From a more complete psychology, we can learn that everything that accelerates human growth forces and forms human growth so that people shoot up and become lanky is connected in a certain sense with the formation of memory. If we require too much of memory, then, within certain limits, we make lanky people out of children. If we require too much from imagination, then we retard people in their growth. Memory and imagination are connected with the human developmental forces in a secret way. We must acquire the proper eye in order to turn our attention to these connections.

For example, the teacher must be able to cast a comprehensive eye upon the class at the beginning of the school year, particularly when the children enter the phases that begin at age nine and twelve.[3] The teacher must review the physical development of the children and notice how they look. At the end of the school year or of another period, the teacher must again review and notice the changes that have occurred. The result of these two reviews must the teacher's realization that one child's growth may not have been enough during this period, and another may have shot up. The teacher must then ask: In the next school year or next period of time, how can I effect a balance between imagination and memory that counters these anomalies?

This is why it is so important that you have the same children during all of the school years, and why it is so idiotic that children have a different teacher every year. However, there is another side to this. At the beginning of each school year and at the beginning of each developmental period (at seven, nine and twelve years of age), teachers slowly come to know the children. They come to know children who are clearly the imagination type who reorganize everything, and they come to know children who are clearly memory types who can remember everything. Teachers must also become familiar with this. They must come to know it through the two reviews I just mentioned. However, teachers must extrapolate from this knowledge, not through an external observation of growth, but through imagination and memory, whether a child indicates the possibility of growing too quickly, which will happen if the child's memory is too good, or if the child is likely to become stocky from too much imagination. Clichés and jargon will not help you to recognize the connection between body and soul; you must instead be able to observe the interconnections between body, soul, and spirit in the growing human being. Children with much imagination grow differently than those gifted with memory.

In modern psychology everything is finished. Memory is there and psychologists describe it. Imagination is there, and it, too, is described. However, in the real world, everything is interconnected, and we can learn to understand these interconnections only if we can make our comprehension comfortable with them. That means we do not use our comprehension only to properly define everything, but instead we make this comprehension flexible so that what it has recognized it can change inwardly, it can change conceptually.

In itself the spirit-soul leads into the physical to a degree where we could say that through affects on the body, through the milk, the genius of nature raises the child at the beginning of life. In the same way, after the change of teeth, we raise children by slowly feeding them with art during elementary school. As children near the end of elementary school, another change occurs: their independent judgment, their own feelings of personality and their desires for independence will slowly sparkle in from a later period. We consider this when we form a curriculum so that we use what should enter in.

12

When we consider the human body, we must bring it into relationship with our physically sensible surroundings, because it exists in a continuous interaction with them, and they support it. When we gaze at our physical surroundings, we perceive minerals, plants, and animals. Our physical body is related to these minerals, plants, and animals. Superficial observation, however, does not immediately reveal the type of relationship; we must delve more deeply into the essence of the natural kingdoms if we want to understand the interaction between human beings and their physical surroundings.

We first perceive the skeleton and muscles of the human physical body. If we penetrate further, we then perceive the circulatory system and the organs associated with it. We perceive breathing and the digestive processes. We can see how the organs, as natural science calls them, develop out of various vessel forms. We perceive the brain, the nerves, the sense organs. Our task is to integrate these various human organs and processes into the world where the human being exists.

Let us begin with what at first seems most complete (we have already seen how it is in reality), that is, let us begin with the human brain and nervous system, and its interconnections with the sense organs. Here we have those human functions and structures that have developed over the longest period, so that they have gone beyond the animal form. The human central nervous system has, in a sense, gone through and beyond that of the animal to a truly human system most clearly expressed as the head.

Yesterday, we spoke of the head's effect on individual human development, that is, the extent to which the formation of the human body arises out of forces emanating from the head. We also saw that the effects of the head in a sense conclude with the change of teeth, around seven years of age. We need to be clear about what actually occurs in the interaction of the human head with the chest and limb organs. We need to answer the question: What does the head actually do in its work with the torso and limbs? It continuously forms. In the first seven years, our life consists of a formative impulse emanating from the head and entering the physical body. After that time, the head continues to assist by preserving the form and filling it with soul and spirit.

The head is connected with human formation, but does the head create our human form? No, it does not. You must get used to the idea that the head always secretly wants to make something of you other than what you are. There are moments when the head wants to form you so that you look like a wolf. There are moments when the head wants to form you so that you look like a lamb, then to make you look like a worm and to change you from a worm to a dragon. All of the forms your head would like to make of you, you can find illustrated in the various animal forms of nature. If you were to look at the animal kingdom, you could say to yourself: There I am; only my torso and limbs continually do me the favor of reforming me from a wolf back to a human being each time my head attempts to make a wolf out of me. You continually overcome what is animalistic. You overcome it such that it does not ever come into existence; instead, you metamorphose and transform it. Through the head, human beings are related to the animal kingdom, but in such a way that in their physical activities, they continually go beyond it. What actually remains in you? You can look at someone. You can imagine someone, and you can create an interesting observation by saying: There is a human being. On top, there is a head, but it moves like a wolf. However, it is not a wolf. The wolf is dissolved by the torso and the limbs. It moves like a lamb, but is dissolved by the torso and limbs.

Animal forms are always active supersensibly in the human being and are then dissolved. What would happen if there were a supersensible photographer who could capture this process? If we could capture this whole process on photographic plates or on continually changing photographic plates, what would they show? What would we see in these photographs? We would see human thoughts. Human thoughts are the supersensible equivalent of what is not expressed sense perceptibly. The continual metamorphosis of animalistic tendencies streaming downward from the head is not expressed sense perceptibly, but those tendencies act supersensibly upon the human being as the thought process. That really exists as a supersensible process. Your head is not just a lazybones sitting on your shoulders. It is actually the thing that would like to keep you an animal. It gives you the forms of the whole animal kingdom and continually wants to create the animal kingdom. However, due to your torso and limbs, you do not allow yourself to become a whole animal kingdom while you are alive; instead, you transform this animal kingdom in your thoughts. That is how we stand in relationship to the animal kingdom. We allow the animal kingdom to arise in us supersensibly, but do not allow it to come to sense-perceptible reality. Instead, we hold it in the supersensible. The torso and limbs do not allow the arising animals into their realms. If the head tends too strongly to create something from those animalistic forms, the remainder of the organism resists it, and the head must resort to migraines and similar conditions to destroy them.[1]

The torso also has a relationship to the environment. However, it is a relationship not to the animal realm, but to the entire plant world.[2] A secret connection exists between the human torso, that is, the chest, and the plant world. In the torso, it occurs primarily in the circulation, breathing and digestion. All of these processes interact with the natural physical activity of the plant world, but within a very unusual relationship.

Let us first look at breathing. What does a person do while breathing? You know that a person takes in oxygen and combines it metabolically with carbon, thereby producing carbon dioxide. Carbon enters the body through metabolized food. The carbon bonds with oxygen, thus forming carbon dioxide. This would be a fine opportunity for people, once they have created carbon dioxide, to retain it rather than to expel it. What would happen if they could separate the carbon from the oxygen? If, after human beings inhaled oxygen and bonded it with carbon to form carbon dioxide, they were then able to release the oxygen but retain and use the carbon, what would then occur. The plant world. A variety of plants would suddenly grow in people. Plants could grow. When you look at a plant, what does it do? Plants do not rhythmically inhale oxygen as people do; they assimilate carbon dioxide. By day, plants are eager for carbon dioxide and give off oxygen. It would be dreadful if plants did not do that since we and animals would then have no oxygen. However, plants retain the carbon and form starch and sugars out of it. They build their entire organism from it. The world of plants exists because plants are formed of carbon separated from the assimilated carbon dioxide. If you look at the plant world, you will see that plants are metamorphosed carbon separated in the assimilation process that corresponds to human breathing. In a way, plants breathe, but differently from the way people breathe. Only superficial observation could assert that plants breathe. They do breathe a little in the night, but to say this is breathing would be the same as if you were to say: Here is a razor blade; I want to cut meat with it. The breathing process in plants is different from that of people and animals in the same way that a razor blade is different from a steak knife. The human breathing process corresponds to the reverse process in plants, namely, assimilation.

Now you can understand how all kinds of plants could grow in you if the process that forms carbon dioxide were to continue, and oxygen were again expelled. If carbon dioxide were transformed into carbon as is done in nature (you have the materials in you), then you could internally achieve the sudden growth of the entire plant world. You would disappear and be replaced by the plant world. The capacity to continually create a world of plants exists in human beings, but they do not allow it to come to completion. The torso has a strong tendency to create the plant world. However, the head and limbs do not allow that to occur; they resist it. Human beings exhale carbon dioxide and inhibit the growth of the plant kingdom in themselves. Instead, they allow the plant kingdom to arise from carbon dioxide in the world outside.

The curious interrelationship of the torso and its sense-perceptible surroundings is that the plant world exists outside people, and that, in order not to become a plant, people must not allow the vegetative process to arise within them. When it occurs, they must immediately expel it. We can, therefore, say that human beings are capable of creating the inverse of the plant kingdom in the torso. If you imagine the plant kingdom as positive, then people create the negative of it. In a sense, they create the reverse of the plant kingdom.

What occurs when the plant kingdom begins to misbehave in people, and the head and limbs do not have sufficient strength to stop it in its tracks? Then, people become ill! In principle, internal illnesses that arise in the torso occur because people are too weak to immediately hinder vegetative growth. If, at the moment when something within us tends toward the plant kingdom, we are not able to expel it immediately and let it create its own kingdom outside us, we become ill. We must seek the nature of illness in the realization that plants begin to grow in people. Of course, people do not become plants because the interior of a human being is not a pleasant surrounding for a lily. However, a tendency for the plant kingdom to arise can occur due to a weakness of the other systems, and then people become ill. If we look at the entire plant world, we must admit that in a certain sense the plant world presents us with pictures of all our illnesses. It is a curious aspect of the human connection to nature that not only can we see pictures of preadolescent human development in plants, as we have discussed on other occasions, but, insofar as plants bear fruit, we can also see pictures of illness.[3] This is something that people may not like to hear because, of course, they love the aesthetics of the plant world. Insofar as the plant world unfolds its nature outside human beings, people are correct in their aesthetic viewpoint. However, when the plant world wants to unfold its nature inside human beings, that is, when human beings want to become plant-like, then what is active in the colorful world of plants outside then becomes the cause of illness inside them. Medicine will become a science when it can bring each illness into correspondence with a plant.[4] It is simply a fact that as people exhale carbon dioxide for the sake of their existence, in reality, they exhale the plant world wanting to develop in them.

You need not be amazed that when plants extend beyond their normal existence and develop poisons, these poisons also have a connection with human health and disease. However, there is also a connection with normal digestion.

Digestion, like breathing, also occurs in the torso, and must be considered in a similar way.[5] In digestion, people ingest their surroundings but do not allow them to remain as they are; they transform them. People transform their surroundings with the help of oxygen brought in through breathing. They join what they eat with oxygen after they transform the food. This process appears to be a process of combustion, making people look as if they continuously burned inside. Scientists often say that a burning, oxidizing process is active in people. However, that is not true. What occurs in people is not a real oxidation process. It is an oxidation process—pay attention to this—that is missing the beginning and end. It is only the middle stage of combustion, and the beginning and end are missing. The beginning and end of the oxidation process must never occur in the human body, only the middle. If the first stage of oxidation took place in the human organism, as it does in the formation of fruit, it would be destructive, as when people eat unripe fruit. People cannot endure the beginning of the combustion process. It cannot exist in them and makes them ill. When people can eat a large amount of unripe fruit, as strong country people can, it is because they have such an extremely strong relationship to the surrounding nature that they can digest unripe apples and pears in the same way they digest fruit cooked to maturity by the sun. Generally, people can endure only the middle part of the process, only the middle oxidizing process of digestion. People are also not able to participate in the concluding stages of the process, which is like what occurs when ripe fruit begins to rot. They cannot take part in the end of the process and must, therefore, excrete the nutritional matter. In fact, natural processes are not completed in people as they are in the environment; only the middle portions are completed in people. They cannot complete the beginning and the ending.

Now we see something very unusual. Consider breathing. It is the opposite of everything that occurs in the plant world. In a sense, it is "anti-plant kingdom." Human breathing is anti-plant kingdom. Inside human beings, breathing joins with digestion, the middle portion of an external process. As you can see, two different things live in our physical torso, namely, the anti-plant process of breathing that always acts with the middle portion of the other, the external, natural processes. These things interact. Here is the connection between body and soul; it is the mysterious connection between body and soul. When the human breathing process connects with the middle part of the remaining natural processes, the soul, that is, the anti-plant process, connects with the humanly physical that is always the middle portion of natural processes. Science will have to think long and hard about the inner connections between body and soul if it does not seek them in the mysterious connection between the ensouled breath and the bodily existence of the middle part of natural processes. These natural processes neither rise nor fall in human beings. They begin outside people and can end only after they are excreted. People are physically connected only with the middle events of the natural processes, and these processes are ensouled by breathing.

Here arises the fine web of processes that the medicine and healthcare of the future must study. In the future, healthcare will need to ask how the various levels of heat interact in the cosmos. What is the effect of heat transferred from a cooler location to a warmer one and vice versa? How does an external heat process affect the human organism when a human being encounters it? An interplay of air and water in the processes of external vegetation has been identified, but its effects on people will need to be studied.

Modern medicine has barely begun to ask such questions. It places much greater value upon the discovery of the bacteria that cause a disease or illness.[6] It is satisfied when it knows this. However, it is much more important that we know how human beings can sometimes internally develop a tiny amount of the vegetative process so that bacteria sense that as a pleasant place to stay. What is important is that we maintain our bodies so they do not present a hospitable place for any kind of vegetative growth. If we do that, then these fine bacterial friends will no longer be able to create such chaos in us.

In considering the relationship of the physical human being to the outer world, we still have the question concerning the relationship of the skeleton and muscles to human vital processes.

Here we come to something that you absolutely must understand if you are to understand the human being, but that remains almost totally unconsidered by modern science. Consider what occurs when you bend your arm. Through contracting your muscles, you cause the lower arm to bend, which is a very mechanical process. Imagine that you held the position shown in this first sketch.

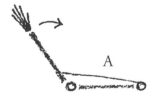

You could attach a string here (A) and roll it up. Then, the lower arm would make this movement. This is a mechanical movement. You also perform such mechanical movements when you bend your knees and walk. In walking, all the machinery of your body moves and forces act continuously, primarily forces of leverage, but forces, nevertheless. Now suppose it were possible to photograph only the forces a person employs walking, but not the person. That is, we could photograph the forces used to lift first one leg and then the other and so forth. We could photograph only the forces, and there would be nothing in the picture of the person. If you developed these photographs of forces, you would see only shadows, or, in the case of walking, a band of shadows. It would be an error to believe that you live with your I in the muscles and flesh. Even when you are awake, you do not live with your I in the muscles and flesh; you live with your I mainly in these shadows that you photographed, that is, in the forces that cause the movement of your body. For example, as odd as it may sound, when you sit down and press your back into the chair, you live with your I in the force that develops in that pressure. When you stand, you live in the force that your feet exert upon the Earth. You are always living in forces. It is untrue that our I lives in our visible bodies. Our I lives in forces. We only drag our visible bodies around with us during our physical earthly life. When we are wakeful, we live only in a force-body. But, what does this force-body actually do? It undertakes an unusual task.

When you eat, you ingest all kinds of mineral matter. Even though you may not salt your soup strongly, you ingest mineral matter (salt is already in the food). Further, you have a need to ingest minerals. What do you do with these minerals? You head is unable to do much with minerals, and the same is true of your torso. But your limbs inhibit minerals from assuming their natural crystal forms within you. If you did not develop the forces in your limbs, you would become a salt block when you ate salt. Your limbs, your skeleton and muscles, always tend to work against the mineral forming capacity of the Earth. That means they tend to dissolve minerals. The human forces that dissolve minerals come from the limbs.

If an illness goes beyond the simple vegetative stage, that is, if the body not only tends to allow the plant world to begin to grow, but also allows the crystallization process to begin, then an extremely destructive form of illness exists, for example, diabetes.[7] Then, the human body is no longer able to dissolve the minerals it takes in from the world as the forces from the limbs should dissolve them. When we are unable to overcome those illnesses arising from disease-causing mineralization in the body, it is often because we are unable to utilize fully the remedies against these illnesses that we all must take from the network of the sense organs or the brain or the nerves. In some form or another, we must use the pseudo-matter (I call it pseudo-matter for particular reasons) that is in the sense organs, in the brain and in the nerves, that decomposing matter, to gain control over such illnesses as gout, diabetes and so forth.[8] People can first become healthy in this area when we understand the relationship of human beings to nature from the standpoint I have discussed today.

We can only understand the human body by first understanding its processes and understanding that people must dissolve what is mineral in themselves, must invert what is plant in themselves and must raise themselves above, that is, spiritualize, what is animal.[9] Everything teachers should know about physical development is based upon such anthropological and anthroposophical considerations as those I have discussed with you here. Tomorrow, we want to discuss what we can build on this pedagogically.

13

I f we use what we have learned in these lectures as a basis, we can comprehend human behavior and understand how to relate to children's behavior. Our task is to use these insights properly. Concerning human behavior, remember that we must keep *two* things in mind, because we can speak of two contrasting human aspects, namely, the aspects of the limbs and head.

Head 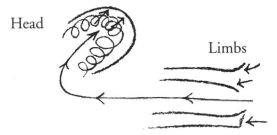 Limbs

We must assimilate the difficult idea that we can comprehend the form of the limbs only when we imagine the head turned inside out like a glove or a sock. The result has tremendous importance for all of human life. If we sketch this, we can say that the head is formed, in a sense, from internal pressure, that it is "inflated" from the inside out. When we think of the human limbs, we can imagine them as being compressed from the outside inward through being turned inside out at the forehead (this is very important in human life). Recall that your inner humanity streams from within toward your forehead. If you look at the palms of your hands and the soles of your feet, you will see that a kind of pressure continuously exists that is the same as the pressure from inside upon your forehead, only in the opposite direction. If you hold the palm of your hand up to the world, or place the sole of your foot upon the ground, the same thing streams in through your palm or your sole as streams from inside against your forehead. That is an extremely important fact. It is important because through it, we can see what the human spirit-soul actually is. You can see that the spirit-soul is a stream that flows through the human being.

What is the human being in relation to this spirit-soul? Imagine a flowing river which is then obstructed so that counterwaves form. In the same way, the spirit-soul breaks and cascades against the human being. Human beings are an obstruction for the spirit-soul wanting to flow unhindered through them; however, they block it and slow it. The spirit-soul backs up in people. However, the effect that I have referred to as a streaming is very strange. I have referred to this effect of the spirit-soul as something that flows through people; but, what is it in relationship to the physical body? It is something that continuously absorbs human beings.

People face the physical world, and the spirit-soul continuously tries to absorb them. For this reason, we are always shedding and peeling on the outside. If the spirit is not sufficiently strong, then we must cut off some parts, such as fingernails, because the spirit wants to destroy them by absorbing them from the outside. It destroys everything, but the body slows the spirit's destructiveness. People must create a balance within themselves between the destructive spirit-soul and the continuous growth of the body. The chest and abdomen are inserted into this stream; they fight against the destruction of the penetrating spirit-soul and fill people with matter. From this you can see that the human limbs extending out beyond the torso are really the most spiritual part of the human being, because in the limbs the process of creating matter occurs the least. The metabolic processes the abdomen and chest send into the limbs are all that make our limbs material. Our limbs are spiritual to a very high degree, and as they move, they consume our body. The body depends upon the development of what people have as tendencies from birth. If the limbs do not move sufficiently or appropriately, then they do not sufficiently consume the body. The torso is then in the lucky position, at least lucky for it, that the limbs do not consume enough of it. It uses what thus remains to create an overabundance of matter. This material surplus then permeates both what people have as a tendency at birth and their proper physicality because they are born beings of spirit-soul. What people need is permeated with something they do not need—matter that is only earthly and does not tend toward the spirit-soul in the true sense of the word; people are filled more and more with fat. However, when people store that fat in an abnormal way, it presents too much resistance to a spirit-soul process, a process of absorption, the consuming process that permeates people, and then the spirit-soul's path to the head becomes more difficult. Therefore, it would be incorrect to allow children to eat too much fattening food. If they do so, since the fat blocks the spirit-soul, the head separates from the spirit-soul and becomes empty. It is our task to develop the tact necessary to work with the complete social situation of children so they do not, in fact, become too fat. Later in life, the tendency to become fat depends upon all sorts of things. However, through correct nutrition it is possible, when the children are not abnormal—that is, when they are not particularly weak children who easily become fat—to help prevent children from becoming too fat.

We are irresponsible if we do not fully appreciate the great meaning of these things. We must realize that we interfere with cosmic evolution when we, for instance, allow a child to become too fat. Cosmic evolution expresses its intent toward human beings in that it allows human beings to be permeated with a spirit-soul stream. We really do interfere with cosmic evolution if we allow a child to become too fat.

You see, something very curious occurs in the human head, namely, as it accumulates, the spirit-soul sprays back like water meeting a weir.[1] That is, the spirit-soul carries matter with it the way the Mississippi carries sand, and where the spirit-soul is obstructed, that matter is sprayed back into the brain so that overlapping waves occur. This pounding of matter against matter causes it to continuously disintegrate in the brain. When matter still permeated with life is beaten back as I have described and then disintegrates, nerves are created. Nerves are always created when matter forced through life by the spirit disintegrates and dies in the living organism. This is the reason that nerves in the living organism are dead material: life is displaced and dammed up in itself, and matter crumbles and disintegrates. That is how channels filled with dead matter—the nerves—are created everywhere in people. There the spirit-soul can course through the human being. The spirit-soul speeds through the human being along the nerves because it needs disintegrating matter. It allows the matter on the surface of people to decompose and peel off. The spirit-soul can only fill people after matter dies in them. Inside human beings, spirit-soul moves parallel to the materially dead nerve pathways.

In this way, we can see how the spirit-soul works in people. We see it approaching from outside—developing an absorbing and consuming activity. We can see it enter, see it dam up, crumble and bring death to matter. We can see how matter decomposes in the nerves and how the spirit-soul approaches the skin from the inside out as it prepares paths through which it can travel. The spirit-soul cannot move through what lives as an organic whole.

How can you get an idea about what is organic and living? You can imagine what lives as something that absorbs the spirit-soul and does not let it through. You can imagine what is dead, what is material, what is mineral, as something that lets the spirit-soul through. From this you can, in a way, define the living body, the skeleton and the nervous system or mineralized matter, in general: What is living and alive is spiritually imper-meable; what is physically dead is spiritually permeable. *Blood is a very special fluid.*[2] The relationship between blood and the spirit is the same as that between opaque matter and light. Blood does not allow the spirit to pass through; it keeps the spirit in itself. The substance of nerves is also a very special sub-stance. It is as transparent glass to light. Just as transparent glass lets light through, in the same way purely physical matter, including the nerves, lets spirit through.

Here you have the difference between two human elements, between what is mineral and is transparent to the spirit, and what is more like an animal, more organically alive, and retains the spirit, causing the spirit to produce forms and to shape the organism.

The difference is very consequential for working with human beings. If people work physically, they move their limbs. That means they swim totally immersed in the spirit. This is not the spirit dammed up in that person, it is the spirit outside. If you chop wood or go for a walk, if you use your limbs simply by moving them for work, whether it be useful or useless work, you are always splashing around in the spirit and you are always connected with the spirit. That is very important. It is also important to ask ourselves what happens when we perform mental work, when we think or read or similar things. Here our connection is with the spirit-soul living within us. Here we no longer splash in the spirit with our limbs; instead, the spirit-soul works in us and uses the life in our body, that is, it is completely expressed as a living bodily process. Through the obstruction within us, matter is continuously deposited. In mental work, our body is excessively active; in contrast, in physical work, our spirit is excessively active. We cannot work with the spirit-soul unless we work inwardly with our body. When we work physically, the spirit-soul within us at most participates by providing us with the thoughts to give direction to our walking or to orient us. However, the spirit-soul outside us does take part. We always work in the spirit of the cosmos. We always connect ourselves with cosmic spirit when we work physically. Physical work is spiritual; mental work is a human bodily function. We must comprehend and understand that physical work is spiritual and that mental work is human activity. When we work physically, we are engulfed by the spirit.[3] When we work mentally, matter is active and excited within us.[4]

We must know these things if we want to think with understanding about work, whether mental or physical, about relaxing and tiring. We cannot knowledgeably think about working, relaxing or tiring if we do not understand what we have just discussed. Imagine, for a moment, someone who works too much with the limbs, someone who does too much physical labor, and what the consequence is. That person would be too closely connected to the spirit. He or she would be continuously immersed in the spirit when working physically. The spirit would thus gain too much power over the person, that is, the spirit that approaches a person from outside. We make ourselves too spiritual if we work too much physically. We make ourselves spiritual from the outside. This results in our having to give ourselves over to the spirit for too long, that is, we must sleep too long. If we work too much physically, we must sleep too long. However, sleeping too long promotes bodily activity too strongly, the activity arising out of the torso, not the head. Excessive sleep excites life too strongly, and we get a fever and become too hot. If we sleep too much, our blood boils and its activity cannot be transformed. And excessive physical work creates a desire to sleep too much.

What about those who are lethargic, who so like to sleep and sleep? This is different and occurs when someone actually cannot stop working. They cannot stop working. Lethargic people do not sleep because they work too little, but because they continually move their legs and fidget with their arms throughout the day. Lethargic people are doing something, and, seen externally, they do nothing different than someone who is industrious, but they do it without any goal. Industrious people turn to the outside world and connect their activity with a goal. That is the difference. Senseless activity, like that done by lethargic people, makes sleep more alluring than purposeful activity. In purposeful activity, we do not just splash about in the spirit; rather, because we act purposefully, we slowly draw the spirit in. When we reach out our hand to purposeful work, we connect ourselves with the spirit, and, therefore, the spirit has less need to work unconsciously in sleep, because we work with it consciously. It is not important for people to simply be active, because this is also true of lethargic people. Rather, what is important is the extent to which people are *purposefully active*. Purposefully active —these words must permeate us if we are to teach children. When are people active senselessly? They are senselessly active if they are active only as the body demands. They are purposefully active if they are active according to the surrounding demands, not simply as the body demands.

We must consider this with children. On the one hand, if we only ask the body what movements to accomplish, we can increasingly guide the child's physical activity toward what is just in the physical body—that is, toward calisthenics. On the other hand, we can guide a child's external movements toward purposeful movements, toward movements filled with purpose, so that the child does not splash around in the spirit, but follows the spirit as the goal. We then develop physical movement in the direction of eurythmy. The more we allow children simply to do calisthenics, the more we lure children into excessive sleep and toward an excessive tendency to become fat. Because people must live in rhythm, the more we allow the pendulum to swing toward the body, the more it will swing back into purposeful exercise, such as eurythmy, where every movement expresses a sound and has meaning. The more we alternate physical education with eurythmy, the more we can bring the need for sleep and wakefulness into harmony.[5] This is how we use the will to maintain balance in the child's life. That we have slowly made something senseless out of gymnastics, have made it into an activity that only exercises the body, is a side effect of the age of materialism. That we want to raise it to the level of a sport, that we want to add nonsense to it, so that it becomes even less than senseless, meaningless movements, reflects a desire to drag people down, not just to the level of materialistic thinking, but also to animalistic feeling. Excessive sport activity is Darwinism in practice.[6] Theoretical Darwinism claims that people developed from animals.[7] Sports are practical Darwinism, and that means setting up the goal of degenerating people back into animals.

We must state these things radically because modern teachers must understand that they are to be not simply teachers of the children entrusted to them. They must also have a social effect that will affect all of humanity so that things do not continually arise that would slowly make people more like animals. This is not false asceticism. It is something derived out of true objective insight and is just as true as any other scientific finding.

However, what is the situation with mental work? Bodily activity and a continuous decomposition, that is, a dying, of organic matter always accompany mental work, thinking, reading, and so on. We have decomposing organic matter in us if we do too much mental work. If we spend our day in nonstop academic activity, by evening we have too much decomposed matter in us—decomposed organic matter. This affects us; it disturbs our peaceful sleep. Excessive mental work destroys sleep the same way excessive physical work makes people drowsy. But, if we strain ourselves mentally, if we read difficult things that we must think about as we are reading (something not particularly enjoyed by modern people), if we want to read thoughtfully too much, we fall asleep. Or, in another instance, if we do not listen to the babbling of popular speakers or others who talk only about what we already know, but instead listen to people whose words we must follow thoughtfully because they are saying something that we don't know, then we become tired and drowsy. It is a well-known occurrence that people who go to lectures or concerts that must be thoughtfully perceived and comprehended, and who are unaccustomed this but go because it is "what you do," such people fall asleep at the first tone or word. They often sleep through the whole of any lecture or concert that they attend because of social convention.

Here again we find two differing aspects. Just as there is a difference between senseless busy-ness and purposeful external activity, there is also a difference between a mechanical thinking activity and a thinking activity accompanied by feeling. If we always connect interest with our mental work, then this interest and attentiveness enlivens our chest activity and does not allow the nerves to die off excessively. The more you simply read along and make no effort to absorb with interest what you read, the more you foster the death of your own inner matter. The more you follow what you read with interest and warmth, the more you foster blood activity and the enlivening of matter, and the more you inhibit the disturbance of your sleep. If you are cramming for a final exam, you are learning much that does not interest you. If you were to learn only what interests you, then, at least under today's conditions, you would fail the final. The result is that cramming for a final disturbs your sleep and brings disorder into your normal life. We must pay particular attention to this with children, and it is best and most in line with the ideal of education to let the congested learning that precedes final examinations fall by the wayside—that is, drop final examinations all together. In other words, the end of the school year should be just like the beginning. As teachers, we might ask ourselves why we should test children at all, because we have had them in front of us and know very well what they do or do not know. Under current conditions, this can, of course, be only an ideal, and I would ask you, in general, not to reveal your rebellious natures too strongly. For the present time, you need to keep what you have to say against modern culture to yourselves, so that you can slowly work (because, in this area, we can only work slowly) toward the goal that people learn to think differently. In that way, society can take on a form other than the one it has now.

You must think of the interconnections between everything. You must know that eurythmy is an activity filled with purpose and is a spiritualizing of physical work, and that interesting instruction literally enlivens intellectual work and supplies it with blood.[8]

We must bring spirit to all external work and our life's blood to all inner and intellectual work. If you think about these two things, then you will see that the first is significant in teaching and social life, and that the second is significant in teaching and health.

14

If, in the interest of developing a true pedagogical art, we consider people as we have until now, then, because of many different things, the threefold aspect of the human physical body becomes apparent. We clearly differentiate between everything connected with the form of the human head and everything to do with the form of the chest, and, in general, the torso, and with the form of the limbs. We need to understand that the limbs are much more complicated than people normally think, because what the limbs represent extends from outside into the human being. We need to differentiate between the forms from-within-outward in human beings, and those inserted into the human body from outside.

If we consider these three parts of the human body, it becomes particularly clear that the human head is a whole human being raised above the animal world.

In the head we have the actual head, and we also have the torso—that is, everything associated with the nose. And we have a limb component that extends into the cavity of the body—that is, everything surrounding the mouth. In this way, we can see how the entire physical human being is present in the head. But, only the head's "chest" is stunted. It is stunted to the degree that we can only vaguely recognize the connection between the nose and lungs. Nevertheless, the nose is related to the lungs. The human nose, to a certain extent, is a metamorphosed lung. The nose transforms the breathing process so that it is directed toward the physical. It would be a mistake to view the lung as less spiritual than the nose. The lung is more artistically formed. The spirit, or at least the soul, permeates it more completely than the nose. If you understand things properly, you will see that, although the nose sits shamelessly in the middle of the human face, the lungs, even though they are more closely connected with the soul, modestly hide their existence.

Everything about the human mouth, with its undeniable relationship to nutrition and the human limbs, is connected with metabolism, digestion and nutrition, and extends the limb forces into the human being. Thus, the human head is a complete human being, only the things not head-like in it are stunted. The chest and abdomen exist in the head, but there they are stunted.

By contrast, when we look at the limb aspect of the human being, everything that the limbs represent in their external form and development is primarily a transformation of the upper and lower jaws. Stunted forms of what your legs and feet, arms and hands are enclose your mouth from above and below. You only have to think of them in the proper way. Now you might interject that when you imagine your arms and hands to be the upper jaw, and your legs and feet, the lower jaw, the question arises about the purpose of what this "jaw" represents. Where does it "bite?" Where is the "mouth?" It is at the points where your upper arm and your upper leg or thighbone join your body. If you imagine that this is the human torso [Rudolf Steiner begins to draw], then you must imagine that somewhere out there is the actual head. The mouth opens on the upper side and the lower side so that you can imagine a curious tendency for the jaws of an invisible "head" to open toward your chest and stomach.

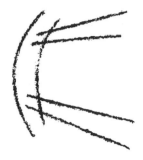

What does this invisible "head" do? It continuously consumes you and spreads its "mouth" open toward you. In this form, you have a wonderful picture of what actually exists. While the real human head is a physical, material head, the head associated with the limbs is a spiritual head. However, it becomes a little material in order to continuously consume the human being. When human beings die, this spiritual head has completely consumed them. It is an amazing fact that our limbs are formed so that they can continuously consume us. Our organism is always slipping into the wide open mouth of our spirituality. The spirit demands of us a continuous sacrifice of devotion, and this sacrifice expresses itself in the form of our bodies. We cannot understand the human form if we cannot see how this sacrifice, devoted to the spirit, is expressed in the relationship between the human limbs and the rest of the human body. The head and the limb natures of the human being exist at extremes, and the chest or torso nature is in the middle, and, in a sense, it creates the balance between these two extremes.

The human chest is head and limb nature as well. The limb and head aspects mix into the nature of the chest. The chest at its upper end always has a tendency to become head and at the lower end, the tendency to adjust itself to the stretched out limbs, to the external world. In other words, the lower end of the torso tends to take on the nature of the limbs. The upper portion of the chest tends to become head and the lower portion tends to become limbs. Although the upper portion of the human torso always wants to become head, it cannot do so. The other head inhibits this, and the chest can only bring forth a likeness of the head, something we might call the beginning of a head. Can we clearly recognize that the upper part of the chest makes a start toward the formation of a head? Yes, the larynx, which people intuitively call the "throat-head," is there [the German, *Kehlkopf,* for larynx, is literally "throat-head"]. The human larynx is, without a doubt, a stunted human head, a "head" that cannot quite become head and, therefore, can only live out its "head" nature through human speech. Human speech is a continual attempt to become a head in the air. When the larynx attempts to become uppermost in the head, it produces the sounds that human nature holds back most strongly. When the larynx attempts to take on the characteristics of the nose, it cannot truly become a nose because the real nose hinders it. It thus brings forth nasal sounds when it attempts to become a nose. In nasal sounds, the actual nose constricts the arising air-nose. It is particularly significant that human speech continually attempts to create parts of the head in the air, and that these parts of the head expand in wave-like movements that the physical head then constricts. This is human speech.

It will certainly not amaze you that the moment the head is physically complete—around the age of seven—the change of teeth presents the opportunity for the soul-head to arise from the larynx, permeated with a kind of skeleton. However, it must be a "soul-skeleton." We do this by ending the wild development of language by imitation and, instead, begin to control speech development of through grammar.[1] We must be aware that when we receive children in elementary school, we need to practice an activity on the soul similar to what is practiced by the body when it produces the second set of teeth. We make the development of speech firm in the soul aspect when we include grammar in a reasonable way, so that what comes from speech enters into writing and reading. We will achieve a proper relationship of feeling to human speech if we know that the words people form tend to become the head.

In the same way that the human chest has an upward tendency to become the head, it also has a downward tendency to become the limbs. Just as speech arises from the larynx as a refined "head," a head caught in the air, everything that continues downward from the human chest toward the limbs has a coarsened limb-nature. In a sense, what the world pushes into people has a thickened and coarsened limb nature. When science begins finally to explore the secret of how the hands and feet, arms, and legs are coarsened and inserted more deeply into people than they appear, it will have discovered the answer to the riddle of sexuality; only then will people find the proper tone to speak of such things. It is not surprising that all of the discussion we hear today about how we should handle sex education really has no meaning. People cannot explain what they do not understand. Modern science has absolutely no understanding of what we have only hinted at about the connection between the human limbs and torso. However, you must know that just as we insert what entered the nature of the teeth before age seven into the soul in the first years of elementary school, so we must, in the final years of elementary school, bring into the child's soul life what comes from the nature of the limbs and is first fully expressed at puberty.

Thus, just as the soul-teeth appear as a capacity to learn to read and write, an activity of imagination and a permeation of inner warmth announces what the soul develops toward the end of elementary school at the age of twelve to fifteen years. You must emphasize particularly anything that depends on the soul's capacity to fill things with inner love, that is, everything expressed by imagination. You must appeal to the power of imagination, particularly in the final years of elementary school. We are more justified in requiring the seven-year-old child to develop intellectuality through reading and writing than we are in neglecting to bring imagination continually into the power of judgment that slowly approaches at the age of twelve. We must teach everything children have to learn in those years by stimulating their imagination. That is how we must teach everything concerning history and geography.

We also appeal to children's imagination when, for instance, we tell them, "Here you see a lens that collects light; you have such a lens in your eye. You are familiar with the camera that makes images of things; your eye is such a camera." Here, too, when we show how human sense organs embody things that exist in the world, we are actually appealing to the children's imagination. What they embody is visible only as a corpse when we remove it from the body; we cannot see it in the living body.

In the same way, all the instruction given for geometry, and even for arithmetic, must not fail to appeal to imagination. We appeal to imagination if we always make an effort to have the children use their imagination, even in geometry and arithmetic. We attempted this in the practical part of this seminar when considering how to make surfaces comprehensible not only to the child's intellect, in such a way that the child would truly comprehend the nature of a surface.[2] As I said yesterday, I am surprised that no one ever thought of explaining the Pythagorean theorem in the following way: Suppose there were three children. One child blows enough powder onto a square to cover it. The second child does the same with a second square, the third with a small square. We can encourage the children's imagination by showing them that the amount of powder that covers the large area equals the combined amounts of powder on the small and middle-sized surfaces. Then we would draw the children's comprehension into the powder blown onto the squares, not through mathematical exactness, but with imagination. The children would follow the surface in their imagination. They would understand the Pythagorean theorem through their imagination and through the flying powder blown onto a square. We cannot, of course, perform this in reality, but we can engage the children's imagination.

In these years we must always take care that, as teachers, we create what goes from us to the children in an exciting way so that it gives rise to imagination. Teachers must inwardly and livingly preserve the subject material; they must fill it with imagination. This is not possible unless we fill it with feeling-will. In later years, this often has a strange effect. What we must emphasize, and what is particularly important toward the end of elementary school, is community life, the harmonious life, between teacher and children. No one can become a good grade school teacher who does not always try to present the lesson with imagination and in a fresh way. It is a fact that when we present things one time filled with imagination and continue to repeat them, they become frozen in the intellect. We must continue keep imagination alive, otherwise, what it produces becomes petrified.

This, however, sheds some light on how teachers themselves must be. They must never, at any time in their lives, be bitter. There are two concepts that never fit together if life is to be fertile: pedantry and the vocation of teaching. If teaching and pedantry come together in life, the result will be an extremely unhealthy marriage, more so than anything else life could offer.

I do not believe we need accept the absurdity that there has ever been a union of pedantry and the vocation of teaching.

You can see, therefore, that teaching has a certain inner morality, an inner responsibility. Teachers truly have a categorical imperative! This categorical imperative is: *Keep your imagination alive.* If you feel yourself becoming pedantic, then say to yourself: For other people pedantry may be bad, but for me, it is immoral! This must be the teacher's attitude. If it is not the teachers, attitude, then teachers must consider learning how to use their knowledge of teaching for another profession. Of course, in life we cannot accomplish these things and achieve completely the ideal; however, we must at least *know* the ideal.

You will not have the proper enthusiasm for pedagogical morality if you do not fill yourself with something fundamental—that is, the recognition that the head itself is already a complete human being with stunted limbs and chest. You must know that each limb of a human being is a complete human being, but with the head and chest stunted, that and in the chest the head and limbs maintain balance. If you use this fundamental thought, then you will receive inner strength from it so that you can fill your pedagogical morality with the necessary enthusiasm.

What forms human intellectuality has a strong tendency to become slow and lazy, and it becomes most lazy when people constantly feed it with materialistic ideas. However, it will take flight when we feed it ideas received from the spirit, but we receive these into our souls only through the indirect path of imagination.

How people ranted and raved against including imagination in education during the late nineteenth century! In the first half of the nineteenth century we had such brilliant people as Schelling, for example, who thought more soundly about education.[3] You should read Schelling's exciting discussions in *Concerning the Method of Academic Study*—which was, of course, not intended for elementary school, but ithe early nineteenth-century spirit of pedagogy lives in it. During the second half of the nineteenth century, people understood this spirit in a masked form. Then, people were cowardly about the life of the soul and complained about whatever entered the human soul through the indirect path of imagination, because they believed that if they accepted imagination, they would fall directly into the arms of untruthfulness. People did not have the courage for independence, for freedom in their thinking and, at the same time, for a marriage to truth instead of lies. People feared freedom in thinking because they believed they would immediately take lies into the soul. To what I just said—that is, to filling their lessons with imagination—teachers must therefore add *courage for the truth*. Without this courage for truth, teachers will achieve nothing with the will in teaching, especially with the older children. We must join what develops as courage for truth with a strong sense of responsibility toward truth.

A need for imagination, a sense for truth, and a feeling for responsibility—these are the three forces that constitute the nerves of pedagogy. Those who would take up education should write this as their motto:

> Enliven imagination,
> Stand for truth,
> Feel responsibility.

NOTES

LECTURE 1

1. Emil Molt (1876–1936), industrialist and Director of the Waldorf-Astoria Cigarette Factory in Stuttgart, created educational opportunities for the workers of his company. Out of this arose the idea of creating a school for the workers' children. He called upon Rudolf Steiner to form and lead the "Waldorf School." In 1919, Molt was one of the most engaged representatives of Rudolf Steiner's Threefold idea. See *Emil Molt and the Beginnings of the Waldorf School Movement: Sketches from an Autobiography,* Christine Murphy, ed./trans., Floris Press, Edinburgh, 1991. See also *Beiträge zur Rudolf Steiner Gesamtausgabe,* Heft Nr. 103 (Notes on Rudolf Steiner's collected works, Vol. 103), Dornach, Michaelmas, 1989.

2. Concerning the connection of self-interest with the question of immortality and the three aspects of the personality, see Rudolf Steiner's lecture on June 12, 1907, in *Ursprungsimpulse der Geisteswissenschaft,* "Die drei Aspekte des Persönlichen" (The original impulse of spiritual science, "The three aspects of the personality"), GA 96.

3. Refer to the discussion with Rudolf Steiner on April 21, 1909, contained in *Spiritual Hierarchies: Inner Realities of Evolution,* Anthroposophic Press, 1996, GA 110.

4. Refer to Rudolf Steiner's, *An Outline of Occult Science,* Chapter 4, "The Evolution of the Cosmos and Man," Anthroposophic Press, 1972, GA 13.

5. Refer to Rudolf Steiner's, *Cosmology, Religion and Philosophy,* Chapter 6, "Transference from the Psycho-Spiritual to the Physical-Sense Life in Man's Development," Anthroposophic Press, 1955, GA 25.

6. Concerning the aspects of the human being, refer to Rudolf Steiner's *Theosophy,* Chapter 1, "The Essential Nature of the Human Being," GA 9, and also *An Outline of Occult Science,* GA 13. See also Rudolf Steiner's *Paths of Experience,* Rudolf Steiner

Press, London, 1983, GA 58, and *Metamorphosis of the Soul,* Rudolf
Steiner Press, London, 1983, GA 59.

7. Translators' note: *Verstandesseele oder Gemütseele* (Comprehension
Soul). Previous translations of these terms for the second aspect of
the human soul have fairly consistently rendered them as "intellectual or mind soul." *Verstand,* although correctly translated as "intellect" in common parlance, literally means "to cease standing still."
Gemüt does not have an English equivalent, but as Rudolf Steiner
uses it, it could be defined as "the warmth that flows between people who have the courage to love one another to the extent that they
understand the other as they understand themselves." Christ is said
to live in the *Gemüt* and in the rhythms of the world. The role of
this part of the human soul *(Verstandesseele oder Gemütseele)* is to
reach into the experiences of the sentient soul and, through the
activity of thinking *independent of the experiences* themselves, lift
these sensations into a relationship with truth. It is thus that we
come to understand Earthly experience in light of what is eternal,
what is true. The work of this part of the human soul can better be
described as an ongoing breathing process than as the analysis so
intimately associated with the words "intellectual" and "mind."
"Intellectual" and "mind" seem to us to be too static as concepts
and not to the point so far as meaning is concerned. We believe this
aspect of the human soul requires a word in English that implies
activity and allows for a kind of understanding that goes beyond the
intellect. We offer "comprehension soul" (literally, "the grasping-
together soul") for its implied movement of reaching out, laying
hold of many things, and bringing them back to the beholder. To
comprehend something requires interest, activity, work, the ability
to make whole what has become separate and, finally, the courage to
take the result into oneself. We do not believe that "comprehension
soul" is a perfect solution, but are hopeful that this term will help
bring the English-speaking reader into a closer relationship to this
aspect of the soul.

8. Translators' note: Refer to *Theosophy,* Chapter 1, "The Essential
Nature of the Human Being." See especially the addendum at the
end of the chapter (pp. 61–62); trans. Catherine Creeger, Anthroposophic Press, 1994.

9. Concerning the relationship of the temporal body to the spirit-soul,
refer to Rudolf Steiner's lectures on June 13, 1921 and June 15, 1921,

contained in *Education for Adolescents,* Anthroposophic Press, 1996, GA 302; his lecture from August 14, 1921, contained in *The Ego as Experience of Consciousness,* typed manuscript, GA 206; and his lecture from November 20, 1922, in *Geistige Zusammenhänge in der Gestaltung des menschlichen Organismus,* "Erziehungskunst durch Menschenerkenntnis" (Spiritual relationships in the formation of the human organism, The art of education based on an understanding of the human organism), GA 218.

10. Concerning the threefoldedness of the natural human being—not the total being—refer to *The Case for Anthroposophy,* "Principles of Psychosomatic Physiology," Rudolf Steiner Press, 1970, GA 21.

11. Refer to Rudolf Steiner's lecture of January 15, 1917, in *The Karma of Untruthfulness, Part 2,* Lecture 20, Rudolf Steiner Press, 1992, GA 174; and the lectures on May 6 and June 1, 1918, contained in *Kunst und Kunsterkenntnis* (Art and the experiencing of art) GA 271.

12. Concerning children's sleep, refer to Rudolf Steiner's lecture of August 7, 1921, contained in *Menschenwerden Weltenseele Weltengeist:* Vol II; "Die kindliche Entwickelung bis zur Geschlechtsreife" (Human evolution, cosmic soul and cosmic spirit, Part 2, Child development until puberty), GA 206.

13. Refer to *An Outline of Occult Science,* Chapter 3, "Sleep and Death."

LECTURE 2

1. Johann Friedrich Herbart (1776–1841), philosopher and educator, teacher in Göttingen. Recognized as the founder of scientific pedagogy that is closely connected with practical philosophy (ethics) and psychology. Among his works are *Allgemeine Pädagogik* (General pedagogy), 1806, *Lehrbuch zur Psycologie* (Introduction to psychology), 1816, and *Umriß Pädagogischer Vorlesungen* (Survey of pedagogical lectures), 1835. Rudolf Steiner speaks about Herbart's world view in the chapter, "Reactionary World Views," in his book *Riddles of Philosophy,* Anthroposophic Press, 1973, GA 18. See also Steiner's lecture of December 4, 1903, in *Spirituelle Seelenlehre und Weltbetrachtung,* (Spiritual soul instruction and view of the world), GA 52.

2. Translators' note: For a concise description of the developmental periods of humanity and the post-Atlantean cultural ages, see Rudolf Steiner's lectures of August 31 and September 1, 1906, in *At the Gates of Spiritual Science,* Rudolf Steiner Press, 1970, GA 95.

3. Refer to the chapter, "The Human Individuality," *Intuitive Thinking as a Spiritual Path: A Philosophy of Freedom*, Anthroposophic Press, 1995.

4. Refer to Rudolf Steiner's lecture of October 10, 1918, in *Die Ergänzung heutiger Wissenschaften durch Anthroposophie* (Supplementation of contemporary science through anthroposophy), GA 73 and his lectures from April 29–30, 1922, in *The Human Soul in Relation to World Evolution*, Anthroposophic Press, 1984, GA 212.

5. Refer to Rudolf Steiner's lecture of January 19, 1924, in *Anthroposophy and the Inner Life*, Waldorf Institute, Adelphi University, 1992; *Anthroposophy: An Introduction*, Rudolf Steiner Press, 1983, GA 234.

6. *"Cogito ergo sum,"* ("I think, therefore I am,") was proposed by the philosopher, mathematician, astronomer and physicist René Descartes (1596–1650), who served as an officer in various armies and lived in Holland for a long time, finally being called by Queen Christine to Sweden, where he died. Refer to his *Principia Philosophiae* (Amsterdam, 1644), particularly paragraphs 1, 7, and 11–14 in Part 1. "While we thus reject all that of which we can possibly doubt, and feign that it is false, it is easy to suppose that there is no God, nor heaven, nor bodies, and that we possess neither hands, nor feet, nor indeed any body; but we cannot in the same way conceive that we who doubt these things are not; for there is a contradiction in conceiving that what thinks does not at the same time as it thinks, exist. And hence this conclusion, *I think, therefore I am*, is the first and most certain of all that occurs to one who philosophises in an orderly way." (Excerpt of paragraph 7 from *The Philosophical Work of Descartes*, Elizabeth S. Haldane and G.R.T. Ross, trans., Vol. 1, Cambridge University Press, 1967, p. 221.) Rudolf Steiner addresses *cogito ergo sum* in Chapter 3, "Thinking in the Service of Knowledge," *Intuitive Thinking as a Spiritual Path: A Philosophy of Freedom*, GA 4; in his lecture of October 12, 1918, in *Three Streams in the Evolution of Mankind*, Rudolf Steiner Press, 1985, GA 184; in his lecture of April 10, 1913, in *Ergebnisse der Geistesforschung*, (Results of spiritual investigation), GA 62; and in the chapter "German Idealism's Picture of the World" in *The Riddle of Man*, Mercury Press, 1990, GA 20. Refer also to the discussion concerning Descartes in the chapter "The World Conceptions of the Modern Age of Thought Evolution" in *The Riddles of Philosophy*, Anthroposophic Press, 1973, GA 18.

7. In the phrase "activity of thinking," the words "of thinking" were inserted by a previous editor of the German edition.

8. In previous German and English editions the sketches contained in the "ditto" copies were used as a basis. A comparison with the typewritten manuscripts of the original stenographic notes showed that Rudolf Steiner demonstrated this point with the sketch given here. The sketch that was in this position in earlier editions is now inserted in the proper location.

9. Refer to Lecture 2, note 5 above; also, refer to Chapter 9, "The Idea of Freedom," in *Intuitive Thinking as a Spiritual Path: A Philosophy of Freedom*; and Rudolf Steiner's lecture from January 17, 1922, "Anthroposophie und die Rätsel der Seele," published in *Zur Pädagogik Rudolf Steiner*, Vol. 5, no. 1, April, 1931; and in *Die Menschenschule*, Vol. 11, no. 7/8, 1937; also to be published in *Das Wesen der Anthroposophie*, GA 80 (The nature of anthroposophy).

10. Concerning thinking and will in connection with life before birth and after death, refer to Rudolf Steiner's lecture of October 18, 1919 in "Spiritual Scientific Knowledge and Social Understanding," typed manuscript, GA 191.

11. Arthur Schopenhauer (1788–1860) studied natural science and philosophy in Göttingen and Berlin and later lived in Jena, Weimar and Dresden without having completed his studies. Finally, alone and embittered because he felt himself misunderstood and rejected, he moved to Frankfurt in 1833. Only in the 1840s did he gain more attention, and he became a popular philosopher in the 1870s. Concerning the will as a germ of the spirit-soul, refer to his main work, *The World as Will and Idea*, 1819, Book 4. Refer also to the introduction Rudolf Steiner wrote for the Cotta edition of *Arthur Schopenhauer's sämtlichen Werken* (Arthur Schopenhauer's complete works), in *Biographien und biographische Skizzen*, (Biographies and biographical sketches, GA 33), the chapter "Reactionary World Conceptions" in *The Riddles of Philosophy*, GA 18; also his lecture from December 4, 1920, in *Die Brücke zwischen der Weltgeistigkeit und dem Physischen des Menschen*, (The bridge between universal spirituality and physical man; not in the English volume of same title), GA 202.

12. *Theosophy*, Chapter 3, "The Three Worlds: I. The Soul World," Anthroposophic Press, 1994. On the same topic, see also the chapter, "Concerning the Ego-Feeling and the Human Soul's Capacity for Love; and the Relation of These to the Elemental World" in *A Road*

to Self-Knowledge and The Threshold of the Spiritual World, Rudolf Steiner Press, 1975, GA 17.

13. This sketch is contained in the typewritten manuscript of the original stenographer's notes and in their ditto copies. The following is the sketch contained in earlier German and English editions.

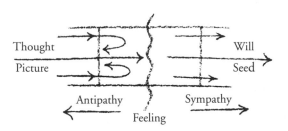

14. This sentence is contained in the typewritten manuscript of the original stenographic notes. The dittoed copies, which have additions from the participant's notes, had instead, "It lives in your antipathy."

15. Refer to Rudolf Steiner's essay, "Frühere Geheimhaltung und jetzige Veröffentlichung übersinnlicher Erkenntnisse," in *Philosophie und Anthroposophie. Gesammelte Aufsätze* 1904–1923 (Earlier secrecy and present publication of supersensible knowledge, *Philosophy and Anthroposophy: Collected Essays*, 1904–1923), GA 35.

16. Refer to Chapter 4, Section 3, "Concerning Abstraction," in *The Case for Anthroposophy*, Rudolf Steiner Press, 1970, GA 21; and Chapter 4, "The World as Perception," in *Intuitive Thinking as a Spiritual Path: A Philosophy of Freedom.*

17. An earlier German editor added "through antipathy."

18. The term "sense perceptions" was contained in the first copies and also in the notes of some of the course participants. In the stenographic notes the term used is "descriptive concepts."

19. Concerning the connection of sympathy, imagination and living pictures, refer to Rudolf Steiner's lecture from December 15, 1911 in *Wisdom of Man, of the Soul and of the Spirit*, Anthroposophic Press, 1971, GA 115. In this lecture, imagination as a higher stage of knowledge is considered. [Translators' note: For a description of the working of what Dr. Steiner calls "normal imagination" above, see the lecture of October 26, 1909 in the same volume.]

20. Refer to Lecture 2, note 12 [*Theosophy*, ch. 3].

21. Translators' note: Motor nerves are conventionally defined as nerves which transmit signals from the brain to parts of the body, thereby stimulating movement. Sensory nerves are said to be nerves that transmit sense perceptions to the brain.

22. In his lecture of November 6, 1916, in *Karma of Vocation*, Anthroposophic Press, 1984, GA 172, Rudolf Steiner speaks about the so-called sensory and motor nerves: "The nerves are all uniformly organized and they all have one function. The so-called motor nerves are different from the so-called sensory nerves in that the sensory nerves serve to perceive the external world whereas the so-called motor nerves serve to perceive one's own organism." Refer also to Chapter 4, Section 6, "Principles of Psychosomatic Physiology," in *The Case for Anthroposophy*, GA 21; Rudolf Steiner's lecture of April 21, 1920, in *The Renewal of Education*, Kolisko Archives 1981, GA 301; lectures of April 23, 1919, June 8 and 9, 1919, in *Spiritual Scientific Considerations of the Social and Pedagogic Questions*, typed manuscript, date unknown, GA 192; lecture of December 7, 1919 in *The Michael Impulse*, typewritten manuscript, date unknown, GA 194; and lecture of December 12, 1919 in *The Mysteries of Light, of Space and of the Earth*, Anthroposophic Press, 1945, GA 194. [Translators' note: The references to GA 192 and 194 are our corrections of references given in error in the German edition.] See also the summary contained in the book by Herbert Hensel and Hans Jürgen Scheurle, *Zur Frage der motorischen und sensitiven Nerven. Auszüge aus Werken Rudolf Steiner* (Concerning the question of motor and sensory nerves: excerpts from Rudolf Steiner's works, Marburg, 1979, new edition 1992). See also Part 2 (documentation appendix) of the publication edited by Wolfgang Schad, *Die menschliche Nervenorganisation und die soziale Frage*, two volumes (The human nervous system and the social question, Stuttgart, 1992).

23. Refer to Rudolf Steiner's lectures on March 20–21, 1911, in *An Occult Physiology*, Rudolf Steiner Press, 1983, GA 128.

24. Earlier editions contained "vertebra" instead of "spinal cord." However, the dittoed copies contained "spinal cord." It is possible that Rudolf Steiner was referring here to the posterior horn of the spinal cord into which the centripetal nerves [called the sensory nerves in English] are drawn, whereas the centrifugal nerves [called the motor nerves in English] extend out from the anterior horn. The typewritten manuscript of the stenographic notes contains the passage,

"Another such leap is to be found in the spinal cord, for example, when one nerve goes toward the anterior horns and the other away from the anterior horns." [Under the entry for *spinal*, Taber's *Cyclopedic Medical Dictionary*, 11th Edition, contains clear illustrations of the spinal cord and the "sensory" and "motor" nerves entering and exiting the opposing horns.]

25. "In our bodies" was added by an earlier German editor.

26. Refer to Lecture 1, note 10.

27. Concerning the connection of the various parts of the body to the cosmos, refer to "Leading Thoughts 32–37" in *Anthroposophical Leading Thoughts*, Rudolf Steiner Press, 1985, GA 26; and Steiner's lecture on November 26, 1920, published as "Shaping the Human Form Out of Cosmic and Earthly Forces," in *Anthroposophical Quarterly*, Vol. 17, no. 1, 1972, GA 202.

28. Rudolf Steiner speaks about this topic in many lectures, particularly in his lecture of October 16, 1923, in *Deeper Insights into Education*, Anthroposophic Press, 1983, GA 302A.

29. See Steiner's lecture of April 10, 1914, in *The Inner Nature of Man* and *Life Between Death and Rebirth*, Rudolf Steiner Press, 1994, GA 153.

LECTURE 3

1. Concerning the Threefold Social Organism, see *Towards Social Renewal*, Rudolf Steiner Press, 1977, GA 23.

2. The Eighth Ecumenical Council took place in 869 in Constantinople [now Istanbul] with the goal of countering Patriarch Photius. Canon 11 of *Canones Contra Photium* states: "While the Old and New Testaments teach that human beings have only an understanding and reasonable soul, and although all fathers and teachers speaking the word of God in this church support this opinion, there are those who have sunken into a frivolousness and unabashedly present the teaching that human beings have two souls and assert, based upon certain unscientific investigations, this is confirmed by the wisdom of their own heresy." The Catholic philosopher Otto Willmann, who was highly regarded by Steiner writes in Section VIII, paragraph 54, "Christian Idealism as a Completion of Antiquity" of his three-volume work *Geschichte des Idealismus* (The history of idealism), Braunschweig, 1894, "The misuse of the Pauline differentiation of the spiritual and physical

human being carried out by the Gnostics when they present one as an expression of their perfection and declare the other as the representative of Christians caught in Church laws, forced the Church to explicitly renounce the Trichotomy." In many lectures, Steiner returns to the importance of this Council's decision. For example, in his lectures on February 5 and April 2, 1918, in *Earthly Death and Cosmic Life*, Garber Press, 1985, (GA 181); the lecture on September 8, 1918, in *Die Polarität von Dauer und Entwickelung im Menschenleben* (The polarity of continuity and change, GA 184); and the lecture on November 21, 1919, in *The Archangel Michael*, Anthroposophic Press, 1995, (GA 194). Concerning this subject, see the essays by Stefan Leber, "Zum Konzil 869" (On the Council of 869) in *Mitteilungen aus der Anthroposophischen Arbeit in Deutschland* (Newsletter of Anthroposophical work in Germany), Easter, 1973, and by Johannes Geyer, "Ein Konzil und seine kulturgeschichtlichen Folgen: Die Abschaffung des Geistes" (A council and its historical effects upon culture: the abolition of the spirit) in *Erziehungskunst*, no. 10/11, 1964; also, the publication *Der Kampf um das Menschenbild. Das achte ökumenische Konzil von 869 und seine Folgen* (The struggle over the picture of the human being: The Eighth Ecumenical Council of 869 and its effects), edited by H. H. Schöffler, Dornach, 1986, which contains these and other essays on this topic.

3. Julius Robert Mayer (1814–1878), German physician and natural scientist, formulated the Law of the Conservation of Energy in 1842 and postulated the equivalence of mechanical movement and heat ("Heat and movement can change from one to the other") in *Bemerkungen über das mechanische Äquivalent der Wärme* (Remarks on the mechanical equivalent of heat), 1851. "Therefore, forces are indestructible, changeable and intangible objects. As incorrect as it would be to conclude that the connection between gravity and movement can be stated by saying that the essence of gravity is movement, it would be just as incorrect to conclude this for heat. Actually, we wish to show the opposite, that in order to have heat, movement, whether it be simple or vibrational, such as light, or radiant heat, etc., must cease to be movement" (in *Bemerkungen über die Kräfte der unbelebten Natur* [Remarks on forces in inanimate nature, 1842]). See also *Robert Mayer über die Erhaltung der Kraft. Vier Abhandlungen* (Robert Mayer and the conservation of energy), edited by Albert Neuburger, Leipzig, which contains both of these essays, and the essays "Die organische

Bewegung in ihrem Zusammenhang mit dem Stoffwechsel" (Organic movement and its connection to metabolism), 1845, and "Über die quantitative und qualitative Bestimmung der Kräfte" (Concerning the quantitative and qualitative determination of forces), 1841. Concerning the importance of Mayer's law, see Steiner's lecture on April 16, 1918 in *Anthroposophical Life Gifts*, typed manuscript, GA 181.

4. See Lecture 8, note 1.

5. Plato (428–348 B.C.): "And of the organs they first contrived the eyes to give light, and the principle according to which they were inserted was as follows: So much of fire as would not burn, but gave a gentle light, they formed into a substance akin to the light of everyday life; and the pure fire which is within us and related thereto they made to flow through the eyes in a stream smooth and dense, compressing the whole eye, and especially the center part, so that it kept out everything of a coarser nature, and allowed to pass only this pure element. When the light of day surrounds the stream of vision, then like falls upon like, and they coalesce, and one body is formed by natural affinity in the line of vision, wherever the light that falls from within meets with an external object" (*Timaeus*, translated by Benjamin Jowett, in *The Dialogues of Plato*, Vol. 3, "*Timaeus* and Other Dialogues," pp. 249–250, Sphere Books, London, 1970). See also Chapter 4, "Plato as Mystic," in Rudolf Steiner's book *Christianity as Mystical Fact*, Garber Communications, 1985; and Steiner's notes on his Berlin Worker's School lecture, "Die griechischen Weltanschauungen" ("The Greek Worldview") in *Über Philosophie, Geschichte und Literatur* (Philosophy, History and Literature, not available in English) GA 51.

6. "Some other similar spiritual activity" is from the early dittoed copies.

7. Rudolf Hermann Lotze (1817–1881), physiologist and philosopher active in Leipzig, Göttingen and Berlin, opposed vitalism in favor of a mechanistic explanation of nature. He referred to his world view as "teleological idealism." He mentions the attributes in the first volume of *Mikrokosmus. Ideen zur Naturgeschichte und Geschichte der Menschheit. Versuch einer Anthropologie,* undated (Microcosmos: Thoughts concerning natural history and the history of humanity: An attempted anthropology) in which he says, "The main reason the soul directs each impression to its particular location in space which it imagines does not lie in the position itself which the impression has in the sense organ . . . the reason lies more in the qualitative attribute which the impression of the nature of the object upon touching the

body provides to its other qualitative attributes. The consciousness can only be accessed by such differences and they serve it as attributes according to which it forms a spacial picture of the impressions." Rudolf Steiner speaks about Lotze in the chapter "Modern Idealistic World Conceptions" in *The Riddles of Philosophy,* Anthroposophic Press, 1973, GA 18; also lecture of January 15, 1914, in *Geisteswissenschaft als Lebensgut,* (Spiritual science in practical life) GA 63.

8. A previous German editor changed "our sense organism" from the original "our lower organism" as contained in the stenographic manuscripts.

9. Compare Chapter 9, "The Idea of Freedom," *Intuitive Thinking as a Spiritual Path: A Philosophy of Freedom,* Anthroposophic Press, 1995.

10. Steiner refers here to the nebular hypothosis of the philosopher and mathematician Emmanuel Kant (1724–1804), according to which the Earth was formed out of a primal fog; also the theories of the French mathematician and astronomer Pierre Simon Laplace (1749–1827), whose theories were developed independently of Kant.

11. In this connection, see Chapter IV, "The Evolution of the Cosmos and Man" in *An Outline of Occult Science,* Anthroposophic Press, 1989.

12. Concerning the meaning of the human corpse for the development of the Earth, see Steiner's lecture of September 22, 1918, in *The Cosmic Prehistoric Ages of Mankind,* typed manuscript, GA 184; the lecture of December 18, 1920, in *The Bridge between Universal Spirituality and Physical Man,* Anthroposophic Press, 1979, GA 202; the lecture on September 4, 1916, in *Faust: The Struggling Human,* typed manuscript, GA 272; and also the lecture cycle *From Jesus to Christ,* Rudolf Steiner Press, 1982, GA 131.

13. See the chapter "Blood and Nerve" in Rudolf Steiner and Ita Wegman's *Fundamentals of Therapy,* Rudolf Steiner Press, 1983, GA 27.

14. An earlier German edition added "bones on the one side and" and "on the other."

15. This text is according to the first dittoed copies. Concerning the difference between animal and human eyes relating to nerve and blood activity, see Steiner's lecture of September 13, 1922, in *The Human Being in Body, Soul and Spirit,* Anthroposophic Press, 1989, GA 347.

16. Eduard von Hartmann (1842–1906) originally began a military career, but a knee injury forced him to leave the military in 1865, and he dedicated himself to philosophical studies. In 1869 he published

his doctoral dissertation, *Die Philosophie des Unbewußten* (The philosophy of the unconscious). In particular, see Chapter 14, "Das Ziel des Weltprocesses und die Bedeutung des Bewußtseins" (The goal of the world process and the meaning of consciousness). On Hartmann's proposal to explode the Earth, see Steiner's lecture of March 26, 1914, in *Geisteswissenschaft als Lebensgut,* (Spiritual science in practical life), GA 63; and lecture of May 14, 1924, in *Philosophers of the Recent Past,* typed manuscript, GA 353. On Hartmann in general, see the chapter "Modern Idealistic World Conceptions" in *The Riddles of Philosophy*; the essay "Eduard von Hartmann. Seine Lehre und seine Bedeutung" (Eduard von Hartmann: teachings and significance) in *Methodische Grundlagen der Anthroposophie* (Foundations of Anthroposophy), GA 30; and his obituary in *Lucifer-Gnosis,* (not available in English), GA 34.

17. See Introduction in *Goethean Science,* Mercury Press, 1988, GA 1; *The Science of Knowing,* Mercury Press, 1988, GA 2; *Truth and Knowledge,* Garber Communications, 1981, GA 3; and *Intuitive Thinking as a Spiritual Path: A Philosophy of Freedom,* Anthroposophic Press, 1994, GA 4.

18. In Chapter 8, "Practical Conclusions," of *Truth and Knowledge,* Steiner writes, "We have seen that the innermost core of the world lives in our knowledge. Cosmic harmony becomes apparent in human cognition." This work, without the Introduction and final chapter, was   Steiner's doctoral thesis at the University of Rostock, Austria, 1891.

LECTURE 4

1. See Steiner's lecture of August 24, 1919, "The Spirit of the Waldorf School," in *The Spirit of the Waldorf School,* Anthroposophic Press, 1995, GA 297.

2. Addition from the original manuscript.

3. See Steiner's essay "The Education of the Child in the Light of Spiritual Science" in *The Education of the Child and Early Lectures on Education,* Anthroposophic Press, 1996, GA 34; and *Soul Economy and Waldorf Education,* Anthroposophic Press, 1986, GA 303 (lectures of December 29 and 30, 1921, and January 1, 2 and 3, 1922).

4. See in particular Chapter 1, "The Essential Nature of the Human Being" and Chapter 2, "Destiny and Reincarnation of the Spirit."

5. Refer to Lecture 1, note 6.

6. Translators' note: Webster's Third New International Dictionary offers the following: "*manes*: 1. The spirits of the dead and gods of the lower world in Ancient Roman belief. Compare Lemures. 2. Ancestral spirits worshiped as gods. Also, the spirit of a dead person regarded as an object to be venerated or appeased." Also of interest is: "*mana*: 1. South Pacific impersonal supernatural force or power that may be concentrated in objects, or persons and that may be inherited, acquired or conferred."

7. Concerning life between death and a new birth, see Chapter 3,"The Three Worlds," *Theosophy,* and Chapter 3, "Sleep and Death," *An Outline of Occult Science;* also the lecture cycles, *The Inner Nature of Man and Life Between Death and Rebirth,* Rudolf Steiner Press, 1994, GA 153; *Between Death and Rebirth,* Rudolf Steiner Press, 1975, GA 141; and *Der Tod als Lebenswandlung* (Death as a metamorphosis of life), GA 182.

8. See Chapter 9, "The Idea of Freedom," in *Intuitive Thinking as a Spiritual Path.* On instinct and drives in children, see *The Education of the Child in the Light of Spiritual Science,* GA 34.

9. "because . . . instinct" is an addition from the original manuscript.

10. For example, Robert Zimmermann, *Philosophische Propädeutik,* 1852. See also Lecture 2, note 1, concerning Herbart.

11. Wilhelm Wundt, 1832–1920, was a philosopher, psychologist and physiologist who founded the first institute for experimental psychology in Leipzig. Rudolf Steiner often mentioned that Wundt's philosophy was influenced by the dogma of the Eighth Ecumenical Council of 869, in which it was determined that the human being consisted only of body and soul (refer to Lecture 3, note 2). See Rudolf Steiner's remarks in "Modern Idealistic World Conceptions," *The Riddles of Philosophy,*; and in his essay "Moderne Seelenforschung" (Modern research on the soul), contained in *Methodische Grundlagen der Anthroposophie* (Foundations of anthroposophy) GA 30.

12. Refer to Chapter 9, "The Idea of Freedom," in *Intuitive Thinking as a Spiritual Path: A Philosophy of Freedom.*

13. See Lecture 2.

14. Rudolf Steiner speaks more completely about psychoanalysis in his lectures of November 10 and 11, 1917, in *Psychoanalysis & Spiritual Psychology,* Anthroposophical Press, 1990, GA 178; and in his lectures of January 22 and March 12, 1918, in *Earthly Death and Cosmic Life,* Garber Press, 1985, GA 181.

15. The textbook example of the woman chased by the carriage is often mentioned by Steiner. Carl Gustov Jung (1875–1961) gives this example in the 1917 edition of his book, *The Psychology of the Unconscious*, Zurich. "I know the case of a young woman who suffered from strong hysteria due to a sudden shock. One evening she was at a social party and was going home around midnight, accompanied by some friends, when suddenly a wagon moving at a fast pace came up from behind them. The others moved to one side; however, frozen by shock, she remained in the middle of the street and ran in front of the horses. The driver snapped his whip and cursed, but this did not help, and she ran down the street that led to a bridge. There her strength gave out and, in order not to be overrun by the horses and due to her desperation, she wanted to jump into the river. But, she was hindered from doing this by some passers-by."

16. Anatole Wassiljewitsh Lunatcharski (1875–1933), Russian author, politician, Commissioner for Public Education in Russia after the October Revolution from 1917–1922 and then President of the Academy of Art in Moscow. In his essay "The Cultural Task of the Working Class," 1919, he says: "The human being who is a *tabula rasa*, that is, an unwritten sheet of paper, begins in early childhood to receive the 'ABCs' of life. The way in which these first impressions of the surroundings, the first effects of other people and the first experiences in working with more distant people are forced to live in the child by the family, the school and the social structure, will determine the full content of each child's soul. The soul is like a crossroads where particular spiritual and sense perceptible forces of social life meet." In his essay "Concerning Elementary Education" (published in 1971), he says: "The dialectic materialism that we represent forces us to build our pedagogy upon exact pedagogical knowledge. We must learn to understand the child from the standpoint of anatomy, physiology and social biology because then it will become clear about what an eight-year-old child consciously brings to school and the surroundings from which this material is derived. . . . We will never gain a healthy generation without proper concern for hygiene in the child's development, without properly organized physical education and sports."

17. Instead of "disappear from the face of the Earth," early editions had "be removed from sovereignty."

18. In the summer of 1905, during a longer stay in Thüringen, Steiner visited a school founded by Dr. Hermann Lietz (1868–1919), the

Deutsche Landerziehungsheim, in Haubinda. Lietz's goal was to create schools for "living personality development." The students were supposed to be independently active in many areas: science, art, handwork, and agriculture. A relationship of comrades should exist between the students and the teachers. The "intellectual excesses of the big cities" were rejected. Steiner also mentions this visit in the conference on June 17, 1921, contained in *Conferences with Teachers*, Michael Hall, 1987, GA 300B.

19. See Lecture 2, August 24, 1919, "The Spirit of the Waldorf School," in *The Spirit of the Waldorf School: Lectures Surrounding the Founding of the First Waldorf School, Stuttgart—1919*, Anthroposophic Press, 1995, GA 297.

LECTURE 5

1. Apparently, the intended meaning here is the first part, "Physiological Colors," in Johann Wolfgang von Goethe's *Theory of Colors*, MIT Press, 1970, trans. Charles Lock Eastlake. See also Steiner's commentaries in *Goethean Science*, Mercury Press, 1988.

2. Changed according to the original notes.

3. Translators' note: The German word used here is *Schwertfortsatz*, which means "ensiform or xiphoid process," a part of the breastbone, not the eye. The correct term would have been *Sichelfortsatz*, or "falciform process," which is a blood-filled structure in the eyes of fish and is similar to the pecten in birds. This same term, which appears in other lectures, seems to have come from information in *Die Augen der Thiere* [The eyes of the animal] by Dr. Otto Thilo. This book, found in Steiner's private library, describes fish eyes as having *Schwertfortsatz* and contains some rough sketches in the margin, apparently from Steiner's hand.

4. An earlier German editor added "few."

5. See *Intuitive Thinking as a Spiritual Path: A Philosophy of Freedom*, especially, Chapter 9, "The Idea of Freedom."

6. "Instinctive impulses" was added from the original stenogram. [In the previous English edition, "instinctive impulses" was simply "impulses."—trans.]

7. Franz Brentano (1838–1917), nephew of Clemens Brentano, was a Catholic theologian and Professor of Philosophy in Würzburg until 1873 when he left the Church and gave up his professorship in

protest against the Dogma of Infallibility. From 1874 on, he was active as a professor in Vienna. In 1917, Rudolf Steiner wrote a memorial to him in *The Case for Anthroposophy* (not contained in the English edition). See also Steiner's essays about him in the collection of articles from *Das Goetheanum* contained in *Der Goetheanumgedanke inmitten der Kulturkrisis der Gegenwart* (The thought of the Goetheanum within the present cultural crisis), GA 36. Brentano's works include *Die Psychologie des Aristoteles* (Aristotle's psychology), Mainz, 1867; *Psychologie vom empirischen Standpunkt* (Psychology from an empirical standpoint), Leipzig, 1874; and *Vom Ursprung sittlicher Erkenntnis* (Concerning the origin of moral cognition), Leipzig, 1889. In the second volume of *Psychologie vom empirischen Standpunkt* in the section entitled "*Von der Klassifikation der psychischen Phänomene*" (On the classification of psychic phenomena) in the seventh chapter, "*Unmöglichkeit, Urteil und Gemütsbeziehung in einer Grundklasse zu vereinigen*" (The impossibility of uniting judgment and feeling relationships into one basic category), Brentano writes, "In the realm of judgment, there exists true and false. However, between them there is no middle ground, just as there is none between existence and nonexistence. This, according to the well-known Law of the Excluded Middle. In contrast, in regard to the Law of Love, there exists not simply a "good" and "bad," rather there is "better" and "less good," a "worse" and a "less bad." This is connected with the peculiarity of preference, which is a particular class of feeling relationship which, as I have shown in my work, "Origin of Moral Cognition," there nothing which corresponds to preference in the realm of judgment. . . . Thus, one desires and often implicitly chooses what is bad, whereby in judging and utilizing the proper method, an untruth is never allowed entrance in order to make the whole more true." "Franz Brentano in Vienna" by Alois Höfler says, "In a way similar to what occurred with the pair of concepts psychological-physical, a strong argument arose about Brentano's discussion of imagination and judgment . . . Brentano is honored (and here I see his major contribution) also in German philosophy to have penetrated into the idea that in a judgment, for instance, the tree is green, the simple connecting of ideas implicit in green tree is not important. Rather, what is important is that what is expressed through the sentence is that I believe, or I am convinced, that the tree is green. Sigwart, Wundt and many others have strongly criticized Brentano's theory of judgment."

8. Christoph von Sigwart (1830–1904) studied Theology and Philosophy in Tübingen, where he was also Professor of Philosophy (1864–1904). He represented the teleological point of view.

9. Richard Wagner (1813–1883), composer, poet, and musicologist. The first draft of *Meistersinger von Nürnberg* was written in the 1840s (first edition, Meinz, 1862) and the first performance was in 1868. Steiner speaks of Richard Wagner in a lecture of March 28, 1907, in *Supersensible Knowledge,* Anthroposophic Press, 1987.

10. Eduard Hanslick (1825–1904), music critic and writer, professor at the University of Vienna. In the preface to his book *Vom Musikalisch Schönen* (Concerning what is musically beautiful), he states, "My passionate opponents accuse me of polemicizing against everything called feeling when, in actuality, every objective and attentive reader can easily recognize that I only protest against the false mixing of feelings into *science,* that I fight against those aesthetic dreamers who only present their harmonious pipe dreams with the pretension of teaching musicians. I am completely of the opinion that the final word concerning what is beautiful always rests upon the evidence of feeling. However, I also maintain the conviction that it is not possible to derive one single law from all the remaining appeals to feeling. This conviction forms one, the *negative principle* of this research. It is first and primarily used against the generally accepted view that music is to 'represent feeling.' . . . In opposition to that *negative principle,* there exists a corresponding *positive principle,* namely, the beauty of a piece of music is *specifically musical,* i.e., the content of the tone relationships without connection to a realm of thinking outside of music. . . . We now also have Richard Wagner's *Tristan, Nibelungenring,* and his teaching of the 'endless melody,' that is, formlessness of the sung and played pipe dream raised to a principle, for which a temple has been opened in Bayreuth." In the text itself, Hanslick states, "Until now, the manner of handling musical aesthetics has suffered from the misconception that it should not be concerned with what is beautiful in music, but more with the feelings that music elicits in us. . . . Therefore, instead of hanging on the secondary and ill-defined effects of music upon the feeling, it is more important to penetrate the inner core of works, and to explain the specific power of musical impressions through the laws of its own organism." Rudolf Steiner speaks of this book in a lecture on

December 3, 1906, in *The Inner Nature of Music and the Experience of Tone,* Anthroposophic Press, 1983, GA 283.

11. For example, see Kant, *The Critique of Pure Reason,* Part 1, "Transcendental Aesthetic." "I do not mean to say that bodies seem only to exist outside, or that my soul seems only to be given in my self consciousness. It would be my own fault, if I changed that, which I ought to count as phenomenal, into mere illusion. . . . Phenomenal predicates can be attributed to the object in its relation to our senses: as for instance to the rose its red color, and its scent. But what is merely illusion can never be attributed to an object as a predicate, for the simple reason that the illusion attributes to the object by itself something which belongs to it only in its relation to the senses, or to a subject in general: as for instance the two handles, which were formerly attributed to Saturn." (Excerpt from *The Critique of Pure Reason,* F. Max Müller, trans., Doubleday Anchor Book, 1966, p. 41.) Rudolf Steiner writes about Kant's theory of cognition in *The Science of Knowing;* in the chapters "Kant's Basic Epistemological Question" and "Epistemology Since Kant" in *Truth and Knowledge;* and in the chapter "The World as Percept" in *Intuitive Thinking as a Spiritual Path: A Philosophy of Freedom.* See also "The Age of Kant and Goethe" in *The Riddles of Philosophy;* and his lecture of October 14, 1909, "The Mission of Spiritual Science, Past and Present" contained in *Metamorphosis of the Soul, Paths of Experience,* Vol. 1, Rudolf Steiner Press, 1983, GA 58.

LECTURE 6

1. In this connection, refer to Rudolf Steiner's lectures of May 9 and 10, 1914, in *How the Spiritual World Penetrates the Physical World,* Anthroposophic Press, 1927, GA 261.

2. Here Rudolf Steiner refers to Solfatara del Pozzuoli, a semi-active volcano on the Gulf of Naples. Sulfur vapors continually rise out of numerous cracks on the volcano and increase noticeably if a piece of burning paper or a torch is placed near the cracks.

3. The wording given in the typed transcript of the original notes is, in itself and in connection with what just precedes it, not quite logical. Previous German editions have resorted to various interpretations and changes in the text. The text given in the present

edition is contained in the first published edition (Dornach 1932), published under the direction of Marie Steiner. In the original transcription, the text is, ". . . awakening in willing means that the human being, to the extent that he is a willing being, through the pain that is otherwise latent and numbed by the sleepiness of the will would be conscious."

4. Translators' note: The German word for "nightmare" is *Alpdruck*, literally, a "goblin pressure" or the feeling of someone sitting on your chest and preventing breathing.

LECTURE 7

1. See Steiner's lecture of February 28, 1907, in *Supersensible Knowledge,* Anthroposophic Press, 1987, GA 55. Concerning "head and heart knowledge" in human life, refer to Steiner's lecture on January 12, 1918, in *Ancient Myths, Their Meaning and Connection with Evolution,* Steiner Book Centre, Vancouver, 1982, GA 180.

2. Concerning Kant's life in old age, see the biography by his long-time secretary, Reinhold Bernhard Jachmann, *Immanuel Kant Geschildert in Briefen an einen Freund,* (Immanuel Kant portrayed in letters to a friend) Königsberg, 1804; and by Jachmann's successor, Eheregott Andreas Wasianski, *Immanuel Kant in seinen letzten Lebensjahren,* (Immanuel Kant in the last years of his life) Königsberg, 1804.

3. Karl Ludwig Michelet (1801–1893), Professor of Philosophy at the University of Berlin, was a representative of the leftist liberal side of the Hegelian school and worked on the publication of Hegel's works. In Steiner's lecture of October 12, 1922, in *The Younger Generation,* Anthroposophic Press, 1984, GA 217, he mentions that Eduard von Hartmann told him this little anecdote. See also the chapter, "The Struggle over the Spirit" in *The Riddles of Philosophy.*

4. Eduard Zeller (1814–1908), historian of philosophy, Professor of Theology in Bern and Marburg and then Professor of Philosophy in Heidelberg and Berlin. Originally a proponent of Hegel, he later distanced himself from this standpoint and attempted to supplement Idealism with a "healthy" Realism.

5. In previous editions the text was "he has sensation."

6. Moriz Benedikt (1835–1920), medical doctor, criminologist and Professor of Nerve Pathology, founded, along with Lombroso, criminal anthropology. He discusses the relationship between sensing and

feeling in "Quellen und Grundlagen des Seelenlebens" (Source and basis of soul life), contained in *Die Seelenkunde des Menschen als reine Erfahrungswissenschaft* (Understanding the human soul as a pure experiential science), Leipzig, 1895. There he writes: "The sensation separated from the impression and arising as a remembrance in consciousness becomes a feeling. Most feelings arise from associated sensations where all or the greatest part of them are already independent of momentary external events and therefore represent simple feelings."

7. Laurenz Müllner (1848–1911), Professor of Philosophy and Chancellor of the University of Vienna, 1894–1895, also teacher of the poet Marie Eugenie delle Grazie. See Rudolf Steiner's description of his personal encounter with Müllner in *An Autobiography,* Garber Communications, 1977, GA 28; and in *The Riddle of Man.*

8. The schoolmate referred to is unknown.

9. Translators' note: In the 1870s, Hungarian schools had a very poor reputation with Austrian and German educators.

10. Translators' note: The schoolmate is here saying that light exists to make things visible, since we cannot see in the darkness. This statement should not be likened to Goethe's observation that the eye is formed in response to the presence of light.

11. Fritz Mauthner (1849–1923), writer and philosopher. Since for him argumentation in philosophy was only an argument about words, he attempted to eliminate terminology through a critique of language. Thus, progress in cognition is only possible when a word grows through "metaphoric" usage. In his *Wörterbuch der Philosophie* (Philosophical dictionary), 1910–1911, under "*geist*" (spirit) he writes, "Now that *spiritus* was finally and completely translated by *geist*, a verb was needed where blowing, breathing, and also surging, fermenting, and frothing would be felt. (This occurred much later with the word *gas* [gas]. The discoverer of the word, van Helmont, was—but only after the discovery—reminded of the word *Chaos* [chaos], which has a similar sound in Dutch. However, he derived it from *gären* [ferment]. Adelung resisted the word "*gas*" and Campe proposed *Luftgeist* [air spirit].)" Concerning this question see also Steiner's lecture of April 23, 1919 in *Spiritual Scientific Considerations of the Social and Pedagogical Questions,* typed manuscript, GA 192.

12. Translators' note: "*Geist*" with "*Gischt*" and "*Gas*."

13. See Steiner's lecture of January 17, 1922, in *Anthroposophie und die*

Rätsel der Seele (Anthroposophy and the riddle of the soul) GA 80, available only in the Swiss journal *Die Menschenschule*, 1937, no. 7.

14. See *Towards Social Renewal*, Rudolf Steiner Press, 1977, GA 23; *Renewal of the Social Organism*, Anthroposophic Press, 1985, GA 24.

LECTURE 8

1. Concerning Rudolf Steiner's views on the senses, see "The Real Basis of Intentional Relation" in *The Case for Anthroposophy*, Rudolf Steiner Press, 1970, GA 21; *Anthroposophy: A Fragment*, Anthroposophic Press, 1996, GA 45; *Wisdom of Man, of the Soul and of the Spirit*, Anthroposophic Press, 1971, GA 115; the lecture of June 20, 1916, "The Twelve Human Senses," contained in *Toward Imagination*, Anthroposophic Press, 1990, GA 169; the lectures of August 12 and September 2, 1916, contained in *The Riddle of Humanity*, Rudolf Steiner Press, 1990, GA 170; the lecture of August 25, 1918, contained in *Mysteries of the Sun and of the Threefold Man*, typewritten manuscript, GA 183; and the lecture of July 22, 1921, contained in *Man as a Being of Sense and Perception*, Steiner Book Centre, Vancouver, 1981, GA 206. Concerning the twelve senses in the relationship to Imagination, Inspiration and Intuition see Rudolf Steiner's lecture of August 8, 1920, in *Spiritual Science as a Foundation for Social Forms*, Anthroposophic Press, 1986, GA 199. In his posthumously published work, *Triertium Catholicum*, Amos Comenius mentions the twelve senses, which he divides into three groups: "Sensus Externi: Tactus, Gustus, Olfactus, Auditus, Visus. Sensus Interni: Attentionis (volgo Communis), Imaginationis, Ratiocinii, Memoriae. Senus Intimi: Lux Mentis/Notitiae Communes, Motus Voluntatis/Instinctus Communes, Vis facultatum/Impetus seu Conscientia."

2. Theodor Ziehen, for example, speaks of a position or movement perception; Frederick Tracy and Joseph Stimpfl mention a sense of temperature, organic and muscle perceptions (inner sense of touch); Josef Klemens Kreibig adds to the usual senses a sense of life, a "static" sense and a movement sense; Robert Zimmermann also mentions the sense of life.

3. See the Appendix to the 1918 edition.

4. See Steiner's lectures in *An Introduction to Eurythmy*, Anthroposophic Press, 1984, GA 277; *Eurythmy as Visible Song*, Rudolf Steiner Press,

1977, GA 278; and *Eurythmy as Visible Speech,* Rudolf Steiner Press, 1984, GA 279.

5. This was corrected in the original German edition. The original transcript read, "We have not only a sense-like consciousness." This sentence was probably not properly recorded, or what Steiner said afterward is missing.

6. See Lecture 3 in this volume.

7. Refer to Steiner's lecture of August 28, 1919 in *Practical Advice to Teachers,* Rudolf Steiner Press, 1976, GA 294.

LECTURE 9

1. Refer to Rudolf Steiner's lecture on July 3, 1921, in *Therapeutic Insights, Earthly and Cosmic Laws,* Mercury Press, 1984, GA 205; and lecture of July 8, 1921, in *Man in the Cosmos as a Being of Thought and Will,* typed manuscript, GA 205.

2. In Aristotle's basic writings on logic in *Organon,* there are three so-called "conclusion figures," which each have four forms, or modi.

3. Concerning concept, "judgment and conclusion" see Steiner's lecture of June 13, 1921, in *Education for Adolescents.*

4. "Memory" was added by an earlier German editor. The original transcript has "from the whole."

5. Hermann Bahr (1863–1934), Austrian poet, writer, theater critic and dramatist, was unusually sensitive and had a great capacity for change. Beginning with naturalism, he became a neo-romanticist, impressionist and finally expressionist. In these areas, he constantly preceded literary development. Rudolf Steiner knew Hermann Bahr as a young student and gave Bahr's path in life considerable attention. See Steiner's lectures of June 6, 1916, in "Ascension and Pentecost," *The Festivals and Their Meaning,* Anthroposophic Press 1958, GA 169; and December 10, 1916, in *The Karma of Untruthfulness,* Part 1, Anthroposophic Press, 1988, GA 173.

6. See Steiner's lecture of August 28, 1919, in *Practical Advice to Teachers,* Anthroposophic Press, 1996, GA 294; and the seminar discussion on August 29, 1919, in *Discussions with Teachers.*

7. An earlier German editor made the change "concepts that are flexible." The original transcript is "such concepts."

8. See the lecture of August 28, 1919, in *Practical Advice to Teachers;* and lecture of August 29, 1919, in *Discussions with Teachers.*

9. See lecture of August 27, 1919, in *Discussions with Teachers*.

10. August Heinrich Hoffmann von Fallersleben (1798–1874), German lyricist in the period preceding the German revolution of 1848, known for his folk songs and also the "Deutschlandlied," which was one of two German national anthems during Rudolf Steiner's lifetime. He studied theology, philology and archeology and was also Professor of German Language and Literature in Breslau. However, he was banned from Germany because of his political activity. Rudolf Steiner reads and discusses his poem about violets in the discussion on August 27, 1919 (see previous note).

11. Curt Friedlein refers to the Socratic method in his *Geschichte der Philosophie* (History of philosophy), Berlin, 1984, as a "way to develop cognition through discussion." He goes on to say, "In the Socratic method, we can distinguish two steps, one following the other, a two-part negative followed by a positive step. At first you hold back your own opinion and go into the viewpoint of your partner in the discussion. You present yourself as unknowing and allow yourself to be taught. In the second part of the negative step, Socrates then performs a kind of cross-examination and draws conclusions from the assertions of his opponent which, in the end, are developed into contradictions. Thus, the opponent is forced to admit, 'I know that I know nothing.' This first part of the method is referred to as Socratic irony. Socrates then begins in the second, positive, stage to develop his own thoughts, not through lecturing, but by allowing the opponent, through a kind of questioning, to come to recognize of himself what it is that Socrates wishes to teach him."

LECTURE 10

1. See Steiner's lecture of August 28, 1919, in *Practical Advice to Teachers*; and lecture of June 13, 1921, in *Education for Adolescents*.

2. See Steiner's lecture, August 28, 1919, in *Practical Advice to Teachers*.

3. This sketch is from Karl Stockmeyer's notes.

4. In the transcript and also in previous editions, this text reads, "the bones of the fore and rear jaw." Apparently, Rudolf Steiner actually said this, since Stockmeyer wrote down the words "fore" and "rear" in his notes. However, two sentences later, Rudolf Steiner clearly speaks of the "upper" and "lower" jawbones and Stockmeyer in conforming

to this wrote these words above "fore" and "rear." Whether this was a slip of the tongue that was corrected two sentences later, or whether Rudolf Steiner here, as has been shown by editors of previous editions, derived the "fore" and "rear" pair from knowledge of embryonic development is no longer ascertainable. The note contained in previous editions regarding this problem is: "From the standpoint of embryonic development, it can be shown that the lower jaw, which comes from a part related to the Branchial Arch, develops from the front toward the rear and the upper jaw has a tendency to develop from the rear toward the front."

5. See Steiner's discussions on Goethe's scientific works in *The Science of Knowing*; and lecture of February 21, 1918, "Goethe als Vater der Geistesforschung" (Goethe as the father of spiritual research) in *Das Ewige in der Menschenseele* (The eternal in the human soul), GA 67.

6. This sketch was contained in the original transcript but not in all of the previous editions.

7. In his diary of 1790, Goethe writes: "As I was walking in the sand dunes of the Lido, as I often did, I came upon a cleaned skull of a sheep that reminded me of a truth that I had earlier recognized, namely that all skulls have arisen through a transformation of the vertebra." He also mentions this, for him, very important discovery in the essay "Bedutende Fördernis durch ein einziges geistreiches Wort" (Important encouragement from a single brilliant word): "In 1791, as I was walking in the sand near Venice, I picked up a cracked sheep's skull and realized that the skull is a development from the vertebra."

8. Translators' note: The German text (1992 edition) reads ". . . the middle of the sphere." We have replaced the word "sphere" with "crescent."

9. Translators' note: An understanding of the concept of counterspace is very helpful in picturing the relationship of the limbs to the universe. On this subject, see Olive Whicher, "The Idea of Counterspace," Anthroposophic Press, n.d., and George A dams and Olive Whicher, *Plant Between Sun and Earth,* Rudolf Steiner Press, 1980.

10. See the lecture of August 28, 1919, in *Practical Advice to Teachers.*

11. See *The Inner Nature of Music and the Experience of Tone,* Anthroposophic Press, 1983, GA 283, especially the lecture of March 7, 1923.

12. See Steiner's cycle *Art as Seen in the Light of Mystery Wisdom,* Rudolf Steiner Press, 1984, GA 275; and *The Arts and Their Mission,* Anthroposophic Press, 1986, GA 276.

13. See Lecture 3, note 2.
14. See Steiner's lecture of March 23, 1920, in *Spiritual Science and Medicine,* Garber Press, 1985, GA 312.
15. See the lecture of August 29, 1919, in *Practical Advice to Teachers.*

LECTURE 11

1. See the lecture of August 29, 1919, in *Practical Advice to Teachers.*
2. A previous German editor added "so that."
3. See lecture of August 29, 1919, in *Practical Advice to Teachers.*

LECTURE 12

1. Concerning migraine headaches, see Rudolf Steiner/Ita Wegman, *Fundamentals of Therapy,* Rudolf Steiner Press, 1983, GA 27; also Steiner's lectures of April 5, 1920, in *Spiritual Science and Medicine,* Garber Press, 1985, GA 312; and July 24, 1924, in *What Can the Art of Healing Gain Through Spiritual Science?,* Mercury Press, 1986, GA 319.
2. Concerning the relationship of human beings to the plant world, see the seminar discussion on August 30 and September 1, 1919, in *Discussions with Teachers.* See also Steiner's lecture of August 6, 1908, in *Universe, Earth and Man,* Rudolf Steiner Press, 1987, GA 105.
3. Refer to the seminar discussion on September 2, 1919, in *Discussions with Teachers.*
4. See Steiner's lecture on December 13, 1914, in *How Does One Bring Reality of Being into the World of Ideas,* typed manuscript, GA 156.
5. Concerning the relationship between breathing and digestion, see Steiner's lecture of April 16, 1921, in *Second Course for Doctors and Medical Students,* Mercury Press, 1991, GA 313.
6. Concerning bacteria, see Steiner's lectures of March 24 and April 7, 1920, in *Spiritual Science and Medicine.*
7. In connection with diabetes, see Chapter 8 in *Fundamentals of Therapy,* GA 27, and to Rudolf Steiner's lectures of April 4, 1920, in *Spiritual Science and Medicine;* November 10, 1923, in *Man as a Symphony of the Creative Word,* Rudolf Steiner Press, 1979, GA 230; and August 9, 1922, in *The Human Being in Body, Soul and Spirit and Early Conditions of the Earth,* Anthroposophic Press, 1989, GA 347.

8. Concerning gout, see Chapter 11 in *Fundamentals of Therapy*, GA 27; and Steiner's lecture of October 9, 1920, in *Physiology and Therapeutics,* Mercury Press, 1986, GA 314; August 9, 1922, in *The Human Being in Body, Soul and Spirit and Early Conditions of the Earth;* and December 12, 1923, in *Nine Lectures on Bees,* Garber Press, 1985, GA 351.

9. Concerning this, see Steiner's lectures on March 24 and April 4, 1920, in *Spiritual Science and Medicine.*

LECTURE 13

1. Translators' note: A *weir* is a partial obstruction or diversion placed in a stream or river. The water thus always meets it at full force, resulting in spray and counterwaves.

2. This is a quote from Goethe's *Faust,* Part I. See also Steiner's lecture of the same title on October 25, 1906, in *Supersensible Knowledge,* Anthroposophic Press, 1987, GA 55.

3. See Steiner's lecture of June 15, 1921, in *Education for Adolescents.*

4. Previous German editions had "sluggish" instead of "excited." "Excited" appears as a result of a new reading of the stenogram.

5. See question and answer session following Steiner's lecture of November 27, 1919, "Spiritual Science and Pedagogy" in *Spirit of the Waldorf School,* Anthroposophic Press, 1995.

6. See Steiner's lecture on December 25, 1921, in *Soul Economy and Waldorf Education,* Anthroposophic Press, 1986, GA 303.

7. Charles Darwin (1809–1882), English natural scientist, physician, geologist and botanist, published *Origin of Species* in 1859, a work that introduced a new era of thinking and scientific ideas. Its high point lies in "proofs" of the theory of descent, which is based upon the mutability of species through external effects, inheritance and overpopulation of living creatures, resulting in a "struggle for survival" and "natural selection." Darwin closes Chapter 15 with the words, "There is grandeur in this view of life, with its several powers, having been originally breathed by the Creator into a few forms or into one." It was only later that this view was also applied to human beings such that it became a truism that people were descended from apes. Rudolf Steiner wrote two articles about Darwin and Darwinism for *Pierers Encyclopedia* (Seventh Edition, 1888) that are contained in *Briefe Band I: 1881–1890* (Correspondence:

1881–1890), GA 38, in which he states, "It should be noted here that neither Darwin nor Haeckel nor any other Darwinist have spoken of an *origin* of human beings from the higher apes, such as the gorilla, but rather claimed that the human being and human-like apes can only be seen as the highest stages of two parallel branches going back to a common origin." Other important works of Darwin are *The Descent of Man* (1871) and *Selection in Relation to Sex* (1871). Steiner discusses the effects of Darwin's works upon nineteenth-century thinking in the chapter, "Darwinism and World Conception," contained in *The Riddles of Philosophy*. See also his lecture of March 28, 1912, in *Menschengeschichte im Lichte der Geistesforschung* (Human history in the light of spiritual investigation), GA 61; and the lecture of December 25, 1921, in *Soul Economy and Waldorf Education*.

8. "Spiritualizing of physical work" is missing in the original notes and early copies; it was added from the notes of a participant at the time of the first publication in 1932.

LECTURE 14

1. The editor of the first edition, published in 1932, added "through grammar."

2. See the lectures of September 1 and 4, 1919, in *Practical Advice to Teachers*; and seminar discussion on September 1 in *Discussions with Teachers*. [See also the lecture of August 16, 1924, in *Kingdom of Childhood*, GA 311, which includes the proof of the theorem.]

3. Friedrich Wilhelm Joseph Schelling (1775–1854), philosopher and proponent of German idealism. His philosophy originated in scientific philosophy and developed from a philosophy of identity into a philosophy of religion. At the age of sixteen, Schelling was accepted to the Academy of Tübingen where he became friends with Hegel and Hölderlin. Following his studies of theology, philology, philosophy, mathematics, and natural science, he was active as a professor in Jena, Würzburg, Erlangen and Munich. His works include *Bruno oder über das natürliche und göttliche System der Dinge* (Bruno, or, on the natural and God-given order of things), Berlin, 1802 and *Vorlesungen über die Methode des akademischen Studiums* (Lectures on the method of academic study), Stuttgart, 1803. In connection with Schelling, see also Steiner's essays "The Classics of the World and

Life Conceptions" in *Riddles of Philosophy,*; and "German Idealism's Picture of the World" in *The Riddle of Man*. See also Steiner's lecture of May 26, 1910, in *Die Philosophie Hegels und ihr Zusammenhang mit der Gegenwart* (Philosophy and Hegel) GA 125.

Acknowledgments

The translators would like to express our feelings of deep gratitude to the following people without whose help our work would have been much more difficult, if not impossible.

First and foremost, we would like to thank Christopher Bamford, our editor, for offering us the project, not flinching when we accepted it and giving us an exceptional level of encouragement, interest and wise counsel along the way. What began as a business relationship has become, for us, a source of warmth and goodwill which has nourished our efforts and which we deeply appreciate.

Secondly, because Lecture Two is both central to the content of the seminar and very difficult to render into intelligible English, we sought the help of Astrid Schmidt-Stegmann, Director of Teacher Training at Rudolf Steiner College. Despite the fact that at the time Astrid was called upon to do about a million other things, she nonetheless read our manuscript word for word, checking it against the German text and her many years of experience teaching *Study of Man*. She then made time to meet with us more than once and went over her suggestions in a way that was genuinely helpful and encouraging. Whatever difficulties remain with our presentation are our responsibility and exist despite her best efforts, for which we are extremely grateful.

Third, we would like to express our sincere appreciation and thankfulness to our dear friend Martin Schmandt, who read the first third of our translation and wrote back general comments, from a more literary perspective, that were so helpful we endeavored to incorporate most of them into the book as a whole. We would also like to thank our friends Paul Goodyear and Jan Tannerome for reading our manuscript and taking the time to share their impressions and suggestions.

It is difficult to convey the extent to which our copy editor, Will Marsh, has contributed to making *The Foundations of Human Experience* a readable, concise and flowing text. This is the second time we have worked with him, and we continue to be amazed by and deeply grateful for the breadth and depth of his expertise.

Finally, we would like to offer a long-distance "thank you" to the editors at the Nachlassverwaltung in Dornach who have worked on this text for many years. Their dedicated research has resulted in both the most accurate text to date and in most of the footnotes offering explanations or pointing to further sources. We deeply value the care they have given the present edition and sustain the hope that the nature and quality of their work will become better known and more widely appreciated.

APPENDIX

The Human Soul and the Human Body
and
Riddles of the Soul and Riddles of the Universe

TWO LECTURES BY RUDOLF STEINER

Translated by Henry Barnes, edited by Henrike Holdrege

FOREWORD

Berlin, March 1917. There might have been a chance, during the preceding months, that the warring powers would have sought a negotiated settlement, but with the collapse of the Czarist regime in Russia in March, and the entry of America into the struggle in April, the die was cast and a continuation of the war was now inevitable. Thus the stage was set for what would come to be seen as the drama of the twentieth century.

When not in Dornach, Switzerland, carving and painting, guiding and inspiring the work on the great building that, in 1917, was nearing completion within sound of French and German guns to the north, Rudolf Steiner was in Berlin.[1] He

---

1. The "great building" referred to is the first Goetheanum, work on which had begun in September, 1913, and continued throughout the War. This enormous edifice, carved from wood, burned to the ground in a tragic fire on New Year's Eve 1922–1923. In its place, a second building, constructed of poured concrete, was erected and dedicated for use in 1928. This Goetheanum, like the first, serves as the headquarters for anthroposophy.

knew that only a thinking that went to the roots of the problems that had made the war inevitable could provide the ground
on which a socially constructive peace might be built. And he
saw that such thinking must reach beyond a one-sidedly spiritual world view or a one-sided materialism, and must show how
the two worlds—soul-spiritual and sense-perceptible—interact
and form a whole.

For thirty years Steiner had pursued his spiritual-scientific
research into the ways that the human soul—as a being of
thinking, feeling, and willing—penetrates the bodily organism.
And, as he said, it was only during the terrible years of war that
the results of this research had finally become clear so that he
was able to give them conceptual form. Therefore, it must have
been with a sense of urgent responsibility that he interrupted
the public lecture series begun in February to hold the two lectures that appear here for the first time in English translation.[2]

He begins the first lecture by drawing attention to the failure
of soul researchers—psychologists—to build a bridge to the
physical, and the failure of natural scientists to find a bridge to
the soul. He then goes on to show that only a science that can
extend the methods of natural science—with its awe-inspiring
achievements—into an investigation of soul and spirit can
hope to build the bridge that is so urgently needed. Only such
a science could show how the human soul, in its totality, penetrates and makes use of the entire human bodily organism as
the instrument for will and feeling, as well as thought.

In the second lecture, Rudolf Steiner links his anthroposophical spiritual-scientific research with the work of those pio-
neering forerunners among the German idealists of the late

---

2. *Geist und Stoff, Leben und Tod* (Spirit and Matter, Life and Death)
(GA66), Seven public lectures held between February 15 and March 31,
1917, in the Achitektenhaus, Berlin.

eighteenth and early nineteenth centuries who came to realize that the life of the organism presupposes an invisible, persistent body of supersensible forces, which unites with, organizes, and sustains the physical organism and survives its dissolution. He goes on to show how the etheric from without, enlivened by the etheric within, gives rise to mental images, to thought representations, and to memory; and how, when rightly intensified, it can lead not only to genuine imagination, but also to hallucinations if the etheric reaches too deeply into the physical organism. In contrast, he describes how in willed activity, when the soul unfolds an impulse of will, the etheric is partially withdrawn from the organism, and the soul works directly through the etheric into the metabolism. When this activity is intensified intuition becomes possible, but when the etheric is bound by the physical, compulsive actions arise. Within the context of these lectures, Rudolf Steiner also makes the challenging assertion that spiritual-scientific research does not reveal any essential difference between the so-called motor and sensory nerves. In this view all nerves are sensory and serve only to perceive the subtle changes in the breathing organism and metabolism that are effected by the soul's intervention in feeling and will.

These few indications may suffice to show the fundamental significance of these two lectures in the evolution of a new and radical anthroposophical anthropology. The insights they embodied were given written form in the volume Steiner published in the following November, and we owe it to Owen Barfield, the distinguished English essayist and critic, that this later volume—*Riddles of the Soul* (*Von Seelenrätseln*) —was made available to English readers some twenty-five years ago.[3] Yet, it

---

3. *The Case for Anthroposophy*, Rudolf Steiner Press, 1970. (Contains selections from *Von Seelenrätseln*. Translated, arranged, and with an Introduction by Owen Barfield.)

is only when one takes the highly concentrated presentation contained in the Commentary Note appended to *Riddles of the Soul,* together with these two earlier lectures, that the full magnitude of these research results becomes apparent. One then realizes, furthermore, that what one finds in its germinal, seed form in 1917 had already expanded and taken root when, two years later, Rudolf Steiner laid the foundation for the establishment of the first Waldorf School in Stuttgart in August, 1919, with the lectures published in the main body of this book. The two lectures presented here, therefore, form an integral part of the wellspring from which Waldorf education flows.

Henry Barnes

1.

THE HUMAN SOUL AND THE HUMAN BODY

in the Knowledge of Nature and Spirit

BERLIN, MARCH 15, 1917

I find myself in a somewhat difficult situation concerning today's lecture, because, due to the nature of the subject, it will be necessary to sketch the results of spiritual-scientific research from a wide spectrum of diverse fields. It might seem desirable for some people to hear details that support and confirm these results, and it will be possible to present such details in later lectures. This evening, however, it will be my task to sketch the field of knowledge we are concerned with. In addition it will be necessary for me to use expressions, ideas, and mental pictures of the soul and body that are grounded in the lectures I have already held here. I shall have to limit myself strictly to the theme, to the characterization of the relationship between the human soul and the human body.

On this subject, one can say that two recent spiritual directions of thought and investigation have led to the greatest possible misunderstanding. And if one becomes engaged in these misunderstandings one finds, on one hand, that the thinkers and researchers who have sought recently to penetrate the field of psychological, of soul phenomena, do not know where to begin when they approach the admirable achievements of natural science—especially in relation to knowledge of the human physical organism. They cannot build a bridge rightly from what they understand as observation of soul phenomena, to the manifestations of the body. On the other hand, it must also be said that those who represent natural-scientific research are, as a rule, so estranged from the realm of soul phenomena, from the observation of psychic experience, that they also cannot build a bridge from the truly awe-inspiring results of modern science to the field of soul phenomena. One finds, therefore, that soul researchers—psychologists, and natural scientists—speak two different languages when they speak about the human soul and the human body; one finds that, basically, they do not understand each other. And because of this, those who seek insight into the great riddles in the soul realm, and the connection between the riddles of the soul and the universal world, are misguided—indeed one could say that they find themselves completely confused.

I want to begin by pointing out where, in fact, the mistake in thinking lies. A curious circumstance has developed—I do not criticize, I only want to present the fact—about how human beings today relate to their concepts to their ideas. Mostly they do not consider concepts, and ideas, no matter how well they may be grounded, to be merely tools for judging reality as it confronts us individually in each and every instance. Human beings today are convinced that when they have mastered an idea, then this idea, this concept, may be immediately applied in the world. The reigning misunderstandings I have characterized are based on this peculiarity of contemporary thinking, which has taken root in all scientific striving. One overlooks the fact that a concept can be entirely mistaken in application. In order to characterize this assumption as a method of thought, to begin with I will clarify this with an example from life. You will agree that one may be justified in the conviction that sleep, healthy sleep, is an excellent cure for illness; this can be an entirely correct concept, a correct idea. If, however, in a particular instance it is incorrectly applied, something like this may happen: Somewhere a man visits an old man who is not well, one who is ill in one way or another. The visitor applies his wisdom to the situation by saying, "I know how very good a healthy sleep can be." When he leaves, perhaps someone says to him, "Now look, this old man sleeps all the time." Or maybe someone else thinks that it's very healthy to take a walk, to just move, for certain illnesses. When he advises someone in this way, however, the other objects, "But, you forget, I am a mail carrier!"

I only want to point out, with this, the principle that one can have thoroughly correct concepts, but these concepts are only useful when properly applied in life.

Also, within various branches of science one can find correct concepts, strictly proven in a way that is difficult to contradict. Yet the question must always be asked—are these concepts also applicable in life? Are they tools that are useful for understanding life? The illness of thought I pointed to and wanted to make clear with these exaggerated examples is enormously widespread in our contemporary thinking. As a result many people are not very aware of where the limits of their concepts are, where it is necessary to extend and broaden their concepts with the facts—whether these facts are physical or spiritual. And there is perhaps no realm where such a broadening of concepts, of ideas, is needed as much as in the sphere we want to speak of today.

Indeed from the perspective of natural science, which is the most important viewpoint today, one has to acknowledge over and again that what has been achieved in this sphere deserves admiration; it is magnificent. And on the other side, significant work has been accomplished in the psychological, the soul realm. But these achievements do not give us insight into the most important soul questions, and, above all, they cannot extend and broaden their concepts so that they can withstand the onslaught of modern natural science, which turns in one way or another against everything of a spiritual nature.

I want to connect what I have to say with two recent literary publications that contain research results in these fields, publications that clearly show the necessity for a vigorous effort toward broadening concepts by extending research. In this regard there is the extraordinarily interesting work of Theodor Ziehen, *Physiological Psychology.*[4] This *Psychology* shows in an outstanding way—although the research results are still inconclusive and hypothetical to a certain extent—how according to modern natural scientific observations one must consider the brain and nervous mechanism in order to get an idea of how the nerve-sense organism functions when we form mental pictures and put those pictures together. This is just the sphere

4. *Leitfaden der physiologischen Psychologie in 15 Vorlesungen,* Jena 1891, fifth edition, Jena 1900. Theodor Ziehen (1862-1950) was a German psychiatrist, physiologist, and psychologist. See Rudolf Steiner *Intuitive Thinking as a Spiritual Path: A Philosophy of Freedom,* pp. 28, 171; also Steiner, *Anthroposophy and Science,* (Spring Valley, NY: Mercury Press, 1991), pp. 81 ff.

where one can see clearly how natural scientific methods of observation, as applied to the realm of soul phenomena, lead to narrowly limited concepts that do not penetrate life. Ziehen demonstrates that, for everything that occurs in the forming of mental pictures, of thinking, something like counter-images can be found within the nerve mechanism. And if one becomes familiar with the research in this field regarding this question, one finds that the school of Haeckel has achieved especially outstanding results in this field. One only needs to draw attention to the excellent work of Max Verworn, Haeckel's pupil, who in the Goettingen laboratory showed what occurs in the human brain, in the human nervous system, when we connect one picture with another—or as one says in psychology, when one mental representation associates with another. Our thinking rests fundamentally on this linking of mental pictures. How to understand this linking of representations, how to think of the arising of memory representations, how certain mechanisms are present that preserve, as it were, these representations so that they can later be recalled from memory—this is all presented in a comprehensive and beautiful way by Theodor Ziehen. When one surveys what he says about the mental life of thinking and about what corresponds with this in the human nervous system, indeed, one can go along with all of this. But then Ziehen arrives at a strange conclusion.

Of course, one knows that the life of the human soul does not just contain the formation of mental images. No matter how one conceives of the connection between other soul activities in the sense of forming mental representations, to begin with, one can not ignore the fact that one must at least recognize other soul activities, or capacities, in addition to representing. We know that besides representing we have feeling, the activity of feeling in its whole wide scope, and in addition to this, the activity of will. Ziehen speaks as if feeling were actually no more than an attribute of representation. He does not speak about feeling as such, but of a feeling quality of sensations or mental pictures. Mental representations are present. They are there, not merely as we think them, but endowed with certain attributes that give them their feeling quality. Thus one could say that such a researcher has no alternative but to say about feeling: What happens in the nervous system does not extend to feeling. As a result one ignores feeling as such and considers it merely as an appendage to representation. One can also say that, in pursuing the nervous system, one does not apprehend within the nerve mechanism the aspect of the soul's life that manifests as the life of feeling. Therefore, one omits the life of feeling as such. However, one also fails to uncover anything in the nerve mechanism that requires a consideration of willing. For this reason, Ziehen completely denies any justification for speaking of the will in relation to knowledge of soul and body within the context of natural science. What happens when a human being wills something? Let us imagine a person walking, in motion. In this regard one says— or such an investigator thinks—the movement, the willing, has its origin in the will. But, in general, what is in fact there? Nothing is there, in the first instance, except the image, the thought of the motion. I imagine, in a sense, what will happen as I move through space; and then nothing happens except what I then see, or feel—in other words, I perceive my movement. The perception of the movement then follows the remembered intention—the remembered image of the intended movement; will, an act of willing, is nowhere to be found. The will is therefore simply eliminated by Ziehen. We see that in pursuing the nerve mechanism one does not arrive at feeling or will; therefore one must leave these soul activities more or less (and in the case of the will, entirely) aside. Then, charitably, one tends to say, "Well, well, we can leave all of this to the philosophers; natural scientists have no grounds for speaking about such things, even if they don't go as far as Verworn, who says, 'The philosophers have imagined quite a bit into human soul life, which, from the perspective of natural science, turns out to be unjustified.'"

A significant researcher of the soul, and Ziehen, who proceeds entirely on the basis of natural scientific data, both come to a similar conclusion. I have frequently mentioned him here, and I have said that he is more significant than one generally assumes. This is Franz Brentano.[5] Brentano, however, proceeds from the soul. He tried in his *Psychology* to investigate the soul life. It is characteristic of this work that only the first volume has appeared, with nothing further since the 1870s. Anyone who knows his circumstances realizes that because Brentano works with the limited concepts—in the sense of the previous characterization—he could not get past the beginning. But one thing is extraordinarily significant about Brentano: he distinguishes *representation* and *feeling* in his attempt to work through the manifestations of the soul, and groups them into certain categories. But in going through the soul from top-to-bottom, so to speak, he never arrives at the will. Willing is, for him, essentially a subordinate aspect of feeling. So a soul researcher also fails to reach the will. Franz Brentano relies on such things as this: language itself shows that how one speaks about soul phenomena indicates that what we generally mean by "will" is really nothing but feeling. Indeed, only feeling is expressed when I say that I have repugnance for this or that. Nevertheless, when I say

---

5. Franz Brentano (1858–1917) was a very influential German philosopher, Catholic priest (1864–1873), who wrote on psychology, logic, ethics, etc. Brentano is considered the father of phenomenology.

that something is repugnant to me, I express instinctively that, within soul life, will belongs with feeling.[6] From this one example you may see how it is impossible for this investigator of the soul to free himself from the limits of a particular conceptual circle. Without a doubt, what Brentano presents is conscientious, careful soul research; yet, equally without a doubt, the experience of the will—the passage within the soul life to outer action, the birth of the external act from the will's impulse—is an experience that cannot be denied. Psychologists, therefore, fail to discover what in itself cannot be denied.

One cannot maintain that every researcher who takes a stand on the basis of natural science and relates the soul life with bodily existence is necessarily a materialist. Ziehen, for example, thinks of matter as a pure hypothesis. But he comes to a very strange point of view—that is, that no matter where we look, there is nothing but the element of soul. There may perhaps be something of the essence of matter out there; this matter must first make an impression on us in its processes—so that, while the material facts make an impression on our senses, what we experience in our sense perception is already a manifestation of soul. Now, we experience the world only through our senses, therefore, everything is fundamentally a manifestation of soul. This is the concept of a researcher like Ziehen. In this sense, the entire realm of human experience is actually of a soul nature, and, in fact, we would only have grounds to say that everything must be considered to have hypothetical reality—except ourselves, except our own experiences of soul. Fundamentally, according to such conceptions, we weave and

---

6. In the original German, Rudolf Steiner used the word *Widerwillen,* "antipathy"; for example, *Ich habe Widerwillen gegen Etwas.* In the ordinary use of language, the word "will" appears as an attribute of feeling.

live within the encompassing realm of soul phenomena and do not get beyond it.

Eduard von Hartmann, at the end of his *Handbook Concerning Soul Knowledge* characterizes this view in an extreme way, and this characterization, though exaggerated, is indeed interesting to contemplate.[7] He says that, in the sense of *panpsychisms*—even constructing such words—one can imagine such an example: two people are sitting at a table and drinking—well, let's say, recalling better times—drinking coffee with sugar. One of them is more distant from the sugar bowl than the other, and in the naive experience of an ordinary human being, it happens that one of them asks the other for the sugar, saying, "Please pass me the sugar." The second person gives the other the sugar. According to Eduard von Hartmann, if the idea of a universal soul element is correct, how can this procedure be viewed? It must be conceived that something occurs in the human brain or nervous system that forms in such a way in consciousness that the mental representation awakes, "I would like to have the sugar." But the one in question hasn't the faintest notion about what is actually out there. Then something that looks like another person links itself to the representation in the soul realm—for what is objectively there cannot actually be known, it only creates an impression—and this "apparent person" then passes the sugar. It is the opinion of physiology, Hartmann says, that what happens objectively is this: in my nervous system, if I am one of the two people, a process unfolds that reflects itself as an illusion in consciousness—

---

7. Karl Robert Eduard von Hartmann (1842–1906), German philosopher who synthesized views of Schopenhauer, Kant, and Hegel into a theory of evolutionary history based on conflict between unconscious will and unconscious reason. He also wrote *Philosophy of the Unconscious*. He was very influential on Steiner's generation.

"I ask for the sugar." Then this same process, which has nothing to do with the nature of consciousness, moves the speech muscles, and once again something objectives arises out there, which one knows nothing about in actuality but, nevertheless, is again reflected in consciousness whereby one receives the impression that one speaks the words, "I would like to have the sugar." Then these movements, called forth as vibration in the air, are transmitted to another person—again assumed hypothetically—and produce vibrations, stimuli, in the nervous system. Because the sensory nerves in this nervous system are stimulated, motor nerves are set in motion. And while this purely mechanical process plays itself out, something like "I am giving this person the sugar bowl" is reflected in the consciousness of the other person. Also reflected is everything else that hangs together with this process, everything that can be perceived, the movement, and so on.

Here we have the peculiar view that everything that occurs in external reality remains unknown to us, is only hypothetical, but appears to be nerve processes that swing, as vibrations in the air, to the other person, and then leaps from the sensory to the motor nerves, with the nerves producing motion, which then accomplishes the perceptible action. This latter is entirely independent of what occurs in the consciousness of the two people, automatically. But in this way one gradually comes to the point where one can no longer gain insight into the connection between what occurs automatically outside and what we actually experience. Because, what we experience—if we assume the standpoint of universal ensoulment has nothing to do with anything, the entire world—is absorbed into the soul. Individual thinkers have countered this with weighty objections. If, for example, a businessman is expecting a telegram with a certain content, only a single word needs to fail and instead of joy, unhappiness, sorrow, and pain may be let loose in his soul. Can one say then that what one experiences within the soul happens only in the soul realm? Or should one not assume that, according to the immediate consequences, something has actually occurred in the external world, which is then experienced also by the soul? On the other hand, if one takes the perspective of this automatism, one might say, "Yes, Goethe wrote *Faust*, that is true; but this only shows that the entire *Faust* lived in Goethe's soul as mental representation. But his soul has nothing to do with the mechanism that described this mental representation. One does not escape from the mechanism of the soul's life to what is outside there in the world."

As a result of all this, the view has gradually formed—which is now widely disseminated—that what is of the nature of soul, in a certain sense, is only a kind of parallel process to what is out there in the world, that it only supplements what is out there, and one can not know what really happens in the world. Fundamentally, one can certainly come to the viewpoint I characterized in my book *The Riddle of Man* as the standpoint that developed in the nineteenth century and, in certain circles, has become more and more dominant—and which I called *illusionism*.[8] One will ask oneself, "Doesn't this *illusionism* rest on very sound foundations?" This may well seem to be the case. It really seems as if one cannot argue with the proposition that there might be something out there that affects my eye, and that the soul only translates what is out there into light and color, so that, indeed, one only has to do with soul experience. It seems justified to assume that one cannot get beyond the limits of the soul realm; that one would never be justified to say, "Something or other out there corresponds to what lives in my soul." Such questions only appear to be insignificant for the

8. Mercury Press, Spring Valley, NY, 1990.

greatest questions concerning the soul—for example, the question of immortality. Indeed, they have a deep significance for us as human beings, and in this regard certain indications can be made today. But I want to begin with this foundation.

The direction of thought I have thus characterized never considers that, in relation to the life of the soul, it only accounts for what occurs when, from outside, through the sense world, impressions are made on the human being who then develops mental images of these impressions through the nerve-sense apparatus. These ways of viewing phenomena do not consider that what occurs in this way applies only to the human being's interaction with the outer sense world. But this ignores the fact that one comes to very particular results—also when one examines this matter in the sense of spiritual-scientific research—when one investigates the interaction with the outer world. Here it becomes evident that the human senses are built up in a very particular way.

However, what I have to propose here about the structure of the senses, and especially about the finer details of this structure, is not yet available to external science. Something is built into the human body, in the organs we use as our senses, that is excluded to a certain degree from the general inner life of the human bodily organism. As a symptomatic example we can consider the human eye. The eye is built into the organization of the skull almost as an entirely independent being and is connected with the interior of the entire organism only through certain organic elements. The whole could be described in detail, but this is unnecessary for today's considerations. However, a certain degree of independence exists, and such independence is indeed inherent to all the sense organs. So, what is never considered is that something very particular happens in sense perception, in sense experience. The sense-perceptible outer world continues by means of the sense organs into our own organism. What occurs there outside through light and color—or better, what occurs *in* light and color—continues its activity into our organism in a way that the life of our organism does not initially participate in its activity. Light and color, therefore, enter the eye in such a way that the life of the organism, as it were, does not hinder the penetration of what occurs out there. In this way the stream of outer occurrence penetrates through our senses into our organism up to a certain point, as if through gulfs or channels.

Now the soul first participates in what flows in because she herself enlivens what at first penetrates in a non-living way from outside. This is an extremely important truth that is revealed through spiritual science. As we perceive with our senses we constantly enliven what continues to penetrate our body from the flow of outer events. Sense perception is an actual living penetration, indeed an enlivening, of what continues its activity within our organism as something dead. In this way we really have the objective world immediately within us in the activity of sense perception, and as we digest it by means of the soul, we experience it. This is the actual process and is extremely important. For in relation to the experience of our senses one cannot say it is merely an impression, that it is only the result of a cause from outside. What occurs outwardly actually enters our inner being as a bodily process, is taken into the soul and permeated with life. In our sense organs we have something that the soul lives within, yet fundamentally, our own body does not live within directly. At some future time one will approach, through natural-scientific considerations, the ideas that I have developed here, and one will understand correctly that in the eyes of certain species of animals—and this can extend to all the senses—certain organs will be discovered that are no longer found in human beings. The human eye is simpler than the eyes of lower animals—indeed even simpler than those of animals close to human beings. One will then ask, "Why, for example, do certain animals still have the so-called "pecten" in their eye, a special organ made up of blood vessels? Why do others have the so-called "sword-form," another organ of blood vessels?" When one asks these questions one realizes that, with these organs penetrating into the senses in the animal organism, the immediate bodily life of the organism still participates in what occurs in the senses as the continuation of the outer world.

The sense perception of an animal, therefore, is definitely not such that one could say the soul directly experiences the outer world as it penetrates the sense organ. For the soul element, within its instrument—the body—still penetrates the sense organ; bodily life permeates the sense organ. The human senses are formed, however, in such a way that they are enlivened by the activity of soul. Through this it becomes clear to anyone who truly grasps sense experience in its essential nature that we actually have outer reality in sense perception. The thinking of Kant or Schopenhauer, all of modern physiology, cannot denying this. These sciences cannot yet allow their concepts to press forward to a true understanding of sense experience. Only when the deeper nervous system, the brain system, takes in what occurs in the sense organ, only then does it enter the sphere where the body's life penetrates directly, and interior bodily processes occur as a result. Thus the human being has the zone of the senses at the periphery, and within this zone of the senses the human being has the zone of direct encounter with the external world where the outer world comes to meet one directly, with no intervention, inasmuch as it approaches through the senses; for, in this process, no intervention occurs. Then, however, when the sense impression becomes mental representation, we are within the deeper nervous system where every process of ideation, of representation, corresponds to a process in the nerve mechanism. When we construct a mental representation drawn from sense perception, an occurrence in the human nervous organism always comes into play.

In this regard, one must acknowledge that we have an admirable accomplishment in what has been accomplished by natural science, especially the discoveries of Verworn concerning the processes that occur in the nervous system and brain when something is represented. Spiritual science has to just be clear about this: when we encounter the external world through our senses we find ourselves confronted by the sequence of what actually exists in the outer world. While we form mental representations—for example, by calling up memories, or thinking about something—without connecting this to something outside ourselves, but inwardly linking impressions that have been derived from outside, in this case our nervous system is unquestionably engaged. And what occurs in our nervous system, which lives in its structures, its processes—the further one investigates this fact, the more one discovers—is truly a wonderfully projected image of the soul realm, the life of representations. One who enters even a little into what can be learned from brain physiology, from nerve physiology, discovers the structure and dynamics of movement within the brain, which reveal the most wonderful insights that one can come to in this world.

However, spiritual science must then be clear, just as we face our own bodily world around us. It is simply that this latter fact is seldom brought to consciousness. But when spiritual-scientific researchers raise their consciousness to what they call *imaginative thinking*, they then recognize that—though the process stays in a dreamy awareness—in the weaving of mental representations, when left to itself, human beings apprehend their inner nerve activity in the brain and nervous system as they otherwise apprehend the outer world. By means of meditations such as I have described, one can strengthen the life of soul, can come to know that one's relationship with this inner nerve world is no different from one's relationship with the outer world of the senses. Except that in the relationship to the external sense world the impression is strong, coming as it does from without, and as a result one forms the judgment that the outer world makes the impression; whereas, what arises from within, out of the bodily organism, does not intrude as forcefully—despite the fact that it constitutes a wonderful play of material processes—and as a result one has the impression that mental representations, mental images, arise of themselves.

What I have said holds true concerning these indications about the human being's interaction with the outer sense world. The soul observes as she penetrates the body, at one time external reality, at another time the play of her own nerve mechanism. Now a certain conceptual view has been concluded from this, and as a result the misunderstanding arises that this is the only way human beings relate with the outer world. When, because of this conception, one asks how the outer world works on the human being, then the answer must come from the standpoint of the wonderful accomplishments of brain anatomy and brain physiology. The question is answered as we have just characterized. One describes what happens when human beings either give their attention to the mental images that arise from the outer world, or as they might later recall them from memory. That is—according to this conceptual view—the only way human beings relate to the outer world. Consequently, this view must conclude that, indeed, all soul life runs parallel to the outer world. For it must certainly be a matter of indifference to the outer world whether we form mental images about it or not; the world goes on as it does, and our mental pictures are merely added on. Indeed, what is valid here is a fundamental principle of this world view—that is, everything we experience is of the nature of soul. But in this soul element the outer world lives at one time and the inner world at another. And, indeed—this is the consequence—at one time, according to the external processes and the next time according to the processes in the nerve mechanism. Now, this view of things proceeds from the assumption that every other soul experience must stand in a similar relation with the external world, in feeling, as well as volition. And if investigators such as Theodor Ziehen[9] are honest with themselves, they do not find such relations. As a result, as demonstrated, they deny the reality of feelings within a mere nerve mechanism, and even less, the will. Franz Brentano doesn't even find the will within the human soul being. Where does this come form?

Some day, spiritual science will shed light on this question after those misunderstandings I described today have vanished, and once the help spiritual science has to offer in these matters has been accepted. Indeed, the fact, which I have only indicated, is this: What we designate as the sphere of feeling within the soul's life—strange as this may sound—as it first arises, has absolutely nothing to do with the life of nerves. I know very well how many assertions of contemporary science this contradicts. I also know very well the well founded objections that can be brought. However, as desirable as it might be to enter into all the details, today I can only present results.

Ziehen is quite right when he fails to find either feeling or willing in the mechanism of the nervous system, when he only finds the forming of mental representations, mental images. Ziehen says in consequence: Feelings are merely tones—that is

---

9. Wrote *Leitfaden der physiologischen Psychologie in 15 Vorlesungen* (*Manual of Physiological Psychology in Fifteen Lectures*), Jena, 1891.

attributes, accentuating the life of representation; for only the life of mental representation is found in the nerves. Willing is altogether non-existent for the natural scientist, because the perception of the movement is linked directly with the mental image of the movement and immediately follows it. There is no will in between. There is nothing of human feeling in the nerve mechanism. This consequence, however, is not drawn, but is within the assumption.

When human feeling, therefore, expresses itself in the bodily organism, what is this connected with? What is the relationship between human feeling and the body, since the relationship between forming mental images and the body is the way I described the relationship between sense impressions and the nerve mechanism? As strange as this still sounds today, spiritual science shows that forming mental images is connected with perception and the interior mechanism of the nervous system, and feeling is connected, in a similar way, with everything that belongs organically with human breathing and related activities—and this will eventually be documented by natural-scientific research, and it can already be presented as a proven result of spiritual science. Feeling as it arises initially has nothing to do with the nervous mechanism, but belongs instead with the breathing organism. However, at least one objection close at hand should be dealt with here—that the nerves, nevertheless, stimulate everything that has to do with breathing. However, just as we perceive light and color by means of our optic nerve, so we perceive the process of breathing itself, although in a more subdued way, through the nerves that connect our breathing organism with the central nervous system. These nerves, usually designated motor nerves in relation to breathing, are nothing but sensory nerves. They are there, like the nerves of the brain, only more dulled, to perceive breathing as such. The origin of feeling in its entire spectrum, from the slightest emotional disturbance up to a quiet, harmonious feeling, is connected organically with all that occurs in the human being as breathing process, and with whatever belongs to it as its continuation in one direction or another in the human organism. One day thinking will be quite different about the bodily characteristics of feeling when people see through the circumstances and no longer insist that certain streams stimulating the breathing process run from a central organ, from the brain, and recognize that, indeed, the opposite is the case. The breathing processes are there, they are perceived by certain nerves; they come in this way to connect with them. But the connection is not of the kind where the origin of the feeling is anchored in the nervous system. And with this we come to a field that has not yet been worked on, despite the admirable natural science of today. The bodily expressions of the feeling life will be wonderfully illuminated when one studies the finer changes in the breathing processes, especially the more subtle changes in the effects of the breathing process while one or another feeling occurs within us.

The process of breathing is very different from the process that plays itself out in the human nerve mechanism. In regard to the nerve mechanism one can say, in a certain sense, that it is a faithful after-image of the human soul life itself. If I wanted to use an expression—such expressions are not yet available to us in our language, and one can, therefore, only use approximations—if I wanted to use an expression for the wonderful way that the soul life is mirrored in the human nervous system, then I might say, "The soul life portrays itself in the life of the nerves; the life of the nerves is a true portrait, a picture, of the soul life. Everything we experience in our soul in relation to our perceptions of the outer world, portrays itself in the nervous system. This is what enables us to understand that even at birth the nervous system, particularly the head, is a faithful reflection of the soul life as it comes from the spiritual world and unites with the bodily life of the organism.

The objections that arise today, just from the perspective of brain physiology, against the union of the soul with the brain—with the head organism, as the soul descends out of the spiritual world—will one day be presented as proof of this connection. Before birth or conception, the soul prepares the wonderful structure of the head from spiritual foundations, which is built up and formed by the human life of soul. The head, for example, grows only four times heavier than it is at birth, whereas the entire organism grows twenty-two times heavier during its later development; thus, at birth the head appears as something thoroughly formed, something complete in itself, as it were. Even before birth it is essentially a picture of the soul's experience, because the soul works on the head from the spiritual world for a long time before any of the physical facts develop in the embryo—facts we are well acquainted with—and this work leads to human existence in the physical world. For the spiritual researcher it is just this wonderful structure of the human nervous system, the projected mirror image of the human life of soul, that confirms both the soul's descent out of the spiritual realm and the fact that forces are active in the spiritual world that make the brain a portrait of the soul life.

Now if I were to express the connection between the feeling life and the breathing life in a way that would similarly characterize the relationship between the life of thought images and the nervous system just characterized, I would say, "The life of the nerves is a picture, a portrait, of the soul's life in its activity of forming mental images, of thought representations," then I would say, "The breathing life, with everything that belongs to it, is an image of the soul's life, which I would compare to pictorial writing, to hieroglyphics." The nervous system is a true picture, a real portrait; the respiratory system is only a hiero-glyph. The nervous system is constructed so that the soul needs only to be completely at one with herself in order to "read" from her portrait (the nervous system) what she wishes to expe-rience of herself. With the pictorial writing, the hieroglyph, one must interpret, one must already know something, the soul must occupy herself more actively with the matter. This is how it is with the respiratory system. The breathing life is less a faithful expression of the soul's experience; if I were to charac-terize this more exactly, I would have to point to the Goethean principle of metamorphosis, but our time today is too short for this. The breathing life is far more the kind of expression I would want to compare to the relationship between pictorial writing and its meaning and significance. The soul's life is, therefore, more inward in the feeling life, less bound to the outer processes. For this reason the connection also escapes a more rudimentary physiology. For the spiritual researcher, however, this is just what makes it clear; just as the breathing, the respiratory life, is connected with the feeling life, so must the feeling life be freer, more independent in itself, because this breathing life is a less exact expression of the feeling.

Thus we understand the body more deeply if we consider it as an expression of the feeling life rather than if we consider it an expression of the life of images. However, because the feel-ing life is connected with the breathing life, the spiritual dwells in a more lively way within the feeling life, more inward, than in the mere life of representation—inasmuch as the life of rep-resentation does not rise to Imagination, but is rather a mani-festation of outer sense experience. Feeling life is not as clear and bright, just as pictorial writing expresses less clearly what it signifies than an actual picture does—I only speak comparatively—but just because of this, what expresses itself in the life of feeling the spiritual is more within than it is in the ordinary life of representation. The breathing life is a less defined tool than the nervous system is.

Now we come to the life of will and find ourselves in the situation where, when we start to speak as spiritual researchers about the facts as we observe them, one may well be discounted as an extreme materialist. But when the spiritual scientist speaks of the relationship between the human soul and the human body, the relationship between the entire soul and the entire body must be considered, not just the soul's relationship to the nervous system, as is normal today. The soul expresses itself in the entire organism, in everything that happens in the body.

If one now wants to consider the life of will, what would be the starting point? One must begin with the most basic, the deepest level of will impulses, which still appear as completely bound to the body's life. Where do we find this will impulse? Such a will impulse manifests very simply when, for example, we are hungry, when certain substances in our organism are used up and must be replaced. We descend into the region where the nourishing processes occur. We have descended from the processes in the nerve organization through the processes in the breathing organism, and we arrive at the processes in the nourishing organism. We find the most basic will impulses bound to the organism for food assimilation and digestion. Spiritual science demonstrates that when we speak of the relationship between willing and the human organism, we must speak of it in relation to the digestive, metabolic system.

The relationship between the process of mental representation and sensation with the nerve mechanism—and between breathing and the life of feeling—is similar to the relationship between the digestive metabolic organism and the life of will in the human soul, except now the relationship is even looser. Indeed, other things, which have further ramifications, are also connected with this. And, in this regard, one must finally become clear about one thing that, basically, only spiritual science speaks of today. For many years in more limited circles I have presented this aspect, which I now present publicly as a result of spiritual-scientific investigation. Contemporary physiology is convinced that whenever we receive a sense impression it stimulates a sensory nerve, and—indeed, if physiology admits the existence of the soul—it is then received by the soul. But then, in addition to these sensory nerves, contemporary physiology recognizes so-called motor nerves, nerves that cause motion. For spiritual science—I know how heretical this is—for spiritual science such motor or motion-producing nerves do not exist. Indeed, I have occupied myself for many years with this matter and, concerning this very point, I know of course that one can refer to much that seems to be well-founded.

Consider, for example, someone who is ill with locomotor ataxia, or whose spinal cord has been pinched and as a result, below a certain organ the lower organism is deadened. These things do not contradict what I am saying, rather, if one indeed sees through them in the proper way they actually substantiate what I am saying. There are no motor nerves. What contemporary physiology sees as motor nerves, nerves that cause motion, will-impulse nerves, are actually sensory nerves. If the spinal column has been damaged in a particular section, then what happens in the leg or foot is simply not perceived, and thus the foot, because it is not perceived, can not be moved; not because a motor nerve has been severed, but because a sensory nerve has been severed that can not perceive what happens in the leg. I can only indicate this because I must press on to the significant consequences in this matter.

One who acquires habits of observation in the realm of soul-bodily experience knows that, for example, what we call "practice"—let's say playing the piano or something similar—has to do with something very different than what is today referred to as "grinding out the motor nerve path." This is not what is happening. In every movement we carry out with the will, nothing is involved as an organic process other than a metabolic process in the organism. What originates as an impulse of will originates from the metabolism. If I move my arm, the nervous system is not involved initially, but the will itself—and the only function of the nerve is to see that the metabolic process, which results from the impulse of will, is perceived through the so-called motor nerve, which is actually a sensory nerve. We have metabolic processes in the entire organism as bodily activators of the processes that correspond to the will. Because every system in the organism interacts, these metabolic processes occur in the brain also, and they are connected with brain processes; nerve processes, in reality, are only related to this in that they transmit the *perception* of the will processes. In the future natural science will recognize this. However, when we consider from one perspective the human being as a "nerve being," and from a another as a "breathing being" with all that goes with this, and from a third perspective as a "metabolic being"—if I may coin the expression—then we have the whole human being. For all the organs of movement, everything in the human body that can move, is connected in its movement with metabolic processes. And the will works directly on the processes of metabolism. The nerve is only there to perceive this occurrence.

In a certain sense one gets into an unhappy situation when having to contradict apparently well-founded assumptions, such as that of the two types of nerves. One at least has support in that until now no one has yet discovered a significant difference between a sensory and a motor nerve, either in their mode of reaction or in their anatomical structure. They are identical in every way. When we acquire an ability in some field through practice, what we acquire through this practice is in learning to master processes in the metabolism through the will. This is what children learn as they master the metabolic processes in finer forms after having at first tossed their limbs in all directions without achieving any ordered movement of the will. And if, for example, we can play the piano or have some similar ability, we learn to move the fingers so that the corresponding metabolic processes with the will are mastered. The sensory nerves, which are actually the otherwise so-called "motor nerves," register more and more what the correct action and movement is, for these nerves are there to feel out, to delineate, what occurs in the metabolism. I would like to ask someone who can really observe soul-bodily processes whether, through such an accurate self-observation, this person feels how what is actually happening is not a "grinding out of motor nerve paths," but a learning to feel out, to perceive, to represent dimly, the finer vibrations of the organism called forth through the will. It is actually self-observation that we exercise. In this whole realm we are dealing with sensory nerves. From this perspective, someone should observe sometime how speech develops from unformed babbling sounds of a tiny child. It is truly based on the will learning how to take hold of the speech organ. And what is learned by the nervous system is only the finer perception of what occurs in the metabolic processes.

In volition we have, therefore, what is expressed organically in the metabolism. The characteristic expressions of the metabolism are movements, even into the bones. This can be easily shown by entering the actual results of today's natural-scientific observations. But the metabolism expresses what transpires in soul and spirit even less than breathing. Just as I have compared the nerve organism with a picture and the breathing organism with a hieroglyph, I can only compare the metabolic organism with a mere writing, an indicative sign, as we have in our alphabet today in contrast to the pictorial script of the ancient Egyptian or Chaldean. These are mere signs, letters, and the soul's activity must become even more inward.

However, because willed activity of soul must become still more inward, the soul—which I would like to say engages itself only loosely in the metabolism—enters the realm of the spirit with the greater part of its being. The soul lives in the spiritual. And thus, just as the soul unites with material substance through the senses, so she unites with the spirit through the will. Also in this regard, again the particular relation of the soul and spirit is expressed, a relationship that spiritual science reveals through the methods I spoke of in the previous lecture. What results is that the metabolic organism as it exists today— to characterize this more exactly I would have to enter into the Goethean idea of metamorphosis—presents only a provisional indication of what is a complete picture in the nervous system, in the head organism.

What the soul accomplishes in the metabolism as she finds, as it were, her right relation to the metabolism, is a preparation of what she will carry through the gates of death into the spiritual world for further life there after death. She carries all of this across with her, of course, through which she lives with the spirit. She is most alive inwardly, as I have characterized it, just where she is most loosely united with the material, so that in this realm the material process acts merely as a sign, an indication, for the spirit; thus it is in relation to the will. For this reason, therefore, the will must be especially developed to become what one designates as actual Intuition—not in the trivial sense, but as I recently characterized it. Feeling can be developed so that it leads to Inspiration; mental representation, thinking, when it is developed in the sense of spiritual scientific research, leads to Imagination. By these means, however, the other element—the spiritual in its actuality—enters objectively into the soul life. For just as we must characterize sense experience in the way the human sense organs are constructed, so that we experience ourselves in them, so in willing we experience the spirit. In willing the spirit sends its being into us. And no one will ever comprehend freedom who does not recognize this immediate life of the spirit in willing.

On the other side one sees how Franz Brentano, who only investigates the soul, is right. He does not reach through to the will; because he only investigates the soul, he arrives at feeling. Modern psychologists do not concern themselves with what the will sends down into the metabolism, because they do not want to become materialists; and materialists do not concern themselves with it because they believe that everything is dependent on the nervous system. However, just as the soul unites itself with the spirit to the degree that the spirit in its archetypal form can penetrate into the human being, project its gulf-like channels into the human being, so also what we can place within the world as our highest, moral willing—what we can place in the world as spiritual willing—is indeed the immediate life of the spirit within the realm of the soul. And because we experience the spirit directly within the soul, the soul element in those mental images—which I characterized in my *Intuitive Thinking as a Spiritual Path* as the basis of free willing—is truly not isolated in itself, but rather, to a very considerable degree, is conscious within the spirit in a higher, and above all, in a different way. It is a denial of this standing within the spirit when physiologists such as Ziehen—and in relation to the will, psychologists also—do not want to hear anything about these finer will impulses, which are indeed a matter of real experience. They cannot, in fact, be found in the realm of soul; but the soul experiences the spirit within herself, and as she experiences the spirit within the will, she lives in freedom.

In this way the human being and the human body are related to each other so that the whole soul is related to the whole body, and not merely to the nervous system. And with this I have characterized for you the beginning of a direction of scientific research, which will become especially fruitful through the discoveries of natural science when these are looked at in the right way. This research will show that the body, where it is considered in its entirety as the expression of the soul, also actually confirms the immortality of the soul, which I characterized from an entirely different point of view in my previous lecture and shall characterize from yet another aspect in my next lecture.

A certain scientific-philosophical direction of recent times has sought refuge in the so-called subconscious, just because it could not come to terms with the soul and bodily life, for the reasons that have been indicated. The main representative of this orientation, apart from Schopenhauer, is Eduard von Hartmann. Now, to assume the existence of a subconscious in our soul life is certainly justified. But the way that von Hartmann speaks of the subconscious, it is impossible to understand reality in a satisfactory way. In the example I quoted of two people sitting opposite one another, of whom one wants the sugar bowl passed by the other, von Hartmann strangely analyzes how consciousness dives down into the subconscious and then what occurs in the subconscious arises again into consciousness. But with such a hypothesis one does not come near the insights that can be gained through spiritual science. One can speak of the subconscious, but one must speak about it in two different ways. One must speak about the subconscious and about the supraconscious. In sense perception something that is unconscious in itself becomes conscious, inasmuch as it is enlivened in the way I characterized today. In this case the unconscious penetrates up into consciousness. Similarly, where the nerve-sense organism is considered in the inner play of mental representations, a subconscious element rises up into consciousness. But one may not speak of an absolute subconscious, rather one must say that the subconscious can rise into consciousness. In this sense the unconscious is also just a matter of time, only unconscious in a relative sense; the unconscious can become conscious. In the same way one can speak of the spirit as the supraconscious that enters the realm of the human soul in the form of an ethical idea or a spiritual-scientific idea, which itself penetrates the spiritual. When this occurs, the supraconscious enters consciousness.

You see how many concepts and mental representations must be corrected to do justice to life. And from the corrections of these concepts insight will, for the first time, be freed to understand the truth in relation to the human soul life. However, the full development of the far-reaching significance of such a way of considering the relationship between soul and body must be reserved for next time. Today, in conclusion, I should only like to draw you your attention to recent developments in education that have tended to lead away from ideas that can shed a clear light on this field. On one hand, it has confined the entire relationship between the human being and the outer world to the aspect that recognizes only the relation between the outer world and the human nervous system. As a result a number of mental pictures that are more or less materialistically colored have arisen in this field; and because our perspective has not been directed to the connections between the soul-spiritual and the bodily, it has become narrowed and confined. And this narrowing of vision has, in fact, been extended to all scientific endeavor as a whole. Consequently, we experience sadness when reading an otherwise relatively good lecture by Professor Dr. A. Tschirch on November 28, 1908, a festival lecture called "Nature Research and Healing," for the occasion of his installation as rector at the University of Bern in Switzerland. Those of my listeners who have attended these lectures more often know that, as a rule, I only attack those whom I genuinely esteem in other connections, and that it is my custom to only express criticism in self-defense. There is a strange confession in this lecture by Professor Tschirch that arises precisely from the misunderstandings and the inability to understand the relationship between soul and body. Here Professor Tschirch says, "It is my opinion, however, that we do not need to trouble our heads today about whether or not we shall, in reality, ever penetrate inner life."

He means, "penetrate the inner aspect of the world." From this attitude everything springs that is present today as antipathy toward potential spiritual-scientific research. In this vein, Professor Tschirch continues, "Indeed, we have more necessary and pressing things to do."

Now, in the face of the great, burning questions that concern the human soul, that someone can say, "Indeed, we have more necessary and pressing things to do"—in regard to such a person, we would have to question the seriousness of his scientific attitude of mind if it were not understandable from the perspective—as it has been characterized—that thinking has taken, and especially when one reads these sentences:

> The "inner aspect of nature," which Haller has somewhat similar thoughts about, and which Kant later called "thing in itself," is for us currently so deep in the "within," that millennia will pass before—always assuming that a new ice age will not destroy our entire civilization—we even come close to it.

These people concern themselves so casually about the spirit, which is actually the inner world, that they can say, "We don't need to concern ourselves about it," but can calmly wait for thousands of years. If this is science's answer to the burning questions of the human soul, then the time has come for an extension of this science, through spiritual science. The mental attitude characterized above has led to the situation where the soul element, as it were, has been summarily discarded, and where the viewpoint has arisen that the soul element is at best an accompanying phenomenon of the bodily organism—a view that the renowned Professor Jodl has proposed almost to the present day; but his is only one among many.[10]

But where does this way of thinking lead? Well, it celebrated a triumphal festival when, for instance, Professor Dr. Jacques Loeb—once again, a man whose positive research achievements I value most highly—lectured on September 10, 1911, at the monistic thinkers' first congress on "Life" in Hamburg. In this instance we see how what actually is based on a misunderstanding is transformed into a general attitude and thus becomes—pardon the expression—brutal toward soul research. The hypothetical conviction that arises from this research becomes a matter of authority, of power. In this sense Professor Jacques Loeb began that lecture by stating:

> The question I intend to discuss is whether, according to the current stance of science, we can anticipate that life—that is the sum total of all living phenomena—can be completely explained in terms of physical and chemical laws. If, after earnest consideration, we can answer this question in the affirmative, then we must build our social and ethical structures of life on purely natural-scientific

---

10. Friedrich Jodl (1849–1924), philosopher and psychologist, professor of philosophy in Vienna.

foundations, and no metaphysician can then claim the right to prescribe modes of conduct for our way of life that contradict the results of experimental biology.

Here you have the striving to conquer all knowledge by means of the science that Goethe has Mephisto say "It makes itself an ass and knows not how!" This is how it appears in the older version of Goethe's *Faust* where the following passage occurs:

> Who will know the living and describe it
> Seeks first to drive the spirit out;
> Then the parts lie in his hand,
> Missing only, sadly! the spirit's band!
> Encheires in Naturae so says our chemistry,
> Mocks thus itself and knows not how it came to be.

Today in *Faust* it reads, "Mocks thus itself and knows not how it came to be," but the young Goethe wrote, "It makes itself an ass and knows not how!"

What has come to be based on these misunderstandings tends to eliminate all knowledge that doesn't merely interpret physical and chemical processes. But no science of the soul will be fortified to withstand such an attack if it cannot claim to penetrate human bodily nature out of its own insight. I appreciate all that has been achieved by such gifted individuals as Dilthey, Franz Brentano, and others. I fully recognize this. I value all these people; but, the ideas they have developed are too weak, too clumsy to hold their ground against the results of today's scientific thinking. A bridge must be erected between the spiritual and the bodily. This bridge must be built in relation to the human being through achieving strong spiritual-scientific concepts that lead to an understanding of the bodily life of the organism. Because the great questions, the question of immortality, the question of destiny, and similar riddles will only be comprehended by understanding bodily life. Otherwise, if a sense for this spiritual science doesn't awaken in humanity, a sense also for the seriousness of these urgent times, then we will find ourselves confronted with views such as the following one expresses. A book can be found by the American scholar Snyder, which has been translated into German. In this book one can read a quaint sentence that nevertheless expresses the attitude and gesture of the entire volume called *The World View of Modern Natural Science*. Translator Hans Kleinpeter in fact particularly shows how this attitude will gradually enlighten present and future times. In conclusion, allow me to quote a sentence—I would say a key and central sentence—from this book:

> Whatever the brain cell of a glow worm may be, or the feeling for the harmonies in *Tristan and Isolde*, their substance is essentially the same; the distinction in their structure is evidently of greater concern than the difference in their substantiality.

And, with this, something essential, something enlightening is thought to have been said! But it is a mental attitude, an inner gesture, that coheres with what I have presented today. And it is deeply characteristic for the present time that such viewpoints can find adherents, that these things can be presented as significant.

I can well appreciate philology as much as the sciences undervalued by many people today. Wherever true science is at work, in whatever field, I can appreciate it. But when someone comes and says to me, "Goethe wrote *Faust*, and sitting next to him was his secretary Seydel who was perhaps writing a letter to his beloved; the difference between *Faust* and Seydel's letter may have been whatever it was, but the ink is the same in both!" Both assertions are on the same level, except that one is considered a great advancement in science, and the other is considered as a matter of fact to be what those in my audience who laughed about it have demonstrated it to be.

In contrast to this, we must reach back and build upon an attitude of mind that is also scientific, has laid the foundations for a science that arises from the whole human soul and from a deep contemplation of the world—an attitude of mind that is also present in Goethe's natural-scientific considerations. The basic elements spiritual science would like to continually develop further are found in Goethe's work, and we find within many of his words, so beautifully and archetypally expressed, the true, genuine attitude of soul that can lead to a truthful contemplation of the world. I would like to close these considerations by presenting Goethe's multifaceted observations of the relationship between spirit and outer matter, and in particular their relationship to the human body. As Goethe contemplated Schiller's skull and, by contemplating this noble soul's fragmentary outer form, sought to feel his way into the relationship between the whole spirit and soul, and the entire human bodily organism, he wrote the words we know in his beautiful poem entitled *On the Contemplation of Schiller's Skull*. From these words we become aware of the attitude of heart and mind necessary for a multifaceted contemplation of spirit and nature:

> What can people win more in life,
> Than that God-Nature reveal to them,
> How she lets solid substance to spirit run,
> How she binds fast what is from spirit won.

And we can apply these words to relation of the human soul and the human body and say:

> What can people win more in life,
> Than that God-Nature reveal to them,
> How she lets matter to spirit run,
> And how in matter spirit self-knowledge is won!

Thus this God-Nature reveals to human beings how the body is the expression, the image, and the signature of the soul, and how the body thus physically proves and reveals the immortal soul and the eternal spirit.

2.

RIDDLES OF THE SOUL

AND RIDDLES OF THE UNIVERSE

BERLIN, MARCH 17, 1917

In the previous lecture I sought to show how, because of misunderstandings, there is so little agreement in today's intellectual culture between those who research the soul and the processes in the soul realm, and those who look at the human organism's material processes that run their course as accompanying phenomena as—whatever terms you use, or as materialism maintains—the necessary causes of soul phenomena. And I sought to portray the causes of such misunderstandings. Today, most of all, I would like to point out how such misunderstandings—as well as misunderstandings in other regards—necessarily arise in the search for true, genuine insight when one fails to consider one aspect—the cognitive process itself, an aspect that forcefully recalls itself to spiritual-scientific research. This appears very odd at first when one says, "In the sphere where world concepts arise—that is in the sphere of insight into spiritual reality, when one tires oneself down to certain points of view, so to speak—a way of looking at the human soul inevitably arises that can be both unequivocally refuted and just as easily proven correct."

Therefore, the spiritual-scientific researcher increasingly tends to abandon the habit of reinforcing one or the other view by applying what would ordinarily be called a proof or a refutation. For, in this sphere, as we've said, everything can be proved with certain reasoning, and with certain reasoning everything can also be contradicted. Materialism, in its totality, can indeed be proven strictly correct, and when it addresses individual questions about life or existence, it can be shown equally correct. And one will not necessarily find it easy to refute one argument or another presented by materialists to support their views by merely trying to refute their conclusions, by proposing opposite viewpoints.

The same thing is true for the one who holds a spiritual view of existence. Therefore, those who truly wish to do spiritual research must, with any world view, not only know everything that speaks *for* the point of view, but also all that speaks *against* it. For the remarkable fact arises that the truth only becomes evident when what speaks both for and against a certain thing is allowed to work on the soul; and those who allow their spirit to fixate on any constellation of concepts, or on one-sided mental pictures of a world view, such people will always be closed to the fact that just the opposite can seem valid to the soul, indeed the opposite must appear correct to a certain extent. Such people can be compared with one who insists that human life can only be sustained by breathing in. Breathing in assumes breathing out; both belong together. So our concepts, our representations, also relate to one another in questions concerning world views. We can present a concept about any matter that confirms it and we can present a concept that refutes it; one requires the other, just as in-breathing requires out-breathing, and vice versa. Therefore, just as real life can only reveal itself through breathing out *and* breathing in, with both present, so the spiritual can also only manifest within the soul when one can enter the *pro* as well as the *con* of a particular matter in an equally positive way.

A supportive, confirming concept is like breathing out within the living wholeness of the soul; a reflecting, denying concept like breathing in; and the element rooted in spiritual reality only reveals itself when these aspects live and work together. Because of this, spiritual science is not concerned with applying the methods we are accustomed to in current literature, where this or that is proved or is refuted. Spiritual scientists realize that what is presented in a positive form concerning world views can, in a certain sense, always be justified, and equally well what appears to contradict it. When one progresses in questions of world views to the immediate life present in positive and negative concepts, just as bodily life lives through in-breathing and out-breathing, one comes to concepts that can truly take in the spirit, one comes to concepts that are equal to reality. However, in doing so, we must often express ourselves very differently than when those who express themselves according to the thought habits of ordinary life. But the way we express ourselves arises from lively inner experience of the spirit. And the spirit can only be experienced inwardly, not perceived outwardly as in material existence.

You know that one of the principal questions of world outlook is what I dealt with in the first lectures I held here this winter—that is, the question concerning matter, about physical substance. As an introduction I shall touch on this question from the viewpoints I have indicated.

We cannot come to terms successfully with questions about substance or matter if we continually attempt to form mental images or concepts about what matter actually is—in other words, when we try to *understand* what matter or substance actually is. Those who have truly wrestled in their souls with such riddles, which are way off the beaten path for many, such people know what is involved in this kind of question. If they have wrestled for some time regarding such a question without yielding to one prejudice or another, they come to a very different viewpoint, a viewpoint that allows them to consider the inner attitude of the soul to be more important when forming concepts about such things as matter. This wrestling of the soul itself is raised into consciousness, and we come to see these riddles in a way that I could characterize as follows:

Those who want to understand matter as it is usually viewed resemble those who say, "I now want to form an impression of darkness, a dark room." What do they do? They turn on the light and consider this the correct method to get an impression of a dark room. Now, you will agree this is just the opposite of the proper way do it. And it is the same—the opposite of the right way, but we have to realize this through the inner wrestling that I mentioned—if we believe that one will come to know and illuminate the nature of matter through the activity of the spirit—that is, to illuminate substance through the spirit. The one and only place where the spirit within the body can silence itself is where an outer process penetrates into our inner life—that is, in sense perception, in sensation, where the life of representation, of forming mental images, ceases. The only way we can allow matter, substance, to truly represent itself within our soul is by letting the spirit come to silence and by experiencing this silence of the spirit.

One does not arrive at such concepts through ordinary logic; or, I would say, if one does come to them through ordinary logic, then the concepts are much too thin to produce a genuine power of conviction. Only when one wrestles within the soul with certain concepts, in the way that has been indicated, will they lead to the kind of result that I have pointed toward.

The opposite is also the situation. Let us assume, someone wants to comprehend spirit. If it is sought, for example, in the purely material external formation of the human body, it is similar to one who extinguishes the light to comprehend it; for the secret in this matter is that external, sense-perceptible nature contradicts the spirit, it extinguishes the spirit. Nature builds the reflected image of the spirit in the same way that an illuminated object throws back, or reflects, the light. But nowhere can we find the spirit in any material processes if we do not apprehend the spirit in *living activity,* because the spirit has transformed itself into just this essential nature of material processes; spirit has incorporated itself into them. If we then try to know the spirit from them, we misunderstand ourselves.

I wanted to give this as a preface so that more and more clarity can be applied to the actual cognitive attitude of heart and mind of the spiritual researcher, and to show how we need a certain breadth and mobility in the life of forming mental images, how we need to be able to penetrate what requires penetration. With such concepts it then becomes possible to illuminate the important questions I touched on last time, and which I will briefly indicate in order to progress to today's considerations.

I said that, as things have developed in recent intellectual education and culture, we have come increasingly to a one-sided view of the relationships between the soul-spiritual and physical body, a view that is expressed in how one really only looks for the soul-spiritual within the part of the human bodily constitution that lies in the nervous system, that is to say in the brain. The soul-spiritual is assigned exclusively to the brain and nervous system, and it is considered the remaining organism when speaking of the soul-spiritual as a, more or less, incidental supplement to the brain and nervous system. I tried to clarify the results of spiritual research in this field by pointing out that we only come to true insight about the relationship between the human soul and the human body when we see the relationship between the entire human soul and the entire bodily constitution.

But this is where it became clear that the matter has an even deeper background—that is, the membering of the wholeness of the human soul into the actual representational thought life, the feeling life, and the will life. For only the actual representational life of the soul is bound to the nervous organism in the way assumed by more recent physiological psychology. In contrast, the life of feeling—let it be properly noted, not insofar as it is represented mentally, but insofar as it *arises*—is related with human breathing, as the life of mental representation is related with the nervous system. Thus we must assign the feeling life of the soul to the breathing organism. And further, what we designate as the life of will is in a similar relationship to what we must designate as the metabolism in the physical body—in its finest ramifications, of course. And inasmuch as one considers the individual systems within the organism to be interacting and interweaving—metabolism, of course, also occurs in the nerves—they interpenetrate, I would say, the three systems interpenetrate at the outermost periphery. But a correct understanding is only possible when we view matters so that the experiences of mental image formation belongs with the human nervous system, that is to say, with the brain.

Matters like this, of course, can only be indicated at first. And for just this reason, objection after objection is possible. But I am very certain that when we no longer approach what has just been presented merely from partial aspects of today's natural scientific research, but from the whole spectrum of anatomical, physiological research, then the result will be in complete harmony with the assertions I have made from the spiritual-scientific viewpoint, and from the assertions of natural science.

Viewed superficially—allow me to cite the following objection only as a characteristic example—objection after objection can be presented against such a comprehensive truth. Someone could say, "Let's agree that certain feelings are connected with the breathing organism; no one can really doubt that this can be very convincingly demonstrated for certain feelings." But someone could also say, "Yes, but what do you have to say about how we perceive certain melodies, how melodies arise in our consciousness—how a feeling of esthetic pleasure is connected with the melodies? In this case, can we speak of any connection between the breathing organism and this, which apparently arises in the head and is thus obviously connected with the nervous organism according to physiological research results?" The moment one considers the matter properly, the correctness of my assertion becomes completely clear. That is, one must consider that with every out-breath an important parallel process occurs in the brain; the brain would rise with the out-breath if it were not prevented from rising by the top of the skull—the breathing carries forward into the brain—and in reverse, the brain sinks with the in-breath. And since it cannot rise or fall because of the skull, a change in the blood stream arises, which is well-known to physiology as *brain-breathing*—that is, certain processes that occur in the surrounding nerves run parallel with the process of breathing. And in the meeting between the breathing process and what lives in us as tone through the ear, an indication occurs that feeling, also in this realm, is connected with the breathing organism, just as the life of mental images is connected with the nervous organism.

I want to show this because it is a relatively remote example, and it can thus provide a ready objection. If one could come to an understanding with someone about all the details given by physiological research, one would find that none of these details contradicts what was presented here last time, or what has been presented again today.

It should now be my task to extend our considerations in a way similar to that of the previous lecture. To do this I must go further into how the human being unfolds the life of sense perception in order to show the actual relationship between the capacity for sense perception, which leads to representations, and the life of feeling and the will—indeed, completely into the life of the human being as soul, body, and spirit.

Through our sense life we connect with the sense-percept-ible environment. Within this sense-perceptible environment natural science distinguishes certain substances—let us rather say, *substance-forms*—because matter depends on these; if I wanted to discuss this with a physicist I would have to say *aggregate-conditions*—solid, fluid, and gaseous. Now, however, as you all know, natural-scientific research also assumes—in addition to the above-mentioned form in which physical sub-stance appears—another condition. When natural science wants to explain light it is not satisfied merely to recognize the existence of the substance-forms that I just mentioned, but science reaches out to include what initially appears to be finer than these kinds of substance; it reaches out to what one usu-ally calls *ether*. The idea of ether is extraordinarily difficult, and one could say that various thoughts have been developed about the ether, and what can be said about it are the most diverse, the most numerous imaginable. Of course, it is not possible to go into all these details, but attention should just be drawn to how natural science feels impelled to postulate the concept of the ether, which means thinking about the world as not just filled with the immediate sense perception of the more solid substances, but thinking of it as filled with ether. It is characteristic that natural science with its current methods fails to rise to an understanding of what the ether actually is. The real activity of natural research always requires material bases. But the ether itself always escapes, in a certain sense, from material foundations. The ether appears united with material processes; it calls forth material processes, but it cannot be grasped, so to speak, by means bound to material foundations. A strange ether-concept has thus developed recently that, essentially, is very interesting. The concept of the ether that one can already find among physicists tends to say that the ether must be—whatever else it may be—something that, at any rate, does not have the attributes of ordinary matter. And in this way, natural-scientific research indicates the recognition of something beyond its own material basis when it says of the ether that it has aspects that research, with its methods, cannot find. Natural-scientific research comes to accept an ether, but cannot, with its methods, fill out this concept of the ether with any content.

Spiritual science yields the following. Natural-scientific research starts with a material foundation; spiritual research with a spirit-soul basis. Spiritual researchers—if they do not remain arbitrarily within a certain limit—are also, like the natural scientist, drawn to the concept of ether, but from the other side. Spiritual investigators attempt to know what is active and effective within the soul. If they were to remain at the standpoint where they can experience inwardly only what takes place in the ordinary soul life, they would, in fact, not advance in this field even as far as the natural scientist, who at least forms the concept of an ether and accepts it for consideration. Soul researchers, if they fail to arrive at a concept of ether, resemble a natural scientist who says, "Why should I bother with anything else that exists? I accept the three basic forms of solid, fluid, gaseous bodies, and I do not concern myself with anything finer than that." For the most part, this is indeed just what the teachings of psychology do.

Not everyone who has been active in the realm of soul research, however, acts this way; and, especially within the extremely significant scientific development based on the foundation laid by German idealism in the first third of the nineteenth century—not in idealism itself, but in what evolved from idealism—one finds the first beginnings leading toward the concept of the ether from the other side, from the spiritual-soul side, just as nature research rises to the idea of ether from the material side. And, if one truly wants a concept of the ether, one must approach it from two sides. Otherwise, one will not properly come to terms with this concept. It is interesting that the great German philosophical Idealists, Fichte, Schelling, and Hegel, despite the penetrating power of their thinking—an ability I have often characterized here— despite this, they did not form the concept of the ether. They could not strengthen, could not empower their inner soul life enough to conceive of the ether. Instead, this concept of the ether arose out of research into the soul's realm within those who allowed themselves to be fructified by this idealism, who, in a sense, allowed the thoughts that had been presented to work further within their souls—even though they were not the great geniuses that their Idealist predecessors were. We first find this ether concept in the work of Immanuel Hermann Fichte, the son of the great Johann Gottlieb Fichte, who was also his father's pupil. He allowed the accomplishments of Johann Gottlieb Fichte and his successors, Schelling and Hegel, to continue working within his soul. Immanuel Hermann Fichte, allowing this thought to condense even more effectively within him, said that when one contemplates the life of soul and spirit, when one, as it were, traverses it in all directions, one comes to say: This soul-spiritual life must flow down into the ether, just as the solid, fluid, and gaseous states flow up into the ether. So the lowest element of the soul must, in a sense, flow into the ether, just as the highest element of matter flows into the ether above. Also characteristic are certain thoughts that Fichte formed about this matter, which he indeed penetrated from the spirit-soul realm and arrived at the boundary of the ether. You will find this passage from his book *Anthropology,* 1860, quoted in my most recent book *The Riddle of Man*:

Within the material elements of substance one cannot find what truly endures—the *uniting* formative principle of the body that reveals itself as operative during our entire life.... Thus we are directed to a second, essentially *different* causative principle in the body.... Inasmuch as this [unifying form principle] contains what actually persists (endures in the metabolism) it is the *true inner body, invisible,* but in all visible substantiality, *present* body. That other, its outward manifestation, which is built from incessantly active metabolism, may be called *bodily* from now on. In fact, this is not what persists, is not the enduring whole, but is the mere result or the after-image of the inner bodily presence that casts one into the constantly changing world of substance, similar to the way a magnetic force makes an apparently solid body out of particles of iron filings, but dissolves in all directions when the force uniting them is withdrawn.[11]

For I. H. Fichte an invisible body lives within the ordinary body consisting of outer material substance,. We might also call this the etheric body, an etheric body that brings the single substantial particles of this visible body into their form, which sculpts them, forms them. Fichte was so certain that this ether body, which he descends to from the soul realm, is not subject to the processes of the physical body, that his insight into the existence of such an etheric body was enough that he could transcend the riddle of death. In this context he says in his *Anthropology:*

It is hardly necessary to ask how human beings, in their essential nature, find themselves in the process of death. Human beings remain after this last, still visible act of the living process, in their *essential being,* entirely the same in

---

11. Quoted in *The Riddle of Man,* p. 51.

spirit and *organizing power* as they formerly were. Their integrity is preserved, because they have indeed lost nothing of what was theirs and belonged to their substance during visible life. In death they only return into the invisible world; or rather, since they never left the invisible world, since this is what actually *endures* within all that is visible, they have simply stripped off a particular form of the visible. "To be dead" only means that one is no longer perceptible to ordinary apprehension through the senses, in the same way that what is actually real, the ultimate ground of bodily manifestation, is also imperceptible to the senses.[12]

I have shown with Fichte how he proceeds from the soul realm to such an invisible body. It is interesting to note that the same thing appears in a number of instances of the after-glow of the spiritual life of German idealism. Some time ago I also drew attention to Johann Heinrich Deinhardt who died in the 1860s,[13] a singular thinker who, as a school director in Bromberg, occupied himself with the question of immortality. Initially he was concerned with the question of immortality as others were, seeking to penetrate the question of immortality through thought and concept. But for him more came of it than for those who merely live in concepts. The publisher of a treatise on immortality, which Deinhardt had written, was able to quote from a letter the author had written to him, where Deinhardt stated that, although he had not gotten far enough to publish it in a book, his inner research had, nevertheless, resulted in the clear recognition that human beings, during all of life between birth and death, work to form an invisible body that is then released into the spiritual world at death.

---

12. Ibid., p. 52.
13. Johann Heinrich Deinhardt (1805–1867).

One could thus point to a variety of other cases of research in this direction within German spiritual life, of ways of seeing and comprehending the world. They would all show that in this direction of research there was an urge not to remain limited by mere philosophical speculation, which results in a mere life of concepts, but rather to strengthen the inner life of the soul so that it presses forward to a degree of concentration that reaches through to the etheric.

Along the paths these researchers entered, the true riddle of the etheric cannot be resolved yet from within, but in a certain sense one can say that these researchers are on the way to spiritual science, because this riddle of the etheric will be resolved when the human soul goes through the inner processes of practical exercise I have frequently characterized here, and are described more exactly in *How to Know Higher Worlds*. When human beings go through these inner soul processes, they indeed gradually reach the etheric from within. The etheric will then be immediately present for them. They are only then, however, really in the position to understand what sense perception is, what really occurs in sense perception.

To characterize this today, I must look for a way into this question, so to speak, from another side. Let us approach what actually happens in the metabolic processes of human beings. Expressed simply, in the human organism we can think of the metabolic processes as occurring so that they are associated essentially with the fluid material element. This can be easily understood if one becomes acquainted, even to a limited degree, with the most accessible natural-scientific ideas in this field. What constitutes a metabolic process lives, as it were, in the fluid element. What breathes lives in the airy, gaseous element; in breathing we have an interchange between inner and outer processes in the air, just as in the metabolism we have an interchange between the processes of substance occurring outside the body and what occurs within the body. What then happens when we perceive with our senses and proceed to form mental representations? What actually corresponds to this? In exactly the same way that fluid processes correspond to metabolism, and airy processes correspond to breathing—what corresponds to perception? Etheric processes correspond to perception. Just as we live, as it were, with our metabolism in the fluid, and live with our breathing in the air, we live with our perceiving in the ether; inner ether processes, inner etheric processes, that occur in the invisible body, also occur in sense perception. The objection is made that, yes, but certain sense perceptions are obviously metabolic processes; this is especially obvious for sense perceptions that correspond to the so-called lower senses, smell and taste. A more accurate consideration shows that, along with what is substantial, what belongs directly to the metabolism, along with every such process, with tasting also, for example, an etheric process occurs, through which we relate to the external ether, just as we relate to the air with our physical body when we breathe. Without the understanding of the etheric world, an understanding of sense perception and sensation is impossible.

What actually happens? Well, one can only really know what happens here when one has gone far enough in the inner soul process so that one experiences the inner etheric-bodily element as a reality. This will happen when one has achieved what I called *imaginative thinking* in recent lectures here. When one's thoughts have been strengthened through exercises in the book already mentioned, so that they are no longer abstract concepts, such as we normally have, but are thoughts and mental representations filled with life, then one can call them *imaginations*. When these representations have become so alive that they are, in fact, imaginations, then they live directly in the etheric, whereas, if they are abstract representations, they live only in the soul. They apprehend the etheric. And then if one has progressed far enough in an inward experimentation, so to speak, so that one experiences inwardly the ether as living reality, then one can know, through experience, what happens in sense perception, in sensation. Sensation as it arises through sense perception—I can only present this today in the form of results—is made up of what the outer environment sends the etheric from the material surroundings into our sense organs, thus making those gulfs of which I spoke the day before yesterday, so that what is external also becomes internal within the sphere of the senses. We have, for example, a "tone" between the life of the senses and the outer world. Because the external ether penetrates into our sense organs, this external ether is deadened. And as the outer deadened ether enters our sense organs, it is brought to life again because the inner ether coming from the etheric body works toward the deadened etheric coming from outside. Here we have the essential being of sense perception and sensation. Just as a death process and an enlivening arise in the breathing process, when we breathe in oxygen and breathe out carbon dioxide, so a process of exchange also takes place between the dead ether and enlivened ether in our sense experience.

This is an extremely important fact that can be discovered through spiritual science; what no philosophical speculations can find, and where philosophical speculations of the last centuries have ship-wrecked countless times, can only be found along the path of spiritual-scientific research. Sense perception can thus be recognized as a fine process of exchange between the outer and the inner ether, the enlivening of the ether, deadened in the sense organ by the forces of the inner etheric body. So, what the senses kill for us from the environment, is made alive again inwardly by the etheric body, and thus we come to what is, indeed, perception of the outer world.

This is very important, because it shows how human beings, when they devote themselves to the sensations arising from sense perception, live not just in the physical organism, but also in the supersensible etheric; and it shows how the entire life of the senses is a living and weaving within the invisible etheric. This is what, in the time already mentioned, the more deeply insightful researchers have always sensed, have inwardly divined, but will be raised to certainty through spiritual science. Among those who recognized this significant truth, I would like still to mention I. P. V. Troxler, who has been almost totally forgotten.[14] In previous years I have mentioned him here in lectures. He said in *Lectures about Philosophy*:

> In earlier times the philosophers had already differentiated a finer, purer soul organism from the coarser body ... a soul, carrying a picture of the bodily organism, that they called *Schema*, and for them was the higher, inner human being. ... More recently, even Kant in his *Dreams of a Spiritual Seer*, dreams earnestly, but jokingly, a whole interior human soul, who bears all the limbs of the outer body in the spirit body; Lavater composes poetically and thinks in a similar vein. ...

These investigators were also clear, however, that the moment one rises above the usual materialistic way of seeing things to the perception of this supersensible organism in us, one has to move from the usual anthropology to a kind of recognition that achieves results by intensifying our inner capacities. It is interesting, therefore, how I. H. Fichte as well as Troxler, for example, are clear that anthropology must rise to something

---

14. Ignaz Paul Vital Troxler (1780–1866), physician and educator in Basil and Berne.

different, if it wishes to comprehend the whole human being. In *Anthropology* Fichte says:

> Consciousness based in sense perception ... together with the whole human life of the senses, has no significance other than to provide a place where that supersensible life of the spirit occurs, by introducing—through one's own free, conscious act—the spiritual content of the ideas (which lives beyond ordinary consciousness) into the world of the senses.... The fundamental comprehension of the human being in this way thus raises *anthropology* in its end result to *anthroposophy*.

We see the premonition of anthroposophy within this stream of German spiritual life, which tends to drive idealism out of its abstraction toward reality. Troxler said that one must assume a super-spiritual sense united with a super-sensible spirit and that, in this way, one can understand the human being in such a way that one is no longer dealing with ordinary anthropology, but with something higher:

> If it is indeed highly welcome that the most recent philosophy—which ... in every anthroposophy ... must reveal itself—climbs upward, nevertheless, it must not be ignored that this idea cannot be the fruit of speculation, and the true ... individuality of the human being may be confused neither with what it postulates as subjective spirit or finite I, nor with what it poses as its opposite, as absolute spirit or absolute personality.

What is presented as anthroposophy in no way arises arbitrarily. Spiritual life necessarily leads to this when concepts and mental pictures are not experienced as mere concepts and mental pictures, but are—I once again wish to use the expression—condensed, instead, to the point where they lead into reality, where they become saturated with reality.

The weakness, or what's lacking, in this research occurs when we merely rise from the physical to the etheric body and do not really find our way; rather we come to a certain boundary that must nevertheless be transcended; for only beyond the etheric lies the soul-spiritual. The essential thing is that this soul-spiritual can relate to the physical only through the mediation of the etheric. We therefore have to look for the actual soul element of the human being, working and impulsing within the etheric in a fully supra-etheric way; working in a way so that the etheric, in its turn, forms the physical, just as it (the etheric) is itself formed, impulsed, enlivened by the soul element.

Let us now try to understand the human being from the other pole, the pole of will. We have said that the will life is directly connected with the metabolism. Inasmuch as the will impulse lives in the metabolism, it lives not just in the external, physical metabolic processes, but since the entire human being is present everywhere within the limits of his or her own being, so the etheric also lives in what is active as metabolism when an impulse of will occurs. Spiritual science shows that what lives in the will impulse is exactly the opposite of what is present in sense perception. In the case of sense perception, the etheric outside of us is, in a certain sense, enlivened by the etheric within us. That is, the inner etheric pours itself into the dead etheric from outside. In the case of an impulse of will, when a will impulse arises from the soul-spiritual, the etheric body is loosened, expelled from the physical body in the areas where metabolism occurs, through the activity of the metabolism and everything connected with it. As a result, here we have the exact opposite: the etheric body pulls back, so to speak, from the physical processes. And this is just where the essential element in will activity lies; in such activity of the will the etheric body draws back from the physical body.

Those in my audience who heard the earlier lectures will remember that, in addition to *imaginative cognition*, I have also distinguished *inspiration* and, finally, actual *intuitive cognition*. Just as imaginative cognition is an intensification and strengthening of soul life, through which one can reach the life of the etheric in the way I have indicated, so is intuitive cognition achieved in the soul's learning to participate, through powerful impulses of will—indeed, to actually call forth—what one can call "the pulling back," the withdrawing, of the etheric body from the physical processes. Thus, in this realm, the soul-spiritual penetrates the bodily-physical. If a will impulse arises originally from the soul-spiritual, it unites with the etheric and the consequence is that this etheric is withdrawn, pulled back, from one or another area of the physical-bodily organism's metabolic activity. And through the soul-spiritual, through the etheric, working on the bodily organism, there arises what we could call the transition of a will impulse into a bodily movement, into bodily activity. This is where one attains one's actual immortal part, when one considers the whole human being in this way; for as soon as one learns how the spirit-soul weaves in the etheric, it becomes clear that this weaving of the spirit-soul in the etheric is also independent of those processes of the physical organism encompassed by birth, conception and death. Thus along this path it becomes possible to truly rise to the immortal within the human through the stream of inheritance, and this continues when one passes through the portal of death, for the eternal spirit is connected through the mediation of the etheric with what is born and dies.

The mental pictures, the ideas, to which spiritual science comes, are powerfully rejected by contemporary thought habits and, as a result, human beings have great difficulty gaining an understanding of them. One could say that one of the hindrances that make it difficult to find this understanding—along with other difficulties—is that one makes so little effort to seek the real connection of the soul-spiritual with the bodily organism in the way indicated. Most people long for something very different from what spiritual science can offer. What actually happens in human beings when they form mental pictures, form representations? An etheric process occurs that only interacts with an external etheric process. In order that human beings remain healthy in soul and body in this regard, however, it is necessary that they become aware of where the boundary is—that is the point of contact between the inner etheric and outer etheric. In most cases this occurs unconsciously. It becomes conscious when human beings rise to imaginative cognition, when they inwardly experience the stirring and the motion of the etheric and its encounter with the external ether, which dies into the sense organ. In this interaction between the inner and outer etheric we have, in a sense, the furthest boundary of the etheric's effectiveness on the human organism. What works in our etheric body affects the organism mainly, for example, in its growth. In growth it forms the organism from within. It gradually organizes the organism so that it adapts itself to the outer world, in the way that we see the child develop. But this inner formative taking-hold of the physical body by the etheric must come up against a certain limit or boundary. When it passes this boundary because of some process of illness, the following occurs: what lives and weaves within the etheric, and should remain contained within the etheric, overreaches and takes hold of the organism so that, as a result, the organism is permeated by what should remain a movement within the etheric. What happens as a result? What should only be experienced inwardly as mental representation now occurs as a process within the physical body. This is what one calls a "hallucination." When the etheric activity crosses its boundary toward the bodily—because the body cannot resist it properly due to a condition of illness—then what one calls a hallucination arises. Very many people who want to penetrate the spiritual world wish, above all, to have hallucinations. This, of course, is something that the spiritual researcher cannot offer them, for a hallucination is no more than a reflection of a purely material process, of a process that from the viewpoint of the soul occurs beyond the boundary of the physical body— that is, it occurs within the body. In contrast, what leads into the spiritual world involves turning back from this boundary, returning to the soul realm, attaining *imagination* instead of hallucination, and imagination is a pure soul experience. Inasmuch as it is a pure soul experience, the soul lives in imagination within the spiritual world. Thus the soul penetrates the imagination in the fully conscious way. And it is important that we understand that imagination—that is the well-founded way to achieve spiritual cognition—and hallucinations are in direct opposition to each other, and, indeed destroy each other. Those who experience the condition of an organic illness, place obstacles in their way to achieving genuine imagination, as do those who attain true hallucinations and imagination, which are mutually exclusive and destroy each other.

The situation is similar at the other pole of the human being, as well. Just as the etheric body can overreach into the bodily organism, sinking its formative forces into the body, thereby calling forth hallucinations, that is calling forth purely organic processes, so also on the other side, the etheric can be drawn out of the organism—as was characterized in relation to the action of the will—improperly. This can happen because of certain pathological formations in the organism, or because of exhaustion or similar bodily conditions. Instead of the etheric being drawn out of the physical metabolism in a particular area of the body, as in a normal, healthy action of the will, it remains stuck within it, and the physical, metabolic activity in that area—as a purely physical activity—reaches into the etheric. Here the etheric becomes dependent on the physical, whereas in a normal unfolding of the will the physical is dependent on the etheric, which, in its turn, is determined by the soul-spiritual. If this occurs because of processes such as I have indicated, then a compulsive action arises—I would say, like the pathological counter picture of an hallucination— because the physical body, with its metabolic activities, penetrates into the etheric, it more or less forces its way into the etheric. And if a compulsive action is called up as a pathological manifestation, one can say that this compulsive activity excludes what is called intuition in spiritual science. Intuition and compulsive activity are mutually exclusive, just as hallucination and imagination exclude one another. Therefore, there is nothing more empty of soul than—on the one hand—a hallucinating human being, for hallucinations are indications of bodily conditions that should not be; and, on the other hand, for example, we have the whirling dervishes. The dance of the dervish arises because the bodily-physical forces itself into the etheric so that the etheric is not effective in its connection with the spiritual-soul element, but rather, characteristic compulsive activities occur. Those who believe that revelations of a soul nature manifest in the whirling dervish dance, such people should consult spiritual science to understand that whirling dervishes are evidence that the spirit, the spirit-soul, has left the body and, therefore, they dance in this way.

And I would like to say that automatic writing, for example, mediumistic writing, is only a somewhat more comprehensive case of the phenomenon of the dervish dance. Mediumistic writing is nothing other than the spirit-soul nature having been completely driven out of the human organism and the physical

body having been forced into the etheric body and there having been allowed to unfold; to unfold itself after being emptied
of the inner etheric under the influence of the outer etheric
surrounding it. These realms lead away from spiritual science,
not toward a science of the spirit, although certainly no objection should be made from the viewpoints that usually object so
much to these things. One can study what a truly artistic dance
should be just in relation to the whirling dervish. The art of
dance should consist of a correspondence between every single
movement and an impulse of will that can rise fully to consciousness in the individual involved, so that one is never
engaged in a mere intrusion of the physical into the etheric
processes. Artistic dance is achieved only when it is spiritually
permeated by mental pictures. The dance of the dervish is a
denial of spirituality. Many may object, however, that it only
reveals the spirit! Yes, but how? Well, you can study a mussel
shell by picking up the living mussel and observing it; but you
can also study it when the living mussel has left, by studying its
shell; the form of the mussel is reproduced in the mussel shell,
a form born from the life of the organism. Thus, one might say
that one also has an after-image of the spirit, a dead after-image
of the spirit, when involved with automatic writing or with
whirling dervishes. For this reason it resembles the spirit as
closely as the mussel shell resembles the living mussel and it
can, therefore, also be easily confused with it. But we can only
achieve a true understanding in these matters when we truly
penetrate inwardly to the genuine spirit.

When we begin with the bodily, ascend through sense perception and sensation to the activity of forming representations, to thinking, which then carries over into the soul-
spiritual, we come along this path to the spiritual-scientific recognition that what is stimulated through sense perception and
sensation is brought to an end at a certain point and becomes

memory. Memory arises as the sense impression continues on its way into the body, so that the etheric is not just effective within the sense impressions themselves, but also engages itself with what is left behind in the body by the sense impression. Thus, what has entered into memory is called up again from memory.

It is not possible, of course, to go into greater detail about these matters in an hour-long lecture. But we will never come to a true understanding of the reality of mental representation and memory, and how they relate to the soul-spiritual, if we do not proceed along the spiritual-scientific path indicated.

On the other hand, there is the whole stream that flows from the spirit-soul life of our will impulses into the bodily physical, which bring about external activities. In ordinary human life the situation is such that the life of the senses goes as far as memory and comes to a halt. Memory places itself in front of the spirit-soul, so to speak, so that spirit-soul is not aware of itself and how it works when it receives sense impressions. Only an indication, a confused indication that the soul weaves and lives in the etheric, arises when the soul, living and weaving in the etheric, is not yet strongly enough impelled in its etheric weaving so that all of this ether-weaving breaks against the boundary of the bodily-physical. Dream arises when the soul-spiritual weaves within the etheric so that what is formed within the etheric does not immediately break against the physical body, but rather restrains itself in the etheric as though it came to the boundary of the physical body, but still remains perceptible in the etheric. When dream life is really studied it will prove to be the lowest form of supersensible experience for human beings; for in their dreams human beings experience how the soul-spiritual cannot unfold as will impulses within what appears as dream pictures, because, within the dream life, the soul-spiritual lacks strength and forcefulness in its working.

And inasmuch as will impulses are lacking, inasmuch as dreaming spirit and soul do not penetrate the etheric sufficiently for the soul herself to become aware of these will impulses, a chaotic tapestry of dreams arises.

On the one hand, what dreams are, on the other hand, those phenomena are, where the will—which comes out of the spirit-soul realm—takes hold of the outer world through the etheric-bodily nature. But, in doing so, the will is as little aware of what is actually going on, as one is aware in the dream that—due to the weak effect of the spirit-soul—the human being weaves and lives in the spirit. Just as the dream is, in a way, weakened sense perception, so something else occurs as the intensified effect of the spirit-soul element, the strengthened effect of the will impulses; and this is what we call *destiny*.

In destiny we do not have insight into the connections, just as in dreams we do not have insight into what actually weaves and exists there as reality. Just as material processes surging up into the etheric are always present as the underlying ground in dreams, so the spirit-soul element anchored in the will storms up against the outer world. But the spirit-soul element in ordinary life is not organized enough that one can perceive the spirit effectively working in what unfolds before us as the sequence of the so-called "destiny experiences." The moment we comprehend this sequence, we learn to know the fabric of destiny, we learn to know how, just as in ordinary life the soul conceals the spirit for itself through the mental representations, so it also conceals the spirit active in destiny for itself through feelings, through sympathy and antipathy with which it receives approaching events in the experience of life. In the moment when, with the help of spiritual-scientific insight, one sees through the veil of sympathy and antipathy, when one objectively takes hold of the course of life experiences with inner equanimity, in this moment one notices how everything that occurs as a matter of destiny in our life between birth and death is either the effect of earlier lives on Earth, or it is a preparation for later Earth lives. Just as, on one hand, external natural science does not penetrate spirit and soul, not even the etheric, when it looks for connections between the material world and our mental images, so also, in regard to the other pole, natural science today fails in its cognitive efforts. Just as, on one side, science remains tied to the material processes in the nervous organism in attempting to explain the life of mental representations, so also, science remains caught at the other pole in unclarity—that, is, I would say, science teeters in a nebulous way between the physical and the realm of soul.

These are just the realms where we must become aware how concepts in a world view allow themselves to be proved as well as to be contradicted. And the positive position has much to be said for it for those who cling rigidly to proof; but, just as inbreathing must accompany out-breathing, we must also be able to think our way through to an experience of the negative. Recently what has come to be known as *analytical psychology* has arisen. This analytical psychology, generally called *psychoanalysis*, attempts to descend from the ordinary soul level to something no longer contained in the soul life normally present, but remains from the soul's earlier experiences. And in much that appears in the soul life as disturbance, as confusion, as some one-sided deficiency or another, the psychoanalyst sees an effect of what surges in the subconscious.

It is interesting, however, to note what psychoanalysts see in the subconscious. We hear them enumerate disappointment in life's expectations, first of all, in this subconscious. Psychoanalysts encounter some human being who suffers from this or that depression. The depression does not necessarily originate in the soul life's present consciousness, but may come from the past; something that occurred in the soul's experience in this life. The person has overcome the experience, though not completely; something is left over in the subconscious. People may have experienced disappointments, for example. Through education or other processes they transcended these disappointments in the conscious life of soul, which then live on, however, in the subconscious, where they surge, as it were, up to the boundary of consciousness. And here they then bring forth an indefinite depression of the soul. Psychoanalysts, therefore, look for what determines conscious life in a dim, unclear way, in all kinds of disappointments—disappointed life hopes and expectations that have been drawn down into the subconscious. They also look for this in what colors the soul's life as rational impulses; they seek a subconscious that only knocks, as it were, against consciousness. But then they come to an even further realm—I am only reporting here—which psychoanalysts try to comprehend by saying that what plays up into conscious life is the fundamental substratum, the primeval, animalistic, residual mud of the soul. We certainly cannot deny that this primeval mud is there.

In these lectures I have already pointed out how certain mystics have had experiences because certain things, such as eroticism, are subtly refined and play into consciousness so that one believes one has had especially high experiences, whereas in reality, only the erotic "primeval, animalistic mud of the soul" surges up and is sometimes interpreted in the sense of profound mysticism. Even in the case of a fine, poetic mystic such as Mechthild von Magdeburg, we can document single details of her mental representations, of her thoughts.[15]

One must clearly comprehend these matters with exactness to avoid errors in the sphere of spiritual-scientific investigation.

---

15. Mechthild von Magdeburg (1212–1285), German mystic, wrote *Das fließende Licht der Gottheit* (*The Flowing Light of the Godhead*).

Those who want to penetrate the realm of the spirit are particularly obligated to know all the possible paths of error—not so they can pursue them, but to avoid them. But those who speak of this animalistic primeval mud of the soul, who only speak about life's disappointed hopes and other similar matters, do not go deep enough into the life of the soul; such people are like someone who walks across a field where there is nothing to be seen yet and believes that only the soil, or perhaps also the fertilizer is present there, whereas this field already contains all the fruits that will soon spring forth from it as grain or another crop. When one speaks of the primeval mud of the soul, one should also speak of everything embedded in it. Certainly, there are disappointed hopes in this primeval mud; but what is embedded there also hides a germinating force that simultaneously represents what makes disappointed hopes into something very different than mere depression—after the human being has passed through the gates of death into the life between death and a new birth, and then enters a new life on Earth. Something in the next life is created, which leads to an "appointment," as it were, leads to a strengthening of soul initiative, not to a "disappointment." Within what psychoanalysts look for in the soul's deepest disappointed life-hopes—if they only go deeply enough into it—is what prepares itself in the present life to take hold in the next life according to the laws of destiny.

If we dig, therefore, over the animalistic, primeval mud without getting our hands dirty— as, regrettably, happens so often with the psychoanalysts—we find everywhere within the soul's spiritual and psychic life the spiritual-soul weaving of destiny that extends beyond birth and death. We have a realm, especially in analytic psychology, where one can learn very well how everything can be right and everything can be wrong when it comes to questions of world views, looked at from one perspective or another. But there is a tremendous amount that

can be presented to support the one-sided assertions of psychoanalysts and, therefore, to disprove these assertions will not
greatly impress those who swear by these concepts. But if one
learns to form judgments according to the method of knowing
characterized at the beginning of this lecture, in which one recognizes what speaks both for and against a viewpoint, then just
from this *for* and *against* the soul, one will experience what is
truly at work. I would like to say that between what one merely
observed in the soul realm, as the psychologists do who are
only concerned with the conscious realm, and what the psychoanalyst finds down below in the animalistic, primeval mud
of the soul—just between these two realms of research is where
the sphere is that belongs to the eternal spirit and soul, and
goes through births and deaths.

Penetration of the whole inner human realm also leads to a
proper relationship with the outer world. More recent natural
science not only speaks in vague, indefinite ways about the
etheric, but also speaks about it in such a way that just this
greatest of world riddles leads one back to it. It is thought that
what became the fixed shapes of planets, suns, moons, and so
on, formed itself out of etheric conditions. What occurs as the
soul-spiritual in the human being is considered to be, more or
less, a mere episode. Dead ether is before and behind. One who
learns to know the ether only from one side will arrive at a
hypothetical construction of world evolution, about which the
sensitive thinker Herman Grimm said something that I have
frequently quoted, but it is significant enough that it is good to
bring it before the soul again and again.[16] As he became

---

16. Herman Grimm (1828–1901), son of Wilhelm Grimm of fairy tale
fame, he was primarily an independent scholar and the center of a cultural
and intellectual circle in Berlin, where Steiner met him. Grimm greatly
admired Ralph Waldo Emerson, who in turn admired Grimm's work.

familiar with the thinking that asserts how life and spirit now unfolds within what arose from the dead cosmic etheric mist, and as he measured this against Goethe's world view, he said:

> Even in his [Goethe's] youth, the great Laplace-Kantian phantasy of the origin and the eventual destruction of the planet Earth had asserted itself for a long time. From the rotating cosmic mist—which even children become familiar with in school—the central gaseous drop forms itself, out of which the Earth emerges, and in the course of unimaginable epochs of time, as a rigidifying sphere, goes through all those phases—including the episode of human habitation—in order to, finally, plunge back into the Sun as a burned-out slag; a lengthy but, for the public in our [Goethe's] time, an entirely comprehensible process, whose origin requires no outer intervention, other than the effort of some external force, to maintain a steady temperature of heat in the Sun. A more fruitless perspective for the future cannot be imagined, one that is to be forced upon us today in the expectation of its scientific inevitability. The bone of a carcass, that even a hungry dog would take a detour around, would be refreshing and appetizing compared to this ultimate excrement of creation, the form in which our Earth would finally plunge back into the sun. The intellectual appetite our generation has for taking up this kind of thing—and feeling impelled to believe it—is a sign of sick fantasy, and the learned scholars of future ages will need much cleverness to explain it as a historical phenomenon of our time.

Once again, what arises here as a feeling born out of a healthy life of soul within German spiritual life, is shown in a true light by spiritual science. For, if one gains knowledge of how the dead etheric is enlivened through the soul element, through the living ether, then through inner experience one moves away from the possibility that our universal structure could ever have arisen out of the dead etheric. And this world riddle takes a very different aspect if one becomes familiar with the corresponding riddle of the soul. One comes to know the ether itself in its living form; one comes to know how the dead ether must first originate from what is living. Thus, as one returns to the origins of the world evolution, one must return to the soul, and recognize that one must look within the realm of the spirit and the soul for the origin of everything that develops today. The spiritual-soul will remain a mere hypothesis, merely thought out, concerning external world riddles, as long as one does not learn, through spiritual science, to know the whole living and weaving of the etheric, by experiencing how the living ether from within meets with the dead ether from without; the world mist itself will only be recognized as being alive, as being of the nature of spirit and of soul, along a path of spiritual science.

So you can also see that a significant perspective of the world questions is gained just by understanding the riddles of the soul. I must close today with this perspective. You see, just by genuinely considering external and inner life from the viewpoint of spiritual science, one is led by way of the etheric into the spirit and the soul, just as much within the soul as the outer world.

Indeed, a man I referred to and named last time expressed a viewpoint that opposes such a cognitive attitude of soul. Today we can have at least the feeling that, from the way spiritual science thinks about human bodily nature, a bridge leads directly to the spirit-soul realm where ethics and morality are rooted in and stem from the spirit—just as the sense-perceptible leads into the spirit. But in its preoccupation with the purely external material world, the attitude of mind developed by science completely denies that ethics is anchored in the spirit. One is still embarrassed to deny ethics as such, but today ethics are spoken of in the following way, as expressed in the conclusion of a lecture by Jacques Loeb that, in referring to its beginning, I presented last time.[17] There, one who comes through natural-scientific research to a brutal disavowal of ethics says:

> If our existence depends on the blind play of forces and only the work of chance; if we ourselves are only chemical mechanisms, how can there be an ethical reality for us? The answer to this is that our instincts form the roots of our ethical being, and our instincts are as subject to heredity as the constituent forms of our body. We eat and drink and reproduce ourselves, not because metaphysicians have attained the insight that this is desirable, but because we are mechanically predisposed to do so. We are active because mechanically we are forced to be so through the processes in our nervous system, and if human beings are not economic slaves, it is instinct, nevertheless, that determines the direction of their activity of successful triggering or successful work. A mother loves her children and cares for them, not because metaphysicians had the bright idea that this would be a lovely thing to do, but because the instinct to care for the offspring is as firmly implanted, presumably through the two sexual chromosomes, as is the morphological character of the female body. We enjoy the company of other human beings because we are compelled by the conditions of our human inheritance to do so. We fight for justice and truth, we are ready to make sacrifices for them, because, instinctively, we desire to see our fellow

---

17. Jacques Loeb (1859–1924), German-born American biophysiologist, author of *The Dynamics of Living Matter*, *The Mechanistic Conception of Life*, etc.

human beings happy. We have only our instincts to thank for our ethical trait, determined for us chemically and through heredity in the same way as the form of our body.

Ethical action leads us back to instinct! Instincts lead back to the effects of physical-chemical activity! This logic is indeed most threadbare. For, as a matter of course, certainly one can say that, with ethical action, one should not wait for the metaphysicians until they have spun out some metaphysical principles; that would be the same as if someone said, "Should one wait with digestion until the metaphysicians or physiologists have discovered the laws of digestion?" I would like just once to recommend to Professor Loeb that he *not* investigate the physiological laws of digestion as he storms with brutality against the metaphysical laws of ethical life.

But we could say that one can be a significant investigator of nature today—but thought habits tend to cut one off from all spiritual life, tend to prevent even a glance in the direction of the life of the spirit. But parallel with this there is always the fact that one can document a defect in thinking, so that one never has the full effectiveness that belongs to a thought.

One can have peculiar experiences in this regard. I recently presented such an experience, but I would like to present it again because it connects with statements by a very significant natural scientist of today, Svante Arrhenius, who belongs with those whom I attack just because I value them very highly in one sphere.[18] This natural scientist has accumulated great

---

18. Svente August Arrhenius (1859–1927), Swedish physicist, chemist, and professor who established the electrolytic dissociation theory for which he receive the 1903 Nobel prize in chemistry; the quote referred to was from the introduction in *Die Vorstellung vom Weltgebäude im Wandel der Zeiten* (*The Changing Picture of Cosmology*).

achievements in the field of astrophysics, as well as in certain other fields of natural scientific research. When he wrote, however, a comprehensive book on the current view of the universe and on the evolution of this world view, in his forward he arrives at a strange statement. He is, in a certain sense, delighted that we are so wonderfully advanced that we can now interpret all phenomena from a natural-scientific perspective, and he points with a certain arrogance, as is customary in such circles, to earlier times that were not yet as advanced. And, in this regard, he calls on Goethe, by saying that whether one can truly say that we live in the best of times, we cannot determine; but that we live in the best of times in regard to natural-scientific knowledge compared to earlier times, in this regard we can call on Goethe, who says:

> Forgive! It does seem so sublime,
> Entering into the spirit of the time
> To see what wise ones, who lived long ago, believed
> Till we at last have all the highest aims achieved.[19]

Therewith a distinguished contemporary natural scientist concludes his exposition by calling Goethe to witness. Except that in doing so he forgot that it is Wagner who makes this assertion, and after Wagner has left Faust remarks:

> Hope never seems to leave those who affirm,
> The shallow minds that stick to must and mold—
> They dig with greedy hands for gold
> And yet are happy if they find a worm.

---

19. Translated by Walter Kaufman.

The distinguished researcher neglected to reflect on what Goethe actually says when he called on Wagner to express how splendidly advanced we are. In this, I would say that we can glimpse where thinking fails in its pursuit of reality.

We could cite many such examples if we were to explore, even a little, current scientific literature. This will surely not be held against me—since, as I have said, I greatly value natural-scientific research, which prides itself on being able to impart information about the spirit—when I try to express the true Goethean attitude of mind and heart. For, we can forgive various monistic thinkers if, out of the weakness of their thinking, they fail to arrive at the spirit.[20] What is dangerous, however, is if this attitude of soul—which arises in Jacques Loeb and Svante Arrhenius who, while considering themselves to be "Goethes," appear as "Wagners"—gains more and more uncritical acceptance in the broadest circles. And this is what is happening. Those who penetrate into what can arise as an attitude of mind and heart from spiritual science—even though it may not seem respectful enough to some, given a statement such as the one made by the natural scientist about Goethe—can perhaps come to the genuinely Goethean attitude if they take up Goethe's words, which I would like to paraphrase in concluding this lecture:

> Forgive! It is a shock indeed
> Entering souls that in their greed
> Cling to matter with all their might
> And for the spirit have no sight.

---

20. *Monism* proposes one ultimate substance or principle—mind (as in *idealism*) or matter (as in *materialism*), even a foundation of both or something beyond these; it holds that there is but one ultimate reality.

BIBLIOGRAPHY

Basic Works by Rudolf Steiner

Anthroposophical Leading Thoughts, Rudolf Steiner Press, London, 1985.

Anthroposophy (A Fragment). Anthroposophic Press, Hudson, NY, 1996.

An Autobiography. Steinerbooks, Blauvelt, NY, 1977.

Christianity as Mystical Fact. Anthroposophic Press, Hudson, NY, 1986.

How to Know Higher Worlds: A Modern Path of Initiation. Anthroposophic Press, Hudson, NY, 1994.

Intuitive Thinking as a Spiritual Path: A Philosophy of Freedom. Anthroposophic Press, Hudson, NY, 1995.

An Outline of Occult Science. Anthroposophic Press, Hudson, NY, 1972.

A Road to Self-Knowledge and The Threshold of the Spiritual World, Rudolf Steiner Press, London, 1975.

Theosophy: An Introduction to the Spiritual Processes in Human Life and in the Cosmos. Anthroposophic Press, Hudson, NY, 1994.

Other Books by Rudolf Steiner

Ancient Myths and the New Isis Mystery, Anthroposophic Press, Hudson, NY, 1994.

Anthroposophy in Everyday Life: Practical Training in Thought; Overcoming Nervousness; Facing Karma; The Four Temperaments, Anthroposophic Press, Hudson, NY, 1995.

Anthroposophy: An Introduction, Rudolf Steiner Press, London, 1983.

Art as Seen in the Light of Mystery Wisdom, Rudolf Steiner Press, London, 1984.

The Archangel Michael, Anthroposophic Press, Hudson, NY, 1995.

Between Death and Rebirth, Rudolf Steiner Press, London, 1975.

The Bridge between Universal Spirituality and Physical Man, Anthroposophic Press, New York, 1979.

The Case for Anthroposophy, Rudolf Steiner Press, London, 1970.

Cosmology, Religion and Philosophy, Anthroposophic Press, New York, 1955.

Earthly Death and Cosmic Life, Steinerbooks, Blauvelt, NY, 1985.

Eurythmy as Visible Song, Rudolf Steiner Press, London, 1977.

Eurythmy as Visible Speech, Rudolf Steiner Press, London, 1984.

The Festivals and Their Meaning, Anthroposophic Press, New York, 1958.

From Jesus to Christ, Rudolf Steiner Press, London, 1982.

Fundamentals of Therapy, Rudolf Steiner Press, London, 1983.

Goethean Science, Mercury Press, Spring Valley, NY, 1988.

How the Spiritual World Penetrates the Physical World, Anthroposophic Press, New York, 1927.

The Human Being in Body, Soul and Spirit and Early Conditions of the Earth, Anthroposophic Press, Hudson, NY, 1989.

The Human Soul in Relation to World Evolution, Anthroposophic Press, Hudson, NY, 1984.

The Inner Nature of Man and Life Between Death and Rebirth, Rudolf Steiner Press, London, 1994.

The Inner Nature of Music and the Experience of Tone, Anthroposophic Press, Hudson, NY, 1983.

An Introduction to Eurythmy, Anthroposophic Press, Hudson, NY, 1984.

The Karma of Untruthfulness, vol. II, Rudolf Steiner Press, London, 1992.

Karma of Vocation, Anthroposophic Press, Hudson, NY, 1984.

Man as a Being of Sense and Perception, Steiner Book Centre, Vancouver, 1981.

Man as a Symphony of the Creative Word, Rudolf Steiner Press, London, 1979.

Metamorphosis of the Soul, Rudolf Steiner Press, London, 1983.

The Mysteries of Light, of Space and of the Earth, Anthroposophic Press, New York, 1945.

Nine Lectures on Bees, Steinerbooks, Blauvelt, NY, 1985.

An Occult Physiology, Rudolf Steiner Press, London, 1983.

Paths of Experience, Rudolf Steiner Press, London, 1983.

Physiology and Therapeutics, Mercury Press, Spring Valley, NY, 1986.

Psychoanalysis & Spiritual Psychology, Anthroposophic Press, Hudson, NY, 1990.

Renewal of the Social Organism, Anthroposophic Press, Hudson, NY, 1985.

The Riddle of Man, Mercury Press, Spring Valley, NY, 1990.

Riddles of Philosophy, Anthroposophic Press, Spring Valley, NY, 1973.

The Science of Knowing, Mercury Press, Spring Valley, NY, 1988.

Second Course for Doctors and Medical Students, Mercury Press, Spring Valley, NY, 1991.

Spiritual Science and Medicine, Steinerbooks, Blauvelt, NY, 1985.

Spiritual Science as a Foundation for Social Forms, Anthroposophic Press, Hudson, NY, 1986.

Supersensible Knowledge, Anthroposophic Press, Hudson, NY, 1987.

Therapeutic Insights, Earthly and Cosmic Laws, Mercury Press, Spring Valley, NY, 1984.

Toward Imagination, Anthroposophic Press, Hudson, NY, 1990.

Towards Social Renewal, Rudolf Steiner Press, London, 1977.

Truth and Knowledge, Steinerbooks, Blauvelt, NY, 1981.

Universe, Earth and Man, Rudolf Steiner Press, London, 1987.

What Can the Art of Healing Gain Through Spiritual Science?, Mercury Press, Spring Valley, NY, 1986.

Wisdom of Man, of the Soul and of the Spirit, Anthroposophic Press, Spring Valley, NY, 1971.

The Younger Generation, Anthroposophic Press, Hudson, NY, 1984.

Books by Other Authors

Adams, George and Whicher, Olive, *Plant Between Sun and Earth,* Rudolf Steiner Press, London, 1980.

Childs, Gilbert, *Steiner Education in Theory and Practice*, Floris Books, Edinburgh, 1993.

Edmunds, L. Francis, *Rudolf Steiner Education: The Waldorf School*, Rudolf Steiner Press, London, 1992.

Gardner, John, *Education in Search of the Spirit*, Anthroposophic Press, Hudson, NY, 1996.

Goethe, Johann Wolfgang von, *Theory of Colors*, MIT Press, 1970.

Murphy, Christine, ed./trans., *Emil Molt and the Beginnings of the Waldorf School Movement: Sketches from an Autobiography,* Floris Press, Edinburgh, 1991.

Whicher, Olive, "The Idea of Counterspace," Anthroposophic Press, NY, n.d.

THE FOUNDATIONS
OF WALDORF EDUCATION

THE FIRST FREE WALDORF SCHOOL opened its doors in Stuttgart, Germany, in September, 1919, under the auspices of Emil Molt, the Director of the Waldorf Astoria Cigarette Company and a student of Rudolf Steiner's spiritual science and particularly of Steiner's call for social renewal.

It was only the previous year—amid the social chaos following the end of World War I—that Emil Molt, responding to Steiner's prognosis that truly human change would not be possible unless a sufficient number of people received an education that developed the whole human being, decided to create a school for his workers' children. Conversations with the Minister of Education and with Rudolf Steiner, in early 1919, then led rapidly to the forming of the first school.

Since that time, more than six hundred schools have opened around the globe—from Italy, France, Portugal, Spain, Holland, Belgium, Great Britain, Norway, Finland and Sweden to Russia, Georgia, Poland, Hungary, Rumania, Israel, South Africa, Australia, Brazil, Chile, Peru, Argentina, Japan etc.—making the Waldorf School Movement the largest independent school movement in the world. The United States, Canada, and Mexico alone now have more than 120 schools.

Although each Waldorf school is independent, and although there is a healthy oral tradition going back to the first Waldorf teachers and to Steiner himself, as well as a growing body of secondary literature, the true foundations of the Waldorf method and spirit remain the many lectures that Rudolf Steiner gave on the subject. For five years (1919–24), Rudolf Steiner, while simultaneously working on many other fronts, tirelessly dedicated himself to the dissemination of the idea of Waldorf education. He gave manifold lectures to teachers, parents, the general public, and even the children themselves. New schools were founded. The Movement grew.

While many of Steiner's foundational lectures have been translated and published in the past, some have never appeared in English, and many have been virtually unobtainable for years. To remedy this situation and to establish a coherent basis for Waldorf Education, Anthroposophic Press has decided to publish the complete series of Steiner lectures and writings on education in a uniform series. This series will thus constitute an authoritative foundation for work in educational renewal, for Waldorf teachers, parents, and educators generally.

RUDOLF STEINER'S LECTURES
(AND WRITINGS) ON EDUCATION

I. *Allgemeine Menschenkunde als Grundlage der Pädagogik. Pädagogischer Grundkurs,* 14 Lectures, Stuttgart, 1919 (GA293). Previously *Study of Man. The Foundations of Human Experience* (Anthroposophic Press, 1996).

II. *Erziehungskunst Methodisch-Didaktisches,* 14 Lectures, Stuttgart, 1919 (GA294). *Practical Advice to Teachers* (Anthroposophic Press, 2000).

III. *Erziehungskunst. Methodisch-Didaktisches,* 15 Discussions, Stuttgart, 1919 (GA 295). *Discussions with Teachers* (Anthroposophic Press, 1997).

IV. *Die Erziehungsfrage als soziale Frage,* 6 Lectures, Dornach, 1919 (GA296). *Education as a Force for Social Change* (previously *Education as a Social Problem*) (Anthroposophic Press, 1997).

V. *Die Waldorf Schule und ihr Geist,* 6 Lectures, Stuttgart and Basel, 1919 (GA 297). *The Spirit of the Waldorf School* (Anthroposophic Press, 1995).

VI. *Rudolf Steiner in der Waldorfschule, Vorträge und Ansprachen,* Stuttgart, 1919–1924 (GA 298). *Rudolf Steiner in the Waldorf School,* (Anthroposophic Press, 1996).

VII. *Geisteswissenschaftliche Sprachbetrachtungen,* 6 Lectures, Stuttgart, 1919 (GA 299). *The Genius of Language* (Anthroposophic Press, 1995).

VIII. *Konferenzen mit den Lehren der Freien Waldorfschule 1919–1924,* 3 Volumes (GA 300). *Faculty Meetings with Rudolf Steiner,* 2 Volumes (Anthroposophic Press, 1998).

IX. *Die Erneuerung der Pädagogisch-didaktischen Kunst durch Geisteswissenschaft,* 14 Lectures, Basel, 1920 (GA 301). *The Renewal of Education* (Kolisko Archive Publications for Steiner Schools Fellowship Publications, Michael Hall, Forest Row, East Sussex, UK, 1981).

X. *Menschenerkenntnis und Unterrichtsgestaltung,* 8 Lectures, Stuttgart, 1921 (GA 302). Previously *The Supplementary Course—Upper School* and *Waldorf Education for Adolescence. Education for Adolescents* (Anthroposophic Press, 1996).

XI. *Erziehung und Unterrricht aus Menschenerkenntnis,* 9 Lectures, Stuttgart, 1920, 1922, 1923 (GA302a). The first four lectures available as *Balance in Teaching* (Mercury Press, 1982); last three lectures as *Deeper Insights into Education* (Anthroposophic Press, 1988).

XII. *Die Gesunde Entwickelung des Menschenwesens,* 16 Lectures, Dornach, 1921–22 (GA303). *Soul Economy and Waldorf Education* (Anthroposophic Press, 1986).

XIII. *Erziehungs- und Unterrichtsmethoden auf anthroposophischer Grundlage,* 9 Public lectures, various cities, 1921–22 (GA304). *Waldorf Education and Anthroposophy I* (Anthroposophic Press, 1995).

XIV. *Anthroposophische Menschenkunde und Pädagogik,* 9 Public Lectures, various cities, 1923–24 (GA 304a). **Waldorf Education and Anthroposophy 2** (Anthroposophic Press, 1996).

XV. *Die geistig-seelischen Grundkräfte der Erziehungskunst,* 12 Lectures, 1 Special Lecture, Oxford 1922 (GA 305). **The Spiritual Ground of Education** (Garber Publications, 1989).

XVI. *Die pädagogisch Praxis vom Gesichtspunkte geisteswissenschaftlicher Menschenerkenntnis,* 8 Lectures, Dornach, 1923 (GA 306). **The Child's Changing Consciousness As the Basis of Pedagogical Practice** (Anthroposophic Press, 1996).

XVII. *Gegenwärtiges Geistesleben und Erziehung,* 4 Lectures, Ilkeley, 1923 (GA 307). **A Modern Art of Education** (Rudolf Steiner Press, 1981) and **Education and Modern Spiritual Life** (Garber Publications, n.d.).

XVIII. *Die Methodik des Lehrens und die Lebensbedingungen des Erziehens,* 5 Lectures, Stuttgart, 1924 (GA 308). **The Essentials of Education** (Anthroposophic Press, 1997).

XIX. *Anthroposophische Pädagogik und ihre Voraussetzungen,* 5 Lectures, Bern, 1924 (GA 309). **The Roots of Education** (Anthroposophic Press, 1997).

XX. *Der pädagogische Wert der Menschenerkenntnis und der Kulturwert der Pädagogik,* 10 Public Lectures, Arnheim, 1924 (GA 310). **Human Values in Education** (Rudolf Steiner Press, 1971).

XXI. *Die Kunst des Erziehens aus dem Erfassen der Menschenwesenheit,* 7 Lectures, Torquay, 1924 (GA 311). **The Kingdom of Childhood** (Anthroposophic Press, 1995).

XXII. *Geisteswissenschaftliche Impulse zur Entwicklung der Physik. Erster naturwissenschaftliche Kurs: Licht, Farbe, Ton—Masse, Elektrizität, Magnetismus,* 10 Lectures, Stuttgart, 1919–20 (GA 320). **The Light Course** (Steiner Schools Fellowship,1977).

XXIII. *Geisteswissenschaftliche Impulse zur Entwicklung der Physik. Zweiter naturwissenschaftliche Kurs: die Wärme auf der Grenze positiver und negativer Materialität,* 14 Lectures, Stuttgart, 1920 (GA 321). **The Warmth Course** (Mercury Press, 1988).

XXIV. *Das Verhältnis der verschiedenen naturwissenschaftlichen Gebiete zur Astronomie. Dritter naturwissenschaftliche Kurs: Himmelskunde in Beziehung zum Menschen und zur Menschenkunde,* 18 Lectures, Stuttgart, 1921 (GA 323). Available in typescript only as "**The Relation of the Diverse Branches of Natural Science to Astronomy.**"

XXV. **The Education of the Child and Early Lectures on Education** (A collection) (Anthroposophic Press, 1996).

XXVI. Miscellaneous.

INDEX

*for the Opening Address and
Lectures One–Fourteen*

DURING THE LAST TWO DECADES of the nineteenth century the Austrian-born Rudolf Steiner (1861–1925) became a respected and well-published scientific, literary, and philosophical scholar, particularly known for his work on Goethe's scientific writings. After the turn of the century he began to develop his earlier philosophical principles into an approach to methodical research of psychological and spiritual phenomena.

His multifaceted genius has led to innovative and holistic approaches in medicine, science, education (Waldorf schools), special education, philosophy, religion, economics, agriculture (Biodynamic method), architecture, drama, new arts of eurythmy and speech, and other fields. In 1924 he founded the General Anthroposophical Society, which today has branches throughout the world.

. . . .

*For an informative catalog of the work of Rudolf Steiner
and other anthroposophical authors please contact*

ANTHROPOSOPHIC PRESS

P.O. Box 799, Gt. Barrington, MA 01230

www.anthropress.org